# BAKE

# BAKE

Beautiful baking recipes
from around the world

·

This edition published by Parragon Books Ltd in 2013

LOVE FOOD is an imprint of Parragon Books Ltd

PARRAGON
Chartist House
15–17 Trim Street
Bath, BA1 1HA, UK
www.parragon.com/lovefood

ISBN: 978-1-4723-1969-2

Printed in China

New recipes written by Edward Gee

Edited by Fiona Biggs

Created by 99 PAGES

Notes for the Reader

This book uses both metric and imperial measurements. Follow the same units of measurement throughout; do not mix metric and imperial. All spoon measurements are level: teaspoons are assumed to be 5 ml, and tablespoons are assumed to be 15 ml. Unless otherwise stated, milk is assumed to be full fat, eggs and individual vegetables are medium, and pepper is freshly ground black pepper. Unless otherwise stated, all root vegetables should be washed in plain water and peeled prior to using.

For best results, use a food thermometer when cooking meat and poultry – check the latest government guidelines for current advice.

Garnishes, decorations and serving suggestions are all optional and not necessarily included in the recipe ingredients or method.

The times given are an approximate guide only. Preparation times differ according to the techniques used by different people and the cooking times may also vary from those given. Optional ingredients, variations or serving suggestions have not been included in the time calculations.

Recipes using raw or very lightly cooked eggs should be avoided by infants, the elderly, pregnant women, convalescents and anyone suffering from an illness. Pregnant and breastfeeding women are advised to avoid eating peanuts and peanut products. Sufferers from nut allergies should be aware that some of the ready-made ingredients used in the recipes in this book may contain nuts. Always check the packaging before use.

# Baking

## THE HISTORY OF HUMANITY

Bread, cakes and biscuits are a central feature of almost every food culture, whether in the Americas, Europe, Africa, Asia or Australasia. In fact, baking is one of the principal achievements in the history of humankind.

*Historians speculate that Egyptians found the existence of natural yeast by chance. On a warm day, the yeasts that occur naturally in flour caused it to ferment before baking. In the Middle Ages, bread baking with yeast was already highly developed. Thousands of recipes from this era still exist in some part of Europe.*

Many customs and traditions have been and still are associated with baking. Baked goods have traditionally been viewed as a symbol of the gods, because ancient cultures believed that the gods invented the art of baking and then taught it to the people. The Greeks worshipped Demeter, the goddess of grain and fertility. The Roman goddess of agriculture was called Ceres. The word 'cereal' derives from her name.

Over the centuries, thousands of recipes for bread have evolved all over the world. Although the origins of baking are unclear, there are few civilizations where baked goods are not a staple food. Ever since we ceased to be nomadic, we have been cultivating cereal grains. The grain obtained was usually eaten raw and whole and was not very easy to digest. At some point people had the idea of grinding the grain between two stones and then mixing it with water. Between BC 6000 and 3000, this method spread throughout the East to Egypt, China and India. By adding water, milk and fat to the ground grain, a dough mixture was made that is still a basic component of the daily diet of 60 per cent of the world's population today.

However, at that time, bread and cakes in the modern sense were unknown. The mixture was baked into small, round cakes on heated stones or placed in hot ashes. Archaeological findings in Bulgaria show that a type of basic oven was already in use around BC 300. One early type of oven was known as a tube oven – these were heated from within and flat bread was placed on the outside. In India, a similar process is still used, with flat bread being cooked on the walls of mud huts that are heated by the sun.

Early flat bread was an ideal food for taking on long-distance journeys as its low water content meant that it kept for a long time. This made it a practical food for Bronze Age hunters in around BC 2000 and it was also later used by the Vikings. In Finland and some Alpine countries, there was also a hole in the centre of the bread that was used for stringing it up to protect the bread from mice. The holes that are still to be found in bagels are a relic of this practical, everyday solution.

Archaeological artefacts from different parts of the eastern Mediterranean suggest that dough mixture was fermented to leaven for the first time in around BC 1800. This discovery is attributed to the Egyptians who noticed that dough that was left standing for longer periods was looser. Their logical conclusion was that a looser dough would produce a softer bake, rather than hard flat breads – this observation led to the development of early leavened breads and, eventually, cake!

In Egypt in BC 1500, clay ovens were developed and they began to be used in people's homes. In BC 1000, portable ovens, which were 1-metre/3-foot tall pots made of stone or metal, were also created. This ground-breaking invention was followed in rapid succession by improvements in milling and baking technology. The Greeks took their lead from the Egyptians and started leavening the flour to produce sourdough. The Germans also got in on the act and introduced leavened bread in BC 800. In around 50 AD, the Romans began to sift the crushed, wholemeal grains. By 400 AD, there were already more than 250 bakeries in Rome, some of them large factories, grinding and processing up to 30 tons of grain daily.

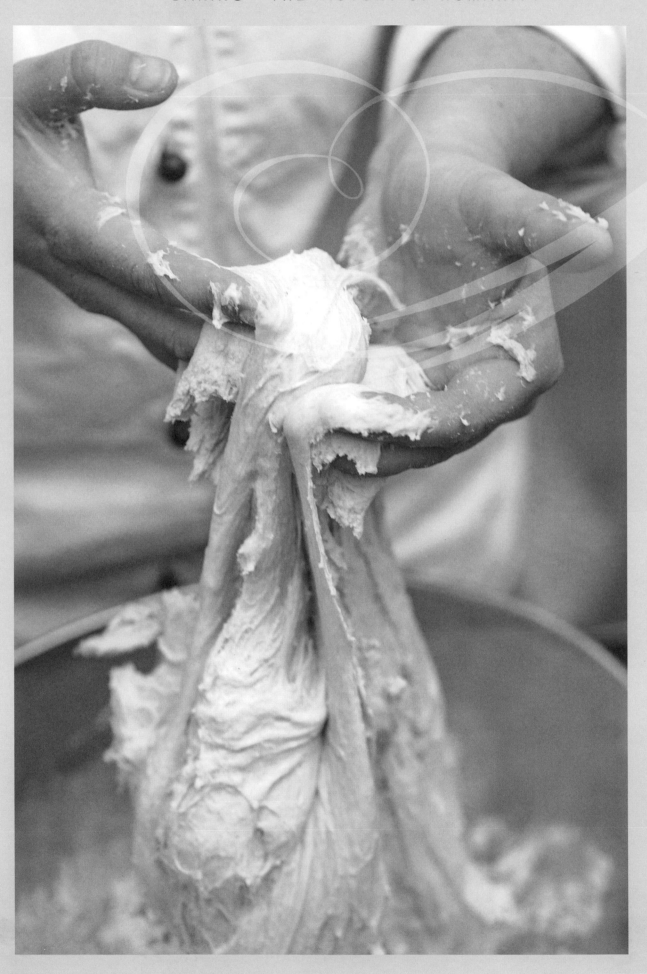

*One of the most recognized and outstanding accomplishments by the German chemist Justus Liebig (1803–1873) was the invention of a nitrogen-based fertilizer. This developed into a product that started to be used in baking instead of yeast, for people who found yeast's strong fermentation flavour undesirable. This product was baking powder, which was revolutionary in home baking.*

However, for the majority of the population, good quality leavened bread still remained out of reach for many hundreds of years. It wasn't until the sixteenth century that flat breads were gradually replaced by leavened breads in Northern and Central Europe, and fine bread was still only eaten at court. This meant that social class could be assessed by the type of bread people ate: the harder and rougher the bread, the lower a person's status.

Documents on brewing beer from the beginning of the sixteenth century provide accurate information about the development of the systematic cultivation of yeast, which meant that leavened bread soon became more widely available. Rapid increases in population brought about the transition from baking at home to baking in commercial bakeries, so as to guarantee a daily supply of bread. Improved sifting devices, mechanized roller mills for grinding the grain and harvest machines all contributed to making the flour finer still.

In the early nineteenth century, German chemist Justus Liebig made the groundbreaking discovery that potassium salt added to soda loosened the batter in a similar way to yeast. This discovery led to the use of baking powder in baking, still an essential ingredient today. It ensures that a mixture rises well, giving a light and fluffy result. This advance led, inevitably, to the baking of cakes on an industrial scale, adding sweetness and luxury to the lives of generations.

The road from the first dough mixture to the bread and elaborate cakes of today was a long and tortuous one. It is no wonder that a food whose production was associated with so much effort has always been held sacred. Grain and bread are often mentioned in the Bible; it shows how people's concern for their 'daily bread' dominated their thoughts. Each crop failure was a threat to their very existence. This explains the line in the 'The Lord's Prayer': 'Give us this day our daily bread'. Bread was, quite simply, a necessity of life. Marriages were often concluded with a symbolic handing over of bread, with the groom giving some bread to the bride at the altar to show his willingness to feed the family in the future. In some cultures a wheat sheaf replaces the bridal bouquet, symbolizing the desire for close ties – an entire life as close and united as the grains in the ear and in the bread. Even today, the beautiful Russian blessing for newlyweds or new homeowners: 'May bread and salt never be missing from your home', is still alive. 'Good luck' bread has a coin baked into it and is given at a christening or to those moving into a new home. Plaited bread is still used to decorate wedding tables, and dough is plaited into wreaths for the harvest festival.

1.

4.

4.

# Black Bottom
## PECAN PIE

SERVES 6–8

PREP TIME: 40 minutes,
plus 1 hour to chill

COOKING TIME: 30 minutes

Pecan nuts are a favourite because of their subtle, nutty-sweet taste and their similarity to the European walnut. Pecan trees grow mainly in the southern United States and are even the official state tree of Texas. The nuts are extremely nutritious and are an excellent source of Vitamin E. In this recipe, pecan nuts and chocolate are brought together to make a delicious sweet pie.

1. To make the pastry, put the flour, salt and sugar into a bowl and mix to combine. Add the butter and mix in with your fingertips or an electric whisk until the mixture resembles coarse bread crumbs. Carefully add the water, 1 teaspoon at a time, until the mixture just begins to crumble. Add more water if necessary to achieve the right consistency.

2. Turn out the pastry on to a lightly floured work surface and knead until pliable. Shape it into a round, sprinkle over a little flour, wrap in clingfilm and chill in the refrigerator for at least 1 hour.

3. Preheat the oven to 180°C/350°F/Gas Mark 4. Grease a 23 cm/9 inch round, fluted tart tin. Remove the pastry from the refrigerator and leave to warm up to room temperature. Roll out the pastry on a lightly floured work surface and ease it into the prepared tin.

4. To make the filling, put the chocolate chips and cocoa powder into a bowl set over a saucepan of barely simmering water and stir until melted. Spread the mixture over the base of the unbaked pastry case.

5. Put the eggs, brown sugar and granulated sugar into a medium-sized bowl and beat to combine. Add the golden syrup and melted butter and mix until incorporated. Stir in the nuts, then pour the filling into the pastry case.

6. Bake in the preheated oven for 30 minutes, or until the filling is just set. Remove from the oven and place on a wire rack to cool in the tin. Serve cold.

## INGREDIENTS

### pastry
*300 g/10½ oz plain flour,
plus extra for dusting*
*1 tsp salt*
*1 tsp sugar*
*225 g/8 oz chilled butter, diced,
plus extra for greasing*
*6–8 tbsp iced water,
plus extra if needed*

### filling
*90 g/3¼ oz milk chocolate chips*
*2 tbsp cocoa powder*
*4 eggs*
*60 g/2¼ oz soft light brown sugar*
*60 g/2¼ oz granulated sugar*
*135 ml/4½ fl oz golden syrup*
*55 g/2 oz butter, melted*
*150 g/5½ oz pecan nuts, halved*

# New York

## CHEESECAKE

SERVES 10

PREP TIME: 40 minutes,
plus 2 hours to cool and
overnight to chill

COOKING TIME: 55 minutes

### INGREDIENTS

*100 g/3½ oz butter,
plus extra for greasing*
*150 g/5½ oz digestive biscuits,
finely crushed*
*1 tbsp granulated sugar*
*900 g/2 lb cream cheese*
*250 g/9 oz caster sugar*
*2 tbsp plain flour*
*1 tsp vanilla extract*
*finely grated zest of 1 orange*
*finely grated zest of 1 lemon*
*3 eggs*
*2 egg yolks*
*300 ml/10 fl oz double cream*

The typical New York style cheesecake is rich, with a dense and particularly creamy consistency. This is because cream or soured cream is added to the batter instead of cottage cheese or cream cheese alone. The brave also add a good pinch of salt to the base to balance out the tender, creamy sweetness of the cake.

1. Preheat the oven to 180 °C/350 °F/Gas Mark 4. Melt the butter in a small saucepan. Remove from the heat and stir in the biscuits and sugar. Press the biscuit mixture tightly into the base of a 23-cm/9-inch round springform cake tin. Place in the preheated oven and bake for 10 minutes. Remove from the oven and leave to cool on a wire rack.

2. Increase the oven temperature to 200 °C/400 °F/Gas Mark 6. Use an electric whisk to whisk the cheese until creamy, then gradually add the caster sugar and flour and whisk until smooth. Increase the speed and whisk in the vanilla extract, orange zest and lemon zest, then whisk in the eggs and egg yolks one at a time. Finally, whisk in the cream. Scrape any excess from the sides and paddles of the electric whisk into the mixture. It should be light and fluffy – whisk on a faster setting if you need to.

3. Grease the sides of the cake tin and pour in the filling. Smooth the top, transfer to the oven and bake for 15 minutes, then reduce the temperature to 110 °C/225 °F/Gas Mark ¼ and bake for a further 30 minutes. Turn off the oven and leave the cheesecake in it for 2 hours to cool and set. Chill in the refrigerator overnight before serving.

4. Slide a knife around the edge of the cake, then unclip and release the springform and transfer the cake to a plate to serve.

1.

1.

3.

2.

2.

4.

# Chocolate *Cupcakes*

At first glance, cupcakes look a lot like muffins. But these little cakes, which as written recipe first appeared in 1928, are sweeter and have a softer batter. They are in fact a completely different experience from a muffin. Covered with a cloud of icing, in this case a chocolate buttercream icing, they provide a taste experience that is hard to beat.

1. Preheat the oven to 180°C/350°F/Gas Mark 4. Place 14 paper cases in a bun tin.

2. Sift together the flour, baking powder and cocoa powder into a large bowl. Add the butter, caster sugar and eggs and beat until smooth. Fold in the melted chocolate.

3. Divide the mixture evenly between the paper cases. Bake in the preheated oven for 15–20 minutes, or until risen and firm to the touch. Transfer to a wire rack and leave to cool.

4. To make the icing, put the chocolate into a heatproof bowl. Heat the cream in a saucepan until boiling, then pour it over the chocolate and stir until smooth. Leave to cool for 20 minutes, stirring occasionally, until thickened. Put the butter in a bowl, stir in the icing sugar and whisk until smooth. Whisk in the chocolate mixture. Chill for 15–20 minutes.

5. Spoon the icing into a piping bag fitted with a large star nozzle. Pipe swirls of icing on top of each cupcake. Decorate with chocolate shapes and gold dragées, if using.

MAKES 14

PREP TIME: 25 minutes, plus time to chill

COOKING TIME: 15–20 minutes

## INGREDIENTS

115 g/4 oz self-raising flour
½ tsp baking powder
1½ tbsp cocoa powder
115 g/4 oz butter, softened, or soft margarine
115 g/4 oz caster sugar
2 large eggs, beaten
55 g/2 oz plain chocolate, melted

### icing
150 g/5½ oz plain chocolate, finely chopped
200 ml/7 fl oz double cream
140 g/5 oz unsalted butter, softened
280 g/10 oz icing sugar, sifted
chocolate shapes and gold dragées, to decorate (optional)

# Apple Pie

**SERVES 6**

PREP TIME: 40 minutes,
plus 30 minutes to chill

COOKING TIME: 50 minutes

## INGREDIENTS

### pastry

350 g/12 oz plain flour,
plus extra for dusting

pinch of salt

85 g/3 oz butter or
margarine, diced

85 g/3 oz lard or white
vegetable fat, diced

6 tbsp cold water

beaten egg or milk,
for glazing

### filling

750 g–1 kg/1 lb 10 oz–2 lb 4 oz cooking
apples, peeled, cored and sliced

125 g/4½ oz caster sugar,
plus extra for sprinkling

½–1 tsp ground cinnamon,
mixed spice or ground ginger

'Mom's apple pie' is the phrase much used for decades on the continent of America to symbolize the warmth of the hearth as the centre of family life. Old-fashioned family values with mother caring for her husband and children by providing delicious comfort food homemade from simple and affordable ingredients are still relevant in today's busy times.

1. To make the pastry, sift together the flour and salt into a bowl. Add the butter and lard and rub in with your fingertips until the mixture resembles fine bread crumbs. Add the water and gather the mixture together into a dough. Wrap in clingfilm and chill in the refrigerator for 30 minutes.

2. Preheat the oven to 220 °C/425 °F/Gas Mark 7. Thinly roll out almost two thirds of the pastry on a lightly floured surface and use to line a deep 23-cm/9-inch pie dish.

3. To make the filling, place the apple slices, sugar and spice in a bowl and mix together thoroughly. Pack into the pastry case to come up above the rim. Add 1–2 tablespoons of water if the apples are not very juicy.

4. Roll out the remaining pastry on a lightly floured surface to form a lid. Dampen the edges of the pie rim with water and position the lid, pressing the edges firmly together. Trim and crimp the edges. Use the trimmings to cut out leaves or other shapes to decorate the top of the pie. Dampen and attach. Glaze the top of the pie with beaten egg, make 1–2 slits in the pastry and place the pie dish on a baking tray.

5. Bake in the preheated oven for 20 minutes, then reduce the oven temperature to 180 °C/350 °F/Gas Mark 4 and bake for a further 30 minutes, or until light golden brown. Serve hot or cold, sprinkled with sugar.

1.

3.

4.

# Chocolate Chip

## COOKIES

The chocolate chip cookie is still a newcomer to the baking world. It was only in 1930 that Ruth Graves Wakefield first concocted these little delights in her Toll House Inn in the village of Whitman, Massachusetts. Apparently some small pieces of chocolate accidentally fell into the dough but she baked the cookies anyway, not wanting to waste the dough. It has been the official cookie of the state of Massachusetts since 1997.

1. Preheat the oven to 190 °C/375 °F/Gas Mark 5. Lightly grease 2 baking trays.

2. Place all of the ingredients in a large mixing bowl and beat them until well combined.

3. Place tablespoons of the mixture on the prepared baking trays, spaced well apart to allow for spreading.

4. Bake in the preheated oven for 10–12 minutes, or until golden brown. Transfer to a wire rack and leave to cool.

**MAKES 8**

**PREP TIME: 10 minutes**

**COOKING TIME: 10–12 minutes**

### INGREDIENTS

*unsalted butter, melted, for greasing*
*175 g/6 oz plain flour, sifted*
*1 tsp baking powder*
*125 g/4½ oz margarine, melted*
*85 g/3 oz light muscovado sugar*
*55 g/2 oz caster sugar*
*½ tsp vanilla extract*
*1 egg, beaten*
*125 g/4½ oz plain chocolate chips*

1.

3.

# Doughnuts

## WITH CINNAMON SUGAR

Doughnuts, or donuts, are omnipresent in the United States and Canada. These doughnuts, with the characteristic hole in the middle, are a tasty and easy variation of fritters. It's possible that American-style doughnuts date back to Polish *pączki*, which have been around in Eastern Europe since the Middle Ages.

1. Sift together the flour, sugar and salt into a mixing bowl and stir in the yeast. Stir in the milk, butter, eggs and lemon rind, mixing to a soft, sticky dough.

2. Turn out the dough on to a lightly floured work surface and knead until smooth. Return to the bowl, cover and leave in a warm place for about 1 hour, or until doubled in size.

3. Turn out the dough on to a lightly floured work surface and knead again for 5 minutes until smooth and elastic. Roll out to a thickness of 1 cm/ ½ inch. Stamp out 7.5-cm/3-inch rounds with a cutter, then cut a 2.5-cm/ 1-inch round from the centre of each.

4. Place the rings on a baking tray lined with greaseproof paper, cover and leave to rise in a warm place for about 1 hour until doubled in size.

5. Heat the oil for deep-frying in a deep-fat fryer or deep saucepan to 180–190 °C/350–375 °F, or until a cube of bread browns in 30 seconds. Add the doughnuts in small batches and fry, turning once, for 3–4 minutes until golden brown.

6. Remove the doughnuts with a slotted spoon and drain on absorbent kitchen paper. Toss the doughnuts in the caster sugar and cinnamon mixture until lightly coated. Serve warm.

MAKES 12–14

PREP TIME: 25 minutes, plus 2 hours to rise

COOKING TIME: 15–20 minutes

INGREDIENTS

*500 g/1 lb 2 oz plain flour, plus extra for dusting*
*85 g/3 oz caster sugar*
*½ tsp salt*
*2¼ tsp easy-blend dried yeast*
*175 ml/6 fl oz lukewarm milk*
*70 g/2½ oz unsalted butter, melted*
*2 eggs, beaten*
*finely grated rind of 1 lemon*
*sunflower oil, for deep-frying*

cinnamon coating
*55 g/2 oz caster sugar*
*1 tsp ground cinnamon*

# BLUEBERRY & CRANBERRY
# *Squares*

MAKES 12

PREP TIME: 20 minutes

COOKING TIME: 25–30 minutes

## INGREDIENTS

*175 g/6 oz unsalted butter, softened,
plus extra for greasing*
*175 g/6 oz caster sugar*
*1 tsp vanilla extract*
*3 eggs, beaten*
*175 g/6 oz self-raising flour*
*55 g/2 oz dried cranberries*
*175 g/6 oz blueberries*

### icing

*200 g/7 oz mascarpone cheese,
or full-fat cream cheese*
*100 g/3½ oz icing sugar*

Blueberries are native to the eastern half of North America. They were once cultivated from low-lying plants in the coastal forests of the new continent. The little berries are rich in nutrients and add a powerful, unique aroma to many bakes, especially when mixed with cranberries, a related fruit.

1. Preheat the oven to 180 °C/350 °F/Gas Mark 4. Grease a shallow 18 x 28-cm/ 7 x 11-inch rectangular cake tin and line with greaseproof paper.

2. Put the butter, sugar and vanilla extract into a bowl and cream together until pale and fluffy. Gradually add the eggs, beating well after each addition.

3. Fold in the flour with a metal spoon, then stir in the cranberries and 100 g/3½ oz of the blueberries.

4. Spoon the mixture into the prepared tin and spread evenly over the base. Bake in the preheated oven for 25–30 minutes, or until risen, firm and golden brown. Leave to cool in the tin for 15 minutes, then turn out and transfer to a wire rack to cool completely.

5. To make the icing, whisk together the mascarpone cheese and sugar until smooth, then spread over the cake with a palette knife.

6. Scatter the remaining blueberries over the cake and cut into 12 squares to serve.

# Fudge Blondies

4.

MAKES 9

PREP TIME: 30 minutes

COOKING TIME: 40–45 minutes

## INGREDIENTS

*125 g/4½ oz butter, softened, plus extra for greasing*

*200 g/7 oz soft light brown sugar*

*2 large eggs, beaten*

*1 tsp vanilla extract*

*250 g/9 oz plain flour*

*1 tsp baking powder*

*125 g/4½ oz soft butter fudge, chopped into small pieces*

*75 g/2¾ oz macadamia nuts, roughly chopped*

*icing sugar, for dusting*

Similar to brownies in shape and texture but made with chunks of fudge and macadamia nuts instead of chocolate.

1. Preheat the oven to 180°C/350°F/Gas Mark 4. Grease a shallow 20-cm/8-inch square cake tin and line with baking paper.

2. Put the butter and brown sugar into a large bowl and beat with an electric whisk until pale and creamy. Add the eggs, one at a time, beating after each addition until combined, then add the vanilla extract and stir to mix. Sift together the flour and baking powder into the mixture and beat until combined.

3. Add the fudge and chopped nuts and stir together until combined. Spoon the mixture into the prepared tin and smooth the surface.

4. Bake in the preheated oven for 40–45 minutes, or until risen and golden brown. Leave to cool in the tin, then dust with sifted icing sugar to decorate and cut into squares.

# Pumpkin Pie

SERVES 8

PREP TIME: 25 minutes

COOKING TIME: 1 hour

## INGREDIENTS

*plain flour, for dusting*

*350 g/12 oz ready-made shortcrust pastry*

*400 g/14 oz canned pumpkin purée or fresh butternut squash purée*

*2 eggs, lightly beaten*

*150 g/5½ oz granulated sugar*

*1 tsp ground cinnamon*

*½ tsp ground ginger*

*¼ tsp ground cloves*

*½ tsp salt*

*350 ml/12 fl oz canned evaporated milk*

### eggnog whipped cream

*350 ml/12 fl oz double cream*

*70 g/2½ oz icing sugar*

*1 tbsp brandy, or to taste*

*1 tbsp light or dark rum, or to taste*

*freshly grated nutmeg, to decorate*

Pumpkin pie is a popular dessert, especially at Halloween, Thanksgiving and Christmas. After all, late autumn is the time of the year when pumpkins, which have been grown in North America for thousands of years, are ready for harvest. The recipe, however, most likely travelled to America from Britain around 1800, where this pie has been baked since the 16th century.

1. Preheat the oven to 200 °C/400 °F/Gas Mark 6. Very lightly dust a rolling pin with flour and use to roll out the pastry on a lightly floured work surface into a 30-cm/12-inch round. Line a 23-cm/9-inch deep pie dish with the pastry, trimming the excess. Line the pastry case with baking paper and fill with baking beans.

2. Bake in the preheated oven for 10 minutes. Remove from the oven and take out the paper and beans. Reduce the oven temperature to 180 °C/350 °F/Gas Mark 4.

3. Meanwhile, put the pumpkin purée, eggs, sugar, cinnamon, ginger, cloves and salt into a bowl and whisk together, then whisk in the evaporated milk. Pour the mixture into the pastry case, return to the oven and bake for 40–50 minutes until the filling is set and a skewer inserted in the centre comes out clean. Transfer to a wire rack and set aside to cool completely.

4. While the pie is baking, make the eggnog whipped cream. Put the cream into a bowl and whisk until it has thickened and increased in volume. Just as it starts to stiffen, sift over the icing sugar and continue whisking until it holds stiff peaks. Add the brandy and rum and beat, taking care not to overbeat or the mixture will separate. Cover and chill until required. When ready to serve, grate some nutmeg over the whipped cream. Serve the pie with the cream.

# Devil's Food

## CAKE

SERVES 10

PREP TIME: 40 minutes,
plus time to cool

COOKING TIME: 35–40 minutes

### INGREDIENTS

140 g/5 oz plain chocolate,
broken into pieces

100 ml/3½ fl oz milk

2 tbsp cocoa powder

140 g/5 oz unsalted butter, softened,
plus extra for greasing

140 g/5 oz light muscovado sugar

3 eggs, separated

4 tbsp soured cream or
crème fraîche

200 g/7 oz plain flour

1 tsp bicarbonate of soda

### icing

140 g/5 oz plain chocolate

40 g/1½ oz cocoa powder

4 tbsp soured cream or
crème fraîche

1 tbsp golden syrup

40 g/1½ oz unsalted butter

4 tbsp water

200 g/7 oz icing sugar

This classic American cake has a moist and dark chocolate sponge smothered in a rich and creamy chocolate icing. It is a lovely cake to serve for a birthday celebration as it can be made in advance and slices beautifully!

1. Preheat the oven to 160 °C/325 °F/Gas Mark 3. Grease two 20-cm/8-inch sandwich tins and line with baking paper.

2. Put the chocolate, milk and cocoa powder into a heatproof bowl set over a saucepan of barely simmering water and heat, stirring, until melted and smooth. Remove from the heat.

3. In a large bowl, whisk together the butter and muscovado sugar until pale and creamy. Whisk in the egg yolks, then the soured cream and the melted chocolate mixture. Sift in the flour and bicarbonate of soda, then fold in evenly. In a separate clean bowl, whisk the egg whites until they hold stiff peaks. Lightly fold into the mixture.

4. Divide the mixture between the prepared cake tins, smooth the surfaces and bake in the preheated oven for 35–40 minutes, or until risen and firm to the touch. Leave to cool in the tins for 10 minutes, then turn out on to a wire rack to cool completely.

5. To make the icing, place the chocolate, cocoa powder, soured cream, golden syrup, butter and water in a saucepan and heat gently until melted. Remove from the heat and sift in the icing sugar, stirring until smooth. Cool, stirring occasionally, until the mixture begins to thicken and hold its shape.

6. Split the cakes in half horizontally with a sharp knife to make four layers. Sandwich the cakes together with about a third of the frosting. Spread the remainder over the top and sides of the cakes, swirling with a palette knife.

2.

3.

5.

# Snickerdoodles

MAKES 40

PREP TIME: 15 minutes,
plus 1 hour to chill

COOKING TIME: 12 minutes

### INGREDIENTS

225 g/8 oz butter, softened
140 g/5 oz caster sugar
2 large eggs, lightly beaten
1 tsp vanilla extract
400 g/14 oz plain flour
1 tsp bicarbonate of soda
½ tsp freshly grated nutmeg
pinch of salt
55 g/2 oz pecan nuts, finely chopped

### cinnamon coating
1 tbsp caster sugar
2 tbsp ground cinnamon

A snickerdoodle is a biscuit with a cracked surface flavoured with cinnamon. It probably originated with the European immigrants to New England who loved giving fanciful names to their recipes. It might also be a corruption of the German *Schneckennudeln*, a larger cinnamon-flavoured baked item, usually made with a yeast dough.

1. Put the butter and sugar into a bowl and mix well with a wooden spoon, then beat in the eggs and vanilla extract. Sift together the flour, bicarbonate of soda, nutmeg and a pinch of salt into the mixture, add the pecan nuts and stir until thoroughly combined. Shape the dough into a ball, wrap in clingfilm and chill in the refrigerator for 30–60 minutes.

2. Preheat the oven to 190 °C/375 °F/Gas Mark 5. Line 2–3 baking trays with greaseproof paper.

3. For the cinnamon coating, mix together the caster sugar and cinnamon in a shallow dish. Scoop up tablespoons of the cookie dough and roll into balls. Roll each ball in the cinnamon mixture to coat and place on the prepared baking trays, spaced well apart to allow for spreading.

4. Bake in the preheated oven for 10–12 minutes, until golden brown. Leave to cool on the baking trays for 5–10 minutes, then use a palette knife to carefully transfer the cookies to wire racks and leave to cool completely.

1.

3.

# Pumpkin

## WHOOPIE PIES

**2.**

**3.**

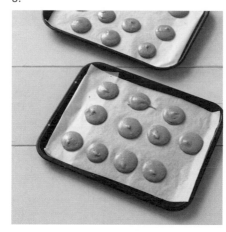

Whoopie pies were born in New England or Pennsylvania and have a sweet creamy filling between two cake halves. Farmers would be given these by their wives as part of their packed lunch – apparently their response was to shout out 'Whoopee!' with joy.

1.  Preheat the oven to 180 °C/350 °F/Gas Mark 4. Line 2–3 large baking trays with greaseproof paper. Sift together the flour, baking powder, bicarbonate of soda, cinnamon and salt.

2.  Put the sugar and oil into a large bowl and whisk with an electric whisk for 1 minute. Add the egg and vanilla extract and beat until incorporated, then beat in the pumpkin purée. Stir in the sifted flour mixture and whisk until thoroughly incorporated.

3.  Pipe or spoon 24 mounds of the mixture on to the prepared baking trays, spaced well apart to allow for spreading. Bake, one tray at a time, in the preheated oven for 8–10 minutes until risen and just firm to the touch. Leave to cool on the trays for 5 minutes, then use a palette knife to transfer the cakes to a wire rack and leave to cool completely.

4.  To make the cinnamon and maple filling, put the soft cheese and butter into a bowl and beat together until well blended. Beat in the maple syrup, cinnamon and icing sugar until smooth.

5.  To assemble, spread or pipe the filling over the flat side of half the cakes. Top with the remaining cakes.

MAKES 12

PREP TIME: 30 minutes

COOKING TIME: 10 minutes

### INGREDIENTS

*275 g/9¾ oz plain flour*
*½ tsp baking powder*
*½ tsp bicarbonate of soda*
*1½ tsp ground cinnamon*
*¼ tsp salt*
*200 g/7 oz soft light brown sugar*
*125 ml/4 fl oz sunflower oil*
*1 large egg, beaten*
*1 tsp vanilla extract*
*115 g/4 oz canned pumpkin purée or fresh butternut squash purée*

### cinnamon & maple filling
*200 g/7 oz full fat soft cheese*
*85 g/3 oz unsalted butter, softened*
*2 tbsp maple syrup*
*1 tsp ground cinnamon*
*85 g/3 oz icing sugar, sifted*

1.

2.

3.

# Key Lime Pie

This pie, going back more than a century, is named after the limes that grow on the Florida Keys. The plant is thornier and its fruit doesn't last as long as the standard lime, but it is a popular ingredient because of its pronounced sour-bitter taste. The Key Lime Pie has been the official pie of the State of Florida since 2006.

1. Preheat the oven to 160°C/325°F/Gas Mark 3. Lightly grease a 23-cm/ 9-inch tart tin, about 4 cm/1½ inches deep. To make the crumb base, put the biscuits, sugar and cinnamon into a food processor and pulse until reduced to fine crumbs – do not overprocess to a powder. Add the melted butter and process until combined.

2. Tip the crumb mixture into the prepared tart tin and press over the base and up the sides. Place the tin on a baking tray and bake in the preheated oven for 5 minutes. Meanwhile, to make the filling, whisk the condensed milk, lime juice, lime rind and egg yolks together in a bowl until well blended.

3. Remove the tart tin from the oven, pour the filling into the crumb base and spread out to the edges. Return to the oven for a further 15 minutes, or until the filling is set around the edges but still wobbly in the centre. Leave to cool completely on a wire rack, then cover and chill for at least 2 hours. Spread with whipped cream and serve.

SERVES 8

PREP TIME: 30 minutes, plus 2 hours to chill

COOKING TIME: 20 minutes

## INGREDIENTS

### crumb base
*175 g/6 oz digestive biscuits or ginger biscuits*

*2 tbsp caster sugar*

*½ tsp ground cinnamon*

*70 g/2½ oz butter, melted, plus extra for greasing*

### filling
*400 ml/14 fl oz canned condensed milk*

*125 ml/4 fl oz freshly squeezed lime juice*

*finely grated rind of 3 limes*

*4 egg yolks*

*whipped cream, to serve*

# Red Velvet

## CAKE

SERVES 12

PREP TIME: 20 minutes

COOKING TIME: 25–30 minutes

### INGREDIENTS

225 g/8 oz unsalted butter,
plus extra for greasing
4 tbsp water
55 g/2 oz cocoa powder
3 eggs, beaten
250 ml/9 fl oz buttermilk
2 tsp vanilla extract
2 tbsp red food colouring
280 g/10 oz plain flour
55 g/2 oz cornflour
1½ tsp baking powder
280 g/10 oz caster sugar

#### icing
250 g/9 oz cream cheese
40 g/1½ oz unsalted butter
3 tbsp icing sugar
1 tsp vanilla extract

The classic reddish-brown colour of this cake comes from the chemical reaction of the anthocyanins found in the cocoa with an acid (for example, buttermilk). To add to the effect, red food colouring is often added to the recipe in North America.

1. Preheat the oven to 190 °C/375 °F/Gas Mark 5. Grease two 23-cm/9-inch sandwich tins and line with baking paper.

2. Place the butter, water and cocoa powder in a small saucepan and heat gently, without boiling, stirring until melted and smooth. Remove from the heat and leave to cool slightly.

3. Whisk together the eggs, buttermilk, vanilla extract and food colouring in a bowl until frothy. Whisk in the butter mixture. Sift together the flour, cornflour and baking powder, then stir quickly and evenly into the mixture with the caster sugar.

4. Divide the mixture between the prepared tins and bake in the preheated oven for 25–30 minutes, or until risen and firm to the touch. Leave to cool in the tins for 3–4 minutes, then turn out on to a wire rack to cool completely.

5. To make the icing, whisk together all the ingredients until smooth. Use about half of the icing to sandwich the cakes together, then spread the remainder over the top, swirling with a palette knife.

2.

3.

4.

# Banana

## BREAD

SERVES 6

PREP TIME: 20 minutes

COOKING TIME: 45 minutes

### INGREDIENTS

225 g/8 oz vegetable fat,
plus extra for greasing
90 g/3¼ oz sugar
150 g/5½ oz plain flour
3 tsp baking powder
1 tsp bicarbonate of soda
1 tsp salt
2 tbsp water
2 eggs
3 ripe bananas, mashed

Banana bread has been a classic in North American cookbooks since the 1930s, when baking powder and bicarbonate of soda became popular raising agents. This quick-to-prepare bread uses fully ripe bananas – the riper the better. The result is moist, sweet, banana deliciousness!

1. Preheat the oven to 160 °C/325 °F/Gas Mark 3. Grease a 450-g/1-lb loaf tin. Put the vegetable fat and sugar into a large bowl and beat together well, then add the flour, baking powder, bicarbonate of soda and salt and mix to combine. Add the water and eggs and beat until light and fluffy.

2. Add the bananas and mix to combine. Spread the mixture in the prepared tin. Use a spatula dipped in a little oil to score an impression along the centre of the loaf.

3. Bake in the preheated oven for 45 minutes until a skewer inserted into the centre comes out clean. Remove from the oven and leave to cool in the tin for 10 minutes, then turn out on to a wire rack and leave to cool completely. Cut into slices and serve.

1.

2.

2.

# Cup

OF HOPE AND

Joy

The cupcake is a traditional American bake that has recently become a phenomenon all over the world. From cupcake cafés to cupcake decorating parties, cupcakes are now everywhere but their spiritual home is the USA.

*Cupcakes makes the world go round! This idea was supported by TV series like 'Sex and the City' and, ever since, the whole world has been talking about cupcakes.*

The well-known theory that chocolate contains substances that make you happy can serve as an excuse to indulge now and again. Probably the same can be said about a treat that has come very much into vogue during the last few years: the cupcake. A small, sweet snack for premeditated bursts of happiness. Cupcakes are colourful, pretty little cakes with sweet decorations and an almost irresistible creamy icing. But contrary to what you would think, they are not a new invention. The first formal reference to them can be found as early as 1928 in Eliza Leslie's American cookbook *Receipts*, though with a quite puritanical formulation: 'The cupcake, as the name already reveals, is fabricated in a cup-like baking pan'. If we left it at that, they would admittedly be just too similar to muffins. But, to begin with, their taste is different. first, their dough is softer and secondly, they are crowned with an opulent and sweet, buttery cream topping decorated with fruit, sugar pearls or sugar flowers. Cupcakes were popular in England and were first known as 'fairy cakes'. The cupcake-euphoria that swept over Europe from the United States at the beginning of the new century has since made cupcakes a popular anytime treat across the capitals of Europe.

The fact is, that these little cakes have by now even found their way into the general vocabulary and that the term 'cupcakes' has become one of the most popular terms of endearment in the United States. Surely the enthusiasm for the television series 'Sex and the City', the first season of which was broadcast in the United States, Britain and Australia in 1997, is partly responsible for this. In an episode in the series, the single Carrie Bradshaw and her friends buy cupcakes from the Magnolia Bakery. Ever since, the whole world has been talking about cupcakes, because they – like any other fashionable accessory – symbolize a little piece of everyday luxury. And the best part is: everyone can afford this luxury, because one can reward oneself without a bad conscience. In other words, personal happiness is within everyone's reach – but especially if it is edible. Cupcakes make the world a happier place.

# Peanut Butter
## S'MORES

SERVES 4

PREP TIME: 5 minutes

COOKING TIME: 1 minute

### INGREDIENTS

*115 g/4 oz smooth peanut butter*
*8 graham crackers or digestive biscuits*
*85 g/3 oz plain chocolate,*
*broken into squares*

Peanut butter, that all-time American favourite, is also an important part of many bakes. In 1884, Canadian Marcellus G. Edson filed a patent for the nutritious, tasty product, but the recipe for peanut butter is mostly attributed to cereal magnate John Harvey Kellogg (1895).

1. Preheat the grill to medium. Spread the peanut butter on one side of each cracker. Place the chocolate pieces on 4 of the crackers and invert the remaining crackers on top.

2. Toast the s'mores under the preheated grill for about 1 minute until the filling starts to melt. Turn carefully. Serve.

# Classic

## VANILLA CUPCAKES

This recipe was once a must-have for American children's parties. Vanilla is the traditional flavour used for these little cakes, which are lighter and sweeter in taste than the muffins they resemble. Plus, they're always topped with icing. Cupcakes were named after the cups in which they were originally baked, although today standard bun tins can be used instead.

1. Preheat the oven to 180°C/350°F/Gas Mark 4. Place 12 paper cases in a bun tin.

2. Put the butter and caster sugar into a bowl and whisk together until pale and creamy. Gradually whisk in the eggs and vanilla extract. Sift in the flour and fold in gently.

3. Divide the mixture evenly between the paper cases and bake in the preheated oven for 15–20 minutes, or until risen and firm to the touch. Transfer to a wire rack and leave to cool.

4. To make the icing, put the butter into a bowl and whisk with an electric whisk for 2–3 minutes, or until pale and creamy. Whisk in the cream and vanilla extract. Gradually whisk in the icing sugar and continue whisking until the buttercream is light and fluffy.

5. Use a palette knife to swirl the icing over the tops of the cupcakes. Decorate with the hundreds and thousands.

MAKES 12

PREP TIME: 25 minutes

COOKING TIME: 15–20 minutes

### INGREDIENTS

175 g/6 oz unsalted butter, softened
175 g/6 oz caster sugar
3 large eggs, beaten
1 tsp vanilla extract
175 g/6 oz self-raising flour

icing
150 g/5½ oz unsalted butter, softened
3 tbsp double cream or milk
1 tsp vanilla extract
300 g/10½ oz icing sugar, sifted
hundreds and thousands, to decorate

2.

5.

3.

4.

5.

# Boston CREAM PIE

SERVES 10

PREP TIME: 40 minutes,
plus time to cool

COOKING TIME: 20–25 minutes

This has been the official cake of the State of Massachusetts since 1996. It was supposedly invented by the French chef at the Parker House Hotel in Boston when it opened in 1856. He replaced the heavy filling between two layers of cake with a light vanilla pastry cream and topped it all with a rich chocolate glaze.

1. Preheat the oven to 180 °C/350 °F/Gas Mark 4. Grease two 23-cm/9-inch sandwich tins and line with baking paper.

2. Place the eggs and sugar in a heatproof bowl set over a saucepan of simmering water. Whisk with a balloon whisk until the mixture is thick and pale and leaves a trail when the whisk is lifted.

3. Sift in the flour and fold in gently. Pour the butter over the mixture in a thin stream and fold in until just incorporated. Divide the mixture between the prepared tins and bake in the preheated oven for 20–25 minutes, or until light golden and springy to the touch. Leave to cool in the tins for 5 minutes, then turn out on to a wire rack to cool completely.

4. To make the pastry cream, whisk together the eggs, sugar and vanilla extract. Blend the flour and cornflour to a paste with 4 tablespoons of the milk, then whisk into the egg mixture. Heat the remaining milk until almost boiling and pour on to the egg mixture, stirring constantly. Return to the saucepan and cook over a low heat, whisking constantly, until smooth and thickened. Pour into a bowl and cover with damp greaseproof paper. Leave until cold, then fold in the whipped cream.

5. To make the glaze, put the chocolate, golden syrup and butter into a heatproof bowl. Heat the cream until almost boiling, then pour it over the chocolate. Leave for 1 minute, then stir until smooth.

6. To assemble, sandwich the sponges together with the pastry cream. Spread the chocolate glaze over the top of the cake.

## INGREDIENTS

*4 large eggs, beaten*
*115 g/4 oz caster sugar*
*115 g/4 oz plain flour*
*40 g/1½ oz butter, melted and cooled, plus extra for greasing*

### pastry cream
*2 eggs*
*55 g/2 oz caster sugar*
*1 tsp vanilla extract*
*2 tbsp plain flour*
*2 tbsp cornflour*
*300 ml/10 fl oz milk*
*150 ml/5 fl oz double cream, softly whipped*

### chocolate glaze
*115 g/4 oz plain chocolate, grated*
*1 tbsp golden syrup*
*25 g/1 oz unsalted butter*
*150 ml/5 fl oz double cream*

# Berry Muffins

MAKES 12

PREP TIME: 20 minutes

COOKING TIME: 20–25 minutes

## INGREDIENTS

*225 g/8 oz plain flour*
*2 tsp baking powder*
*55 g/2 oz ground almonds*
*125 g/4½ oz caster sugar,*
*plus extra for sprinkling*
*150 g/5½ oz butter, melted*
*100 ml/3½ fl oz milk*
*2 eggs, beaten*
*250 g/9 oz mixed berries, such as*
*blueberries, raspberries,*
*blackberries and redcurrants*

The American muffin is the result of the invention of baking powder in 1856 by Harvard professor Eben Norton Horsford, one of the founders of modern nutritional science. With berries added to the batter, this muffin bursts with the warmth and freshness of summer.

1. Preheat the oven to 190 °C/375 °F/Gas Mark 5. Place 12 paper cases in a bun tin.

2. Sift together the flour and baking powder into a large bowl and stir in the ground almonds and sugar. Make a well in the centre of the dry ingredients.

3. Whisk together the butter, milk and eggs and pour into the well. Stir gently until just combined; do not over-mix. Gently fold in the berries.

4. Divide the mixture evenly between the paper cases. Bake in the preheated oven for 20–25 minutes, or until light golden and just firm to the touch. Serve warm or cold, sprinkled with sugar.

2.

3.

4.

# Black & White
## BISCUITS

MAKES 20

PREP TIME: 20 minutes

COOKING TIME: 15 minutes

### INGREDIENTS

*115 g/4 oz unsalted butter,
softened, plus extra for greasing*
*1 tsp vanilla extract*
*175 g/6 oz caster sugar*
*2 eggs, beaten*
*300 g/10½ oz plain flour*
*½ tsp baking powder*
*200 ml/7 fl oz milk*

### icing
*225 g/8 oz icing sugar*
*125 ml/4 fl oz double cream*
*⅛ tsp vanilla extract*
*75 g/2¾ oz plain chocolate,
broken into pieces*

These biscuits originated in New York State, where they are also known as half moons. They come in different taste variations, but what sets them apart is their black-and-white icing. Only one question remains: which side do I bite first? Or should I just bite them both at the same time?

1. Preheat the oven to 190 °C/375 °F/Gas Mark 5. Grease 3 baking trays. Put the butter, vanilla extract and caster sugar into a large bowl. Beat with an electric whisk until light and fluffy, then add the eggs, one at a time, beating after each addition until combined.

2. Sift together the flour and baking powder and fold into the creamed mixture, loosening with milk as you go until both are used up and the mix is of dropping consistency. Drop heaped tablespoons of the mixture on the prepared baking trays, spaced well apart to allow for spreading. Bake in the preheated oven for 15 minutes, or until turning golden at the edges and light to the touch. Transfer to wire racks to cool completely.

3. To make the icing, put the icing sugar into a bowl and mix in half the cream and the vanilla extract. The consistency should be thick but spreadable. Using a palette knife, spread half of each biscuit with white icing. Put the chocolate into a heatproof bowl set over a saucepan of barely simmering water and heat until melted. Remove from the heat and stir in the remaining cream. Spread the dark icing over the uncoated biscuit halves.

1.

2.

3.

# MISSISSIPPI
# Mud Pie

This dish was created by home bakers in Mississippi and was only published for the first time in the 1970s. The pie is made using ingredients that are close to hand, and leftover biscuits are often used in the recipe for the base. This sticky chocolate pie is good with vanilla ice cream.

1. Preheat the oven to 200 °C/400 °F/Gas Mark 6. To make the pastry, sift the flour and cocoa powder into a bowl and stir in the sugar. Rub in the butter with your fingertips until the mixture resembles fine bread crumbs. Add just enough water to bind to a dough.

2. Roll out the dough on a lightly floured work surface to a round large enough to line a 3-cm/1¼-inch deep, 20-cm/8-inch round tart tin. Use the pastry to line the tin. Prick the base with a fork, cover with a piece of greaseproof paper and fill with baking beans, then bake in the preheated oven for 10 minutes. Remove from the oven and take out the greaseproof paper and beans. Reduce the oven temperature to 180 °C/350 °F/Gas Mark 4.

3. Put the chocolate and butter into a saucepan and heat over a low heat, stirring, until melted. Put the sugar and eggs into a bowl and whisk together until smooth, then stir in the chocolate mixture, cream and vanilla extract.

4. Pour the chocolate mixture into the pastry case and bake in the oven for 20–25 minutes or until just set. Leave to cool.

5. To make the topping, whip the cream until it just holds its shape, then spread over the pie. Put the chocolate into a bowl set over a saucepan of barely simmering water and heat until melted, then spoon into a piping bag and pipe decorations over the cream. Serve cold.

SERVES 6–8

PREP TIME: 30 minutes, plus time to cool

COOKING TIME: 35–40 minutes

## INGREDIENTS

*85 g/3 oz plain chocolate*
*85 g/3 oz unsalted butter*
*85 g/3 oz light muscovado sugar*
*2 eggs, beaten*
*100 ml/3½ fl oz single cream*
*1 tsp vanilla extract*

### pastry
*175 g/6 oz plain flour,*
*plus extra for dusting*
*25 g/1 oz cocoa powder*
*40 g/1½ oz light muscovado sugar*
*85 g/3 oz unsalted butter*
*2–3 tbsp cold water*

### topping
*250 ml/9 fl oz whipping cream*
*85 g/3 oz plain chocolate*

# Chocolate Chip
## MUFFINS

MAKES 12

PREP TIME: 20 minutes

COOKING TIME: 20–25 minutes

### INGREDIENTS

*300 g/10½ oz plain flour*
*5 tsp baking powder*
*75 g/2¾ oz chilled butter, diced*
*100 g/3½ oz caster sugar*
*175 g/6 oz milk chocolate, chopped into chunks*
*2 large eggs, beaten*
*225 ml/8 fl oz buttermilk*
*1 tsp vanilla extract*

American muffins have a standard shape and batter, and they have to be made following a special 'muffin method'. The dry and wet ingredients are mixed separately and then stirred together very briefly. If mixed for too long, too much gluten will be activated and the batter will become heavy. Muffins with chocolate chips are a classic.

1. Preheat the oven to 200 °C/400 °F/Gas Mark 6. Put 12 muffin cases into a 12-hole bun tin.

2. Sift together the flour and baking powder into a large bowl. Add the butter and rub in to make breadcrumbs. Stir in the sugar and the chocolate chunks.

3. Beat together the eggs, buttermilk and vanilla extract in a separate bowl. Make a well in the centre of the dry ingredients and pour in the beaten liquid ingredients. Gently stir until just combined. Do not over-mix.

4. Divide the mixture evenly between the paper cases. Bake in the preheated oven for 20–25 minutes, or until risen, golden and just firm to the touch. Leave to cool in the tin for 5 minutes, then transfer to a wire rack to cool completely.

2.

2.

4.

2.

3.

3.

# Maple & Pecan
## BUNDT CAKE

SERVES 10

PREP TIME: 30 minutes,
plus time to cool

COOKING TIME: 45–50 minutes

The Bundt cake tin is a ribbed cake tin with a hole in the middle (like the German Gugelhupf). It became popular in 1950s North America after kitchen appliance manufacturers Dalquist used it as part of their logo. This recipe with maple syrup and pecan nuts gives this all-American cake shape an all-American taste. And, of course, it simply must have icing on top.

1. Preheat the oven to 160 °C/325 °F/Gas Mark 3. Grease a 2-litre/3½–pint Bundt tin and lightly dust with flour.

2. Put the butter and brown sugar into a bowl and whisk together until pale and fluffy. Gradually whisk in the eggs, then stir in the nuts, maple syrup and soured cream. Sift in the flour and fold in thoroughly.

3. Spoon the mixture into the prepared tin and gently smooth the surface. Bake in the preheated oven for 45–50 minutes, or until the cake is firm and golden and a skewer inserted into the centre comes out clean. Leave to cool in the tin for 10 minutes, then turn out on to a wire rack to cool completely.

4. To make the icing, mix together the icing sugar, maple syrup and enough water to make a smooth icing. Spoon the icing over the top of the cake, allowing it to run down the sides. Decorate with the chopped nuts and leave to set.

## INGREDIENTS

200 g/7 oz butter, softened, plus extra for greasing

200 g/7 oz soft light brown sugar

3 large eggs, beaten

55 g/2 oz pecan nuts, very finely chopped, plus extra, roughly chopped, to decorate

4 tbsp maple syrup

150 ml/5 fl oz soured cream

225 g/8 oz self-raising flour, plus extra for dusting

### icing
85 g/3 oz icing sugar, sifted

1 tbsp maple syrup

1–2 tbsp lukewarm water

# CHOCOLATE & CHERRY

# Brownies

MAKES 12

PREP TIME: 30 minutes

COOKING TIME: 45–50 minutes

## INGREDIENTS

*175 g/6 oz plain chocolate,
broken into pieces*

*175 g/6 oz butter, plus extra
for greasing*

*225 g/8 oz caster sugar*

*3 large eggs, beaten*

*1 tsp vanilla extract*

*125 g/4½ oz self-raising flour*

*175 g/6 oz fresh cherries, stoned*

*85 g/3 oz white chocolate,
roughly chopped*

This brownie is rich and sweet with a moist, dense centre. This is because it contains more chocolate than flour. The cherries add a sweet freshness and heighten the typical brownie experience.

1. Preheat the oven to 180 °C/350 °F/Gas Mark 4. Grease a shallow 24 x 20-cm/ 9½ x 8-inch cake tin and line with baking paper.

2. Put the plain chocolate and butter into a large, heatproof bowl set over a saucepan of barely simmering water and heat until melted. Remove from the heat and leave to cool for 5 minutes.

3. Whisk the sugar, eggs and vanilla extract into the chocolate mixture. Sift in the flour and fold in gently. Pour the mixture into the prepared tin. Scatter over the cherries and white chocolate.

4. Bake in the preheated oven for 30 minutes. Loosely cover the tops of the brownies with foil and bake for a further 15–20 minutes, or until just firm to the touch. Leave to cool in the tin, then cut into pieces.

2.

3.

3.

# Canadian
## BUTTER TARTS

MAKES 16

PREP TIME: 30 minutes,
plus 30 minutes to chill

COOKING TIME: 15 minutes

### INGREDIENTS

*1 egg*
*100 g/3½ oz soft light brown sugar*
*2 tsp golden syrup*
*1 tbsp butter*
*1 tsp vanilla extract or 1 vanilla pod,
scraped*
*125 g/4½ oz sultanas*

### pastry

*300 g/10½ oz plain flour,
plus extra for dusting*
*1 tsp salt*
*225 g/8 oz vegetable fat*
*1 egg*
*3 tbsp cold water*

These little tarts are among the few recipes that are uniquely Canadian in origin and are a highlight of the early cuisine of this North American country. In this version, the inside is filled with a rich mixture of golden syrup, brown sugar and sultanas – a true Canadian original.

1. To make the pastry, sift together the flour and salt into a large bowl, then add the vegetable fat and mix until the mixture resembles bread crumbs. Mix together the egg and water in a separate bowl and add to the flour mixture, working it in until smooth. Wrap the pastry in clingfilm and chill in the refrigerator for 30 minutes.

2. Preheat the oven to 200 °C/400 °F/Gas Mark 6. Turn out the pastry on to a lightly floured work surface, roll out and use a 7.5-cm/3-inch cutter to cut out 16 rounds, re-rolling the trimmings if necessary. Press the rounds into 16 tartlet tins and trim the edges.

3. Put the egg, sugar, golden syrup, butter and vanilla extract into a sauce-pan and heat over a medium heat, stirring constantly, until the butter has melted. Divide the sultanas among the tartlet cases. Pour over the filling so that the pastry cases are almost filled. Bake in the preheated oven for 10 minutes until light golden brown. Remove from the oven and serve hot or cold.

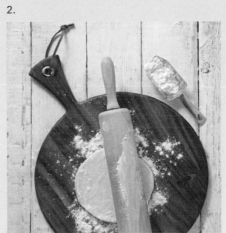

2.

2.

3.

2.

4.

5.

# MINI
# Cherry Pies

The annual cherry harvest coincides with Canada Day (1 July) and the US Independence Day (4 July). These patriotic celebrations at the height of summer are great occasions for these wonderful fruity pies, especially when served with vanilla ice cream or whipped cream. Thanks to the freezer, these dark cherry pies can now be enjoyed year-round.

1. Preheat the oven to 180°C/350°F/Gas Mark 4. Grease two 12-hole bun tins.

2. Put the cherries into a mixing bowl. Stir in the cornflour, jam and lime rind.

3. Thinly roll out half the pastry on a lightly floured work surface. Use a 6-cm/2½-inch fluted cookie cutter to stamp out 24 rounds. Press the rounds gently into the prepared tins, re-rolling the trimmings as needed.

4. Brush the top edges of the pastry cases with a little of the egg yolk and water mixture, then spoon in the filling.

5. Thinly roll out the remaining pastry on a lightly floured work surface. Use a 5-cm/2-inch round cutter to cut out 24 rounds, re-rolling the trimmings as needed. Attach the rounds as lids to the rim of the pies, wet the edges with a little water, then press together to seal. Use a heart-shaped cutter to cut out mini hearts from the pastry and attach them to the lids with a little water. Brush the egg glaze over the pastry and sprinkle with caster sugar.

6. Bake in the preheated oven for 15 minutes, or until golden. Leave to cool in the tins for 10 minutes, then loosen with a round-bladed knife and transfer to a wire rack to cool. Whip the cream until it holds soft peaks, then fold in half the lime rind and the icing sugar. Sprinkle with the remaining lime rind. Serve spoonfuls of the cream with the pies.

MAKES 24

PREP TIME: 25 minutes

COOKING TIME: 15 minutes

## INGREDIENTS

butter, for greasing
350 g/12 oz cherries, roughly chopped
2 tsp cornflour
2 tbsp cherry jam
grated rind of 2 limes
450 g/1 lb ready-made sweet shortcrust pastry, chilled
plain flour, for dusting
1 egg yolk mixed with 1 tbsp water, for glazing
caster sugar, for sprinkling

### to serve
225 ml/8 fl oz double cream
grated rind of 2 limes
2 tbsp icing sugar

# BREAKING
## *bagels*

A bagel is only a good bagel when the hole in the middle is the right size. It has to be round, 5 centimetres (2 inches) high and about two and a half fingers across.

The ingredients? Very simple: Flour, salt, water, yeast and malt. That's it. The whole thing is first boiled and then baked, so that at the end a golden ring comes out, weighing pretty much exactly 125 grams/4½ ounces. Not more, but not much less. And when you bite into it, there should be a slightly crunchy sound. If not, then the bagel is not really a good bagel. As is always the case with legendary recipes, the strangest stories are woven around its origins. In the case of the bagel, scientists and researchers have been trying for years to reconstruct its origins as accurately as possible. Yale University in New Haven, Connecticut, even went as far as to sponsor a Polish author named Maria Balinska in her research. The result was an entire book telling the 'surprising history of a modest bread'. Of course, Jewish bakers had something to do with it and claim to have invented the bagel to celebrate the end of the Turkish siege of

*The bagel's history is long and has plenty of surprising facts. Some of them seem to be an invention, some of them are proven. It is very much influenced by Jewish heritage.*

Vienna. This is doubtless part of the many legends and anecdotes surrounding the history of the bagel. It's now certainly beyond dispute that the bagel has a Jewish background. Linguists have finally concluded that the term comes from the Yiddish word *beigen* (bay-gen), meaning 'to bend'. According to another legend, the Polish baking family Beigel invented the bread for purely practical reasons. This version is based on the Jewish commandment to wash one's hands before eating bread. Since so many Jews were often on the road and the bagel dough was boiled before being baked, the bagel could no longer be considered bread per se, but rather a sort of pasta. This meant that it could be eaten while travelling when clean water was often not available to wash one's hands.

The first time the ring-shaped bread was officially mentioned was in a 1610 regulation from the Jewish community of Krakow, Poland, which prescribed exactly what could and could not be eaten at the celebration of a boy's circumcision ceremony.

With the European emigration wave to the United States, the bagel not only travelled to the new world, but it also took on a life of its own. In the early 1900s, a bakery in Manhattan's Lower East Side with a staff of 300 and a baker's union determined the ingredients to be used for the bagel and how it was supposed to taste. The influence of the bagel bakers of Local 338 can also be measured by the fact that all of the bakeries in New York and the surrounding area in the 1920s meticulously adhered to the specifications for making the 'original New York bagels'. Although the Bagel Bakers Union has since disappeared with the appearance of bagel-baking machines in the 1950s, the making of a real bagel was, and still remains, an unwritten law. The New Yorkers themselves make sure that nothing changes in the good old bagel tradition.

On one occasion, when an attempt was made – for production reasons – to do away with the typical hole in the bread, a great outcry ensued in the press. Such aberrations were not real bagels and not worthy of New Yorkers, the writers declared. In fact, for a long time, the distribution of the bagels was limited to New York with its strong Jewish community. It was only with the emergence of fast-food chains that bagel sandwiches began to spread all over the country. It should be noted that the bagel has nothing to do with its competitor, the doughnut. Although it has a similar shape, doughnuts are made of a completely different type of dough and are deep-fried in fat.

Today, little remains to remind us that the bagel's humble origins were in Europe. In Austria, there is a croissant filled with nuts is still called a beugel. And in Hungary one can find the beigli, a poppy seed stollen, on supermarket shelves for Christmas.

# Sourdough Bread

MAKES 2 LOAVES

PREP TIME: 30 minutes, plus 4–5 days for starter and 2 hours 30 minutes to rise

COOKING TIME: 30 minutes

## INGREDIENTS

*450 g/1 lb wholemeal flour*
*4 tsp salt*
*350 ml/12 fl oz lukewarm water*
*2 tbsp black treacle*
*1 tbsp vegetable oil,*
*plus extra for brushing*
*plain flour, for dusting*

### starter
*85 g/3 oz wholemeal flour*
*85 g/3 oz strong white flour*
*55 g/2 oz caster sugar*
*250 ml/9 fl oz milk*

This was the most important bread for the gold prospectors in California and Canada because the sourdough, which relies on natural yeasts in the air to rise, was easy to make even out in the wilderness. In comparison with standard yeast breads, it has a distinctive, slightly sour taste.

1. For the starter, put the wholemeal flour, strong white flour, sugar and milk into a non-metallic bowl and beat well with a fork. Cover with a damp tea towel and leave to stand at room temperature for 4–5 days, until the mixture is frothy and smells sour.

2. Sift together the flour and half the salt into a bowl and add the water, treacle, oil and starter. Mix well with a wooden spoon until a dough begins to form, then knead with your hands until it leaves the side of the bowl. Turn out on to a lightly floured work surface and knead for 10 minutes, or until smooth and elastic.

3. Brush a bowl with oil. Form the dough into a ball, put it into the bowl and put the bowl into a polythene bag or cover with a damp tea towel. Leave to rise in a warm place for 2 hours, or until the dough has doubled in size.

4. Dust two baking trays with flour. Mix the remaining salt with 4 tablespoons of water in a bowl. Turn out the dough on to a lightly floured work surface and knock back, then knead for a further 10 minutes. Halve the dough, shape each piece into an oval and place the loaves on the prepared baking trays. Brush with the saltwater glaze and leave to stand in a warm place, brushing frequently with the glaze, for 30 minutes.

5. Meanwhile, preheat the oven to 220 °C/425 °F/Gas Mark 7. Brush the loaves with the remaining glaze and bake in the preheated oven for 30 minutes, or until the crust is golden brown and the loaves sound hollow when tapped on the base. If they need longer cooking, reduce the oven temperature to 190 °C/375 °F/Gas Mark 5. Transfer to wire racks to cool.

1.

3.

4.

1.

2.

4.

5.

7.

# Stromboli

## WITH SALAMI, PEPPERS & CHEESE

This bread, which resembles a rolled-up pizza, is named after the volcano in Sicily. The dough and the ingredients are typically Italian, which makes sense, given that Italian immigrants to the United States invented the recipe in the 1950s.

1. Mix together the flour, yeast and 1½ teaspoons of the salt, then stir in the oil with enough water to make a soft dough.

2. Knead the dough on a lightly floured work surface for about 10 minutes. Cover and leave in a warm place for 1 hour, or until doubled in volume.

3. Lightly knead for 2  3 minutes until smooth. Cover and leave for a further 10 minutes.

4. Roll out the dough to a 38 x 25-cm/15 x 10-inch rectangle with a thickness of 1 cm/½ inch.

5. Preheat the oven to 200 °C/400 °F/Gas Mark 6. Spread the salami over the dough and top with the mozzarella cheese, basil and peppers. Season to taste with pepper.

6. Grease a baking tray. Firmly roll up the dough from the long side, pinch the ends and place on the baking tray, join underneath. Cover and leave to stand for 10 minutes.

7. Pierce the roll deeply with a skewer several times.

8. Brush with oil and sprinkle with the remaining salt. Bake in the preheated oven for 30–35 minutes, or until firm and golden. Transfer to a wire rack and leave to cool. Serve the bread fresh and warm, cut into thick slices.

MAKES 1 LOAF

PREP TIME: 20–25 minutes, plus 1 hour 10 minutes to rise

COOKING TIME: 30–35 minutes

### INGREDIENTS

*500 g/1 lb 2 oz strong white flour, sifted, plus extra for dusting*
*2¼ tsp easy-blend dried yeast*
*2 tsp sea salt flakes*
*3 tbsp olive oil, plus extra for brushing*
*350 ml/12 fl oz lukewarm water*

### filling
*85 g/3 oz thinly sliced Italian salami*
*175 g/6 oz mozzarella cheese, chopped*
*25 g/1 oz basil leaves*
*2 red peppers, roasted, peeled, deseeded and sliced (or ready-roasted peppers from a jar)*
*pepper*

2.

3.

4.

5.

5.

# Bagels

MAKES 12

PREP TIME: 60 minutes,
plus 2 hours 20 minutes to rise

COOKING TIME: 25 minutes

A bagel is the only bread in the world that combines fire and water as it is cooked in boiling water before being baked. Bagels were supposedly invented during the Turkish siege of Vienna in 1683. A Jewish baker wanted to please the horse-mad king and made a bread that looked like a bügel, the original German word for 'stirrup'.

## INGREDIENTS

525 g/1 lb 4 oz strong white flour, plus extra if needed and for dusting

1½ tsp salt

3 tbsp sugar

2¼ tsp easy-blend dried yeast

225 ml/8 fl oz lukewarm water, plus extra if needed

3 tbsp malt extract

1 egg, beaten

25 g/1 oz butter, melted

1 egg white, beaten

poppy seeds, sesame seeds and sunflower seeds, for sprinkling

butter and jam, to serve

1.  Dust a baking tray with flour. Put the flour, salt, sugar and yeast into a large bowl. Mix together with your hands and make a well in the centre.

2.  Put the water into a bowl with 2 teaspoons of the malt extract, the egg and butter, and stir to combine. Pour into the well and mix into the flour with your hands. The dough should be soft but sticky. If it is too dry, add a little more water. If it is too wet, work in a little more flour. Cover the bowl with a damp tea towel and leave to rise for about 10 minutes.

3.  Turn out the dough on to a lightly floured work surface and knead for 10 minutes until very smooth. Return to the bowl and leave to stand at room temperature for 1–2 hours, until doubled in size. Turn out the dough on to a floured work surface, divide it into 12 pieces and roll each piece into a ball. Cover with a dry tea towel and leave to stand for 10 minutes.

4.  Lightly press the balls to flatten them, then use a floured finger to make a hole through the centre of each ball. Gently rotate the bagel on your finger until the hole is 2.5 cm/1 inch in diameter.

5.  Preheat the oven to 200 °C/400 °F/Gas Mark 6. Bring a large saucepan of water to the boil and stir in the remaining malt extract. Carefully drop the bagels into the boiling water and poach for 30 seconds on each side. Use a slotted spoon to lift them out of the water, shaking off any excess, then arrange them on the prepared tray. Lightly brush them with egg white, sprinkle over the seeds and bake in the preheated oven for 20–25 minutes until golden brown. Remove from the oven and transfer to a wire rack to cool. Serve with butter and jam.

# Courgette Bread

**SERVES 6**

**PREP TIME:** 20 minutes

**COOKING TIME:** 40–50 minutes

## INGREDIENTS

*butter, for greasing*
*240 g/8½ oz plain flour*
*135 g/4¾ oz caster sugar*
*1¼ tsp bicarbonate of soda*
*1 tsp salt*
*½ tsp ground cinnamon*
*1 egg*
*6 tbsp vegetable oil,*
*plus extra for greasing*
*1 tsp vanilla extract or 1 vanilla pod,*
*scraped*
*½ tsp ground nutmeg*
*125 ml/4 fl oz buttermilk*
*145 g/5¼ oz courgettes, grated*
*45 g/1½ oz walnuts, finely chopped*

This bread is a cake in disguise: like carrots, courgettes can be used to make not overly sweet bakes, especially in the summer when the vegetable grows in abundance. The bread is extremely soft and very moist, and it freezes well.

1. Preheat the oven to 160 °C/325 °F/Gas Mark 3. Grease a 900-g/2-lb loaf tin. Sift together the flour, sugar, bicarbonate of soda, salt and cinnamon into a large bowl. Put the egg, oil, vanilla extract and nutmeg into a separate large bowl and mix to combine. Add the sifted ingredients and the buttermilk and mix well.

2. Gently stir in the courgettes and walnuts. Do not over-mix.

3. Pour the batter into the prepared tin and bake in the preheated oven for 40–50 minutes, or until a skewer inserted into the centre of the bread comes out clean.

4. Leave to cool in the tin for 20 minutes, then turn out on to a wire rack and leave to cool completely.

1.

2.

3.

1.

2.

4.

5.

5.

# Spring Onion & Parmesan
## CORNBREAD

Cornbread dates back to Native American recipes and is a traditional basic foodstuff in the rural United States, especially in the South, because corn is cheaper than wheat. Formerly baked in a cast-iron frying pan over an open fire, the bread is typically baked in a tin in the oven. This bread is made with spring onions and Parmesan cheese and is a hearty accompaniment to other dishes.

1. Preheat the oven to 190 °C/375 °F/Gas Mark 5. Grease a 23-cm/9-inch square cake tin.

2. Sift together the cornmeal, flour, baking powder, celery salt and pepper into a bowl and stir in 40 g/1½ oz of the cheese.

3. Beat together the eggs, milk and butter.

4. Add the egg mixture to the dry ingredients and stir well to mix evenly.

5. Stir in the spring onions, then spread the mixture evenly in the prepared tin.

6. Sprinkle the remaining cheese over the mixture. Bake in the preheated oven for 30–35 minutes or until firm and golden.

7. Cut the cornbread into 16 squares and serve warm.

SERVES 16

PREP TIME: 15 minutes

COOKING TIME: 30–35 minutes

## INGREDIENTS

*oil, for greasing*
*140 g/5 oz fine cornmeal or polenta*
*140 g/5 oz plain flour*
*4 tsp baking powder*
*2 tsp celery salt*
*55 g/2 oz freshly grated Parmesan cheese*
*2 eggs, beaten*
*400 ml/14 fl oz milk*
*55 g/2 oz butter, melted*
*1 bunch spring onions, chopped*
*pepper*

# THE LATIN FLAVOUR

From the historic sights of Machu Picchu to the Carnival in Rio, South America offers a wide range of attractions as diverse as its food culture. The culinary selection ranges from filled burritos, Argentine steaks and beans to sweet biscuits and fruity cakes. The influence of European colonial rulers can often be detected in the way these bakes are made, but they are still characterized by different eating habits and a huge variety of exotic ingredients. Maize is one of the staple foods of South America, and cornflour is often used for pastries and cakes. So, in Colombia, the traditional stone-baked arepas are served for breakfast, and in the afternoons people have coffee with the traditional mantecada pound cake made from corn flour. A speciality is dulce de leche, a confection that was said to have healing properties by ancient ayurvedic medicine. Dulce de leche is prepared by cooking milk, sugar and vanilla for hours and is a component of many sweet foods. The traditional alfajores biscuits and the many layers of the torta de hojas are coated with this sweet flavour.

*Bright colours and full of life: Latin America's baking culture is very much influenced by its colonial history. However, its own style has developed over the last few decades and the area now has many of its own baking traditions.*

# Tres Leches

## CREAM CAKE

SERVES 12

PREP TIME: 30 minutes,
plus 30 minutes to stand

COOKING TIME: 30 minutes

### INGREDIENTS

*butter, for greasing*
*4 eggs*
*170 g/5¾ oz granulated sugar*
*125 g/4½ oz plain flour*
*1 tsp baking powder*
*¼ tsp salt*
*5 tbsp milk*
*1 tsp vanilla extract or
1 vanilla pod, scraped*
*2 egg whites*
*350 ml/12 fl oz evaporated milk*
*350 ml/12 fl oz sweetened
condensed milk*
*4 tbsp whipping cream*
*chopped glacé cherries,
to decorate*

### topping
*600 ml/1 pint whipping cream*
*3 tbsp caster sugar*

Different versions of this cake are found throughout the countries of Latin America. The Spanish name refers to the three types of milk used to soak the typical spongy dough. The method probably originates in Europe where, for example, tiramisù is made in the same way.

1. Preheat the oven to 180 °C/350 °F/Gas Mark 4. Grease a 23-cm/9-inch round cake tin. Put the eggs and sugar into a large bowl and whisk together until doubled in volume. Slowly add the flour, baking powder and salt, mixing well with a wooden spoon. Stir in the milk and the vanilla extract. Whisk the egg whites until they hold stiff peaks, then gently fold into the mixture.

2. Pour the mixture into the prepared tin, smoothing the surface. Bake in the preheated oven for 30 minutes. Remove the cake from the oven, prick all over with a fork, then transfer to a wire rack to cool.

3. Meanwhile, thoroughly mix together the evaporated milk, condensed milk and cream.

4. Gradually pour the mixture over the top of the cooled cake, pausing after each addition to allow it to be absorbed, until the cake is completely saturated. Leave to stand for 30 minutes.

5. Meanwhile, to make the topping, whip the cream with the sugar until it holds stiff peaks. Just before serving, spread the cream over the cake, cut into 12 pieces and decorate each piece with chopped glacé cherries.

1.

2.

4.

1.

3.

7.

# Oaxacan
## COCONUT & CARAMEL CAKE

This dessert from the Mexican state of Oaxaca is a kind of crème caramel. When removed from the tin, the liquid caramel attractively decorates this pudding.

1. Preheat the oven to 160 °C/325 °F/Gas Mark 3. Put a 20-cm/8-inch square cake tin into the oven. Put the sugar and water into a cast-iron non-stick saucepan and heat over a medium heat swirling the pan gently (do not stir) until all the sugar has dissolved. Turn up the heat and continue to swirl the pan gently while the syrup darkens to a deep amber.

2. Remove the hot tin from the oven (do not turn off the oven) and pour in the hot caramel, turning the tin around so that the caramel coats the base and sides as much as possible. Reserve any remaining caramel. Any parts of the tin that remain uncovered will need to be greased when the tin has cooled down.

3. Increase the oven temperature to 180 °C/350 °F/Gas Mark 4. Put the eggs and egg yolks into a medium-sized bowl and whisk to combine, then add the rum and mixed spice.

4. Put the cream, milk and coconut cream into a small saucepan over a medium heat, and bring to the boil, stirring constantly. Slowly pour the liquid into the egg mixture, stirring constantly.

5. Pour the mixture into the cake tin together with the reserved caramel. Place the tin in a deep roasting tin and then half fill the roasting tin with very hot water (not boiling) and carefully put in the preheated oven.

6. Bake for 35 minutes until a cocktail stick inserted into the centre comes out clean. Remove from the oven and leave to cool in the tin, then transfer to the refrigerator to chill overnight.

7. Just before serving, use a knife to gently separate the custard from the sides of the tin and turn it out on to a plate. The liquid caramel will cover the custard. Sprinkle over the coconut, decorate with a Cape gooseberry, if using, and serve.

SERVES 6–8

PREP TIME: 30 minutes, plus 8 hours to chill

COOKING TIME: 45 minutes

## INGREDIENTS

butter, for greasing, if needed
70 g/2½ oz granulated sugar
70 ml/2¼ fl oz water
6 eggs
3 egg yolks
70 ml/2¼ fl oz dark rum
½ tsp ground mixed spice
350 ml/12 fl oz whipping cream
350 ml/12 fl oz milk
350 ml/12 fl oz coconut cream, well stirred
150 g/5½ oz toasted desiccated coconut, for sprinkling
1 Cape gooseberry, to decorate (optional)

# Mexican

## WEDDING BISCUITS

MAKES 30

PREP TIME: 20 minutes

COOKING TIME: 20 minutes

These very delicate biscuits are part of the Mexican wedding tradition, and they can be baked in different shapes. For special occasions, the biscuits are made with high quality butter, very fine sugar and choice nuts. Pecan nuts are the key ingredient of these biscuits from Mexico. When made with walnuts, they are called Russian tea cakes; with almonds and vanilla, they are the German Vanillekipferl (vanilla crescent biscuits).

1.  Preheat the oven to 150 °C/300 °F/Gas Mark 2. Line two baking trays with baking paper. Put the nuts into a dry frying pan over a medium heat and cook, tossing occasionally, until toasted. Take care that they do not burn. Leave to cool, then put them into a food processor with 2 teaspoons of the icing sugar and pulse until finely chopped.

2.  Put the butter, the remaining sugar and the vanilla extract into a large bowl and whisk with an electric whisk until creamy. Stir in the flour and the nuts.

3.  With floured hands, form the dough into 30 finger-sized rolls, then shape into crescents and place on the prepared trays. Bake in the preheated oven for about 20 minutes until lightly browned. Leave to cool slightly, then roll in icing sugar to coat. Sprinkle again with icing sugar just before serving.

### INGREDIENTS

115 g/4 oz pecan nuts

50 g/1¾ oz icing sugar, plus extra for coating and sprinkling

225 g/8 oz butter, softened

1 tsp vanilla extract or 1 vanilla pod, scraped

250 g/9 oz plain flour, plus extra for dusting

3.

# Torta de Hojas
## LAYER CAKE

4.

SERVES 4

PREP TIME: 35–45 minutes

COOKING TIME: 3 hours 15 minutes

### INGREDIENTS

*700 ml/1¼ pints canned sweetened condensed milk*

*500 g/1 lb 2 oz plain flour*

*2 tsp baking powder*

*200 g/7 oz butter, softened*

*3 egg yolks*

*250 ml/9 fl oz milk*

*50 ml/2 fl oz brandy*

*50 ml/2 fl oz water*

*100 g/3½ oz walnuts, roughly chopped*

This 'thousand leaves cake' is a popular dessert in Chile. It is a true labour of love, because each layer has to be baked individually and then they all have to be put together. Make the cake the day before you eat it. It will have set and will be easier to cut.

1.  Heat the unopened cans of condensed milk in a saucepan of boiling water for 3 hours, taking care that the water covers the cans and remembering to top up the water, if needed, during the cooking. Carefully remove the cans from the heat and leave to cool for 10–15 minutes.

2.  Preheat the oven to 180 °C/350 °F/Gas Mark 4. Line several baking trays with baking paper. Mix together the flour and baking powder and set aside. Put the butter into a large bowl and whisk until creamy, then add the egg yolks, one at a time, whisking after each addition until combined. Add the flour mixture and the milk and mix until a firm dough forms.

3.  Divide the dough into 10 pieces and shape each piece into a ball. Flatten each ball into a 23-cm/9-inch round. Place on the prepared baking trays and prick all over with a fork. Bake in the preheated oven for 5 minutes, then turn over and bake for a further 5 minutes until golden brown. You may have to do this in batches. Remove from the oven and transfer to a wire rack to cool.

4.  Mix together the brandy and water in a small bowl. Place a pastry layer on a serving plate. Sprinkle with 1 tablespoon of the brandy mixture, then spread with 1½ tablespoons of the cooled condensed milk. Sprinkle with 1 tablespoon of the nuts. Repeat until all the layers have been used.

# SWEET CARAMEL
# Pasteles

4.

**MAKES 14**

**PREP TIME:** 25 minutes, plus 30 minutes to chill

**COOKING TIME:** 15–20 minutes

## INGREDIENTS

*385 g/13½ oz plain flour, plus extra for dusting*

*40 g/1½ oz icing sugar*

*1 tsp baking powder*

*¼ tsp salt*

*225 g/8 oz chilled butter, diced, plus extra for greasing*

*6–7 tbsp iced water*

*425 g/15 oz soft caramel sweets*

*2 tbsp milk*

*35 g/1¼ oz desiccated coconut*

*1 egg, beaten*

Caramel means 'burnt sugar' in Spanish. The dry sugar, when heated, remains sweet but it also acquires its typical roasted aroma. In Argentina, pasteles are usually filled with soft and sweet caramel. This is a treat that's worth a little effort!

1. Put the flour, sugar, baking powder and salt into a large bowl and mix together thoroughly. Add the butter and rub it in with your fingertips until the mixture resembles breadcrumbs. Add the iced water, a teaspoon at a time, until the pastry comes together. Cover with clingfilm and chill in the refrigerator for 30 minutes.

2. Heat the caramel with the milk in a heatproof bowl set over a saucepan of simmering water, stirring constantly, until the caramel has completely dissolved. Remove from the heat, stir in the coconut and leave to cool.

3. Preheat the oven to 200 °C/400 °F/Gas Mark 6. Line a baking tray with greased baking paper. Roll out the pastry on a lightly floured work surface and use a 7.5-cm/3-inch cutter to cut out 14 rounds, re-rolling the trimmings, if necessary.

4. Place 1 teaspoon of the caramel mixture in the middle of each round and fold it in half. Seal the edges with a fork. Place the pastries on the prepared baking tray and brush them with the beaten egg. Bake in the preheated oven for about 10 minutes until golden brown. Remove from the oven, transfer to a wire rack and leave to cool.

# Guava Bars

The guava tree is native to South America, but now it is also grown in other tropical regions. Its fruit is soft, juicy and slightly pitted. Guavas have a sweet and sour flavour and are slightly reminiscent of pears or strawberries. As they only keep for a few days, they are mainly used for making marmalade, desserts or juice – the basis for this recipe.

1. To make the guava paste, put the guava juice and granulated sugar into a saucepan and bring to the boil. Add the jam sugar and stir to combine, then pour into a flat mould and leave to cool to a firm paste.

2. Preheat the oven to 200 °C/400 °F/Gas Mark 6. Lightly grease a 20 x 30-cm/ 8 x 12-inch baking tin.

3. Mix together the flour, sugar, bicarbonate of soda, salt and oats. Add the butter and rub in until the mixture resembles bread crumbs. Add the honey and mix well. Press half the crumble mixture into the prepared tray.

4. Cut the guava paste into thin strips and lay them on top of the crumble. Cover with the remaining crumble mixture and lightly press into place using the back of a fork. Bake in the preheated oven for 30 minutes until golden brown. Remove from the oven and leave to cool in the tray.

5. Cut into strips about the size of a muesli bar and serve. The bars will keep in an airtight container for up to 1 week.

MAKES 8–10

PREP TIME: 30 minutes, plus time to cool

COOKING TIME: 30 minutes

## INGREDIENTS

*250 g/9 oz plain flour*
*350 g/12 oz soft light brown sugar*
*½ tsp bicarbonate of soda*
*¼ tsp salt*
*150 g/5½ oz porridge oats*
*225 g/8 oz butter, softened, plus extra for greasing*
*150 ml/5 fl oz clear honey*

### guava paste
*300 ml/10 fl oz guava juice*
*70 g/2½ oz granulated sugar*
*50 g/1¾ oz jam sugar*
*or*
*425 g/15 oz ready-made guava paste, sliced*

1.

# Mexican

## SOPAPILLAS

SERVES 4

PREP TIME: 20 minutes,
plus 2 hours 20 minutes to rise

COOKING TIME: 3–5 minutes

### INGREDIENTS

*2 tsp easy-blend dried yeast*
*3 tbsp lukewarm water*
*150 ml/5 fl oz milk*
*85 g/3 oz granulated sugar, plus extra*
*for sprinkling*
*1 tsp salt*
*25 g/1 oz butter*
*1 egg, beaten*
*500 g/1 lb 2 oz plain flour,*
*plus extra for dusting*
*oil, for deep-frying*

The name of this pastry probably comes from the Spanish word *sopaipa* – a term for sweet fried dough. Unlike South American sopapillas, which are a type of tortilla, the Mexican variant puffs up like a doughnut on account of the special dough. They are also made in savoury versions and are an important feature of the local cuisine that developed well over 200 years ago.

1. Put the yeast into a large bowl with the water, stir to dissolve and leave to stand in a warm place. Put the milk, sugar and salt into a saucepan over a medium heat, bring to the boil, then add the butter and stir. Remove from the heat and leave to cool slightly. Stir into the yeast mixture, add the egg and mix to combine, then gradually mix in the flour. Cover the bowl with a damp tea towel and leave to rise for 1–2 hours.

2. Turn out the dough on to a lightly floured work surface and knock back, then leave to rise for 20 minutes. Roll out the dough to a thickness of 1 cm/½ inch, then use a pizza cutter or pastry wheel to cut it into 20 cm x 5-mm/8 x ¼-inch strips.

3. Heat enough oil for deep-frying in a large saucepan or deep-fat fryer to 180–190 °C/350–375 °F, or until a cube of bread browns in 30 seconds. Drop small batches of the dough strips into the oil and fry for 3–5 minutes until light brown, turning to cook on both sides.

4. Remove from the oil and place on absorbent kitchen paper to drain. Sprinkle with sugar and serve immediately.

**1.**

**2.**

**3.**

# Happy Hour
## AT THE CEMETERY

It is the day of the dead celebration: Every year in Mexico, on the night of the 1st of November, the dead are released from their eternal rest for a short time, and so begins the *Dia de los Muertos…* the Day of the Dead.

On 'Dia de los Muertos', which is also cele-brated exuberantly by Hispanics in Chicago, Los Angeles and New York around the same time as Halloween, the cemeteries become a place with strange decorations and special dinner parties for the dead.

On the Day of the Dead, nothing can persuade the dead to stay in their graves and tombs, because, according to an old belief, at the end of the harvest they return to Earth from the afterlife to cel-ebrate a joyful festival with the living. With loud music, lively danc-ing and good food, the dead have something to laugh about and the living can remember those who have passed away.

Their souls are long awaited guests and are welcomed with bizarre death symbols. Brightly painted skeletons, glowing plastic bones and skulls made of sugar and chocolate bearing the name of the deceased on the forehead leave no doubt as to the date: it is *Dia de los Muertos* (Day of the Dead), one of the most important feast days and liveliest folk festivals in honour of the dead. All the streets are decorated with a welcoming carpet of yellow and orange flowers to guide the dead on the way home from the cemetery. Better safe than sorry, because, after such a long absence, it is easy to lose one's way. The bright orange cempasuchil, also called 'flower of the dead', is supposed to be easy to identify, even for the dead with their poor eyesight. The *Dia de los Muertos* is by no means a mournful occasion. According to ancient Mexican belief, the dead are returned from the afterlife. Spanish missionaries, however, found this rather blasphemous. They unsuccessfully tried to abolish the celebration, but eventually had to resign themselves to the fact that Christianity had mingled with Aztec beliefs.

From the point of view of baking history, pan de muerto is a bread made from a soft dough, which is similiar in consistency to the brioche from France. Pan de muerto probably developed from the empanada, a filled pastry popular through-out South America. Housewives took great pride in their skill in braiding pan de muerto in honour of their deceased ancestors. In Mexico, pan de muerto is such an important product that there are cookery competitions and television programmes where professionals and amateurs vie for the title of 'Best Pan de Muerto Baker'. These loaves try to depict skeletons in as much real-life detail as possible. And no one shies away from the copious use of red icing. Although it had its origins in religious ritual, the pan de muerto, artistically decorated with bones and skeletons, is just the thing to bring along when visiting friends, even when it is not the Day of the Dead. On the night before the 2nd November, after the souls have been received at home, there is a farewell ceremony to the dead that takes place in the cemeteries. The pan de muerto is eaten there along with other foods. And naturally there is a lot of drinking, music and dancing. On the stroke of midnight the dead return to the afterlife. Rest at last, until next year!

# CHILEAN

# Pineapple Cake

Pineapple is a much-loved fruit all over the world that has been grown in most tropical regions since the 16th century. However, it originally comes from Latin America, where it was already being cultivated before Christopher Columbus brought it to Europe. The pineapple was given to him as a welcome gift in Guadeloupe in 1493. Its sharp taste gives this typical north Chilean cream cake a special kick.

**SERVES 8–10**

**PREP TIME: 50 minutes, plus 30 minutes to chill**

**COOKING TIME: 30 minutes**

## INGREDIENTS

*6 eggs*
*250 g/9 oz caster sugar*
*150 g/5½ oz plain flour, sifted*
*80 g/2¾ oz cornflour*
*2 tsp baking powder*
*butter, for greasing*
*250 ml/9 fl oz whipping cream*
*100 g/3½ oz icing sugar*
*150 g/5½ oz canned pineapple chunks and their can juices*
*3 tbsp pineapple juice*
*desiccated coconut, to decorate*

1. Put 3 of the eggs into a large bowl with the caster sugar and whisk with an electric whisk for 30 minutes. This long whisking will ensure that enough air is beaten in to keep the cake light. Sift together the flour, cornflour and baking powder into a bowl, then fold into the egg mixture. Separate the remaining eggs and whisk the egg whites until they hold stiff peaks. Gently fold into the flour mixture, making sure that it remains light and fluffy. Add the egg yolks, one at a time, stirring gently after each addition.

2. Meanwhile, preheat the oven to 160 °C/325 °F/Gas Mark 3 and grease a 23-cm/9-inch round cake tin. Pour the mixture into the prepared tin and bake in the preheated oven for about 30 minutes. Remove from the oven, transfer to a wire rack and leave to cool completely. Cut the cooled cake into two horizontal layers.

3. Meanwhile, whip the cream until it holds stiff peaks, then gently fold in the icing sugar. Transfer to the refrigerator to chill until you are ready to assemble the cake.

4. Mix together the can juices and the pineapple juice and set aside.

5. To assemble the cake, place 1 cake layer on a plate. Spread with a thick layer of the whipped cream and arrange some of the pineapple chunks on top. Spread a thinner layer of whipped cream over the pineapple.

6. Pour the pineapple juice over the second cake layer and place on top of the whipped cream. Top with the remaining cream, then decorate with the remaining pineapple and the coconut. Chill in the refrigerator for 30 minutes. Serve chilled.

1.

2.

5.

2.

4.

4.

# Pan de Muerto

## SWEET BREAD

SERVES 8

PREP TIME: 30 minutes,
plus 2 hours 30 minutes to rise

COOKING TIME: 25–30 minutes

Pan de Muerto is the 'bread of the dead': it is baked in Mexico at the end of the harvest season, prior to the 'Day of the Dead'. This important and popular festival is celebrated every year on the 1st and 2nd of November. The sweet, soft bread is often decorated with pieces of dough in the shape of bones, which symbolize the loss caused by death.

1. Put the yeast into a large bowl with the water, stir to dissolve and leave to stand for about 5 minutes. Meanwhile, put the milk into a saucepan set over a medium heat, bring to the boil, then remove from the heat and add the butter, 50 g/1¾ oz of the sugar and the salt. Stir until dissolved. Add the milk mixture to the yeast mixture.

2. Add 1 egg and the flour to the liquid ingredients, mix to combine, then knead until a smooth, silky dough forms. Transfer the dough to a clean bowl, cover with clingfilm and leave to rise in a warm place for 2 hours.

3. Turn out the dough on to a lightly floured work surface and divide into 4 pieces. Set 1 piece aside. Using the palms of your hands, shape each of the remaining pieces into 3 ropes of equal length.

4. Line a baking tray with baking paper and lightly grease the paper. Weave the 3 dough ropes into a plait and join the ends to make a round loaf. Take the reserved piece of dough and shape it into 2 bones and a skull. Arrange these on top of the loaf and press lightly. Place on the prepared baking tray and leave to rise for 30 minutes.

5. Meanwhile, preheat the oven to 180 °C/350 °F/Gas Mark 4. Mix together the anise, cinnamon and the remaining sugar in a small bowl. Whisk the remaining egg and brush it on to the plaited dough (do not brush the skull and bones), then sprinkle with the anise mixture.

6. Bake in the bottom of the preheated oven for 20–25 minutes until golden. If it is browning too quickly, cover with baking paper or foil. Remove from the oven and place on a wire rack to cool.

## INGREDIENTS

*3 tsp easy-blend dried yeast*
*4 tbsp lukewarm water*
*4 tbsp milk*
*60 g/2¼ oz butter, diced,*
*plus extra for greasing*
*60 g/2¼ oz granulated sugar*
*½ tsp salt*
*2 eggs*
*425 g/15 oz plain flour,*
*plus extra for dusting*
*½ tsp ground star anise*
*¼ tsp ground cinnamon*

# Brigadeiros

## CHOCOLATE SWEETS

MAKES 25

PREP TIME: 35 minutes,
plus 4 hours to chill

COOKING TIME: 15 minutes

### INGREDIENTS

*400 ml/14 fl oz canned sweetened
condensed milk*

*25 g/1 oz butter,
plus extra for greasing*

*2 tbsp whipping cream*

*2 tsp golden syrup*

*2 tsp cocoa powder*

*85 g/3 oz plain chocolate chips*

*200 g/7 oz chocolate vermicelli*

During World War II imported goods were scarce in Brazil. The country drew on its own resources and made the most of being a major producer of cocoa. At the same time, the Swiss manufacturer Nestlé introduced condensed milk to the market there. The combination of the two resulted in these Brazilian chocolate truffles, named after Brigadier Eduardo Gomes, who was a popular military man and politician in Brazil at the time.

1. Pour the condensed milk into a small saucepan and heat over a low heat, taking care that it does not boil. Add the butter, cream and golden syrup, stirring constantly.

2. When small bubbles start to appear in the mixture, add the cocoa powder and chocolate chips. Simmer for about 10 minutes until thickened, then remove from the heat.

3. Pour the mixture into a bowl and leave to cool to room temperature.

4. Meanwhile, put the chocolate vermicelli into a shallow bowl and lightly grease your hands. Roll the cooled mixture into 2.5-cm/1-inch balls or other shapes and toss in the vermicelli until completely coated. Place the brigadeiros in paper cases and chill in the refrigerator for 4 hours, or until ready to serve.

1.

2.

4.

# Garibaldi BISCUITS

MAKES 24–30

PREP TIME: 15 minutes

COOKING TIME: 15 minutes

### INGREDIENTS

*140 g/5 oz plain flour*

*100 g/3½ oz icing sugar,
plus extra for dusting*

*1 tsp finely grated lime zest*

*115 g/4 oz butter, softened,
plus extra for greasing*

*pinch of salt*

Garibaldi biscuits, named after the Italian revolutionary, are also popular in Britain. In this South American version, the raisins or soft fruit are left out, and fine lime zest and icing sugar are used instead.

1. Preheat the oven to 180 °C/350 °F/Gas Mark 4. Lightly grease a baking tray. Put the flour, sugar and lime zest into a medium-sized bowl and mix to combine. Add the butter and salt and beat to a smooth dough.

2. Turn out on to a lightly floured work surface, roll out into a large rectangle and cut this into about 3 wide strips. Use your hands to roll the strips into tubes, then cut them into 2-cm/¾-inch pieces. Roll into small balls, then place on the prepared tray. Pinch with your fingers to create a ridged shape on each biscuit, then bake in the preheated oven for about 15 minutes until golden brown.

3. Remove from the oven, sprinkle with sugar and serve.

1.

1.

2.

1.

2.

# Mantecada

RING
CAKE

SERVES 6–8

PREP TIME: 15 minutes

COOKING TIME: 30–40 minutes

This sponge cake is very popular in Colombia and Venezuela, and its batter consists mainly of butter, sugar, cornmeal (you can use polenta) and eggs – and just a little flour. It is based on a kind of muffin from Spain, and the rum and orange rind are essential ingredients. It is often served with a scoop of ice cream, cream or fresh fruit.

1. Preheat the oven to 180 °C/350 °F/Gas Mark 4. Grease a cake ring tin. Put the butter, sugar, flour and baking powder into a bowl and whisk with an electric whisk until slightly fluffy. Add the eggs, one at a time, stirring after each addition, then sift the polenta into the mixture. Continue to whisk until smooth. Add the rum and the orange zest, stirring well.

2. Pour the mixture into the prepared tin and bake in the middle of the preheated oven for 30–40 minutes.

3. Remove the cake from the oven and carefully turn out of the tin. Serve hot or at room temperature.

## INGREDIENTS

*450 g/1 lb butter,
plus extra for greasing*
*450 g/1 lb granulated sugar*
*100 g/3½ oz plain flour*
*3 tsp baking powder*
*10 eggs*
*400 g/14 oz fine yellow polenta*
*2 tsp rum*
*finely grated zest of 1 orange*

# AMARANTH
# *Alegrias*
## BISCUITS

2.

MAKES 10–15

PREP TIME: 15 minutes

COOKING TIME: 15 minutes

2.

### INGREDIENTS

*450 ml/16 fl oz water*

*800 g/1 lb 12 oz jaggery or
soft dark brown sugar*

*3 tbsp clear honey*

*juice of 2 lemons*

*115 g/4 oz amaranth, toasted
(available in health-food shops)*

*85 g/3 oz raisins*

*55 g/2 oz skinned, unroasted
peanuts*

Amaranth has been considered sacred for a long time: the Incas believed the plant to be a source of great power. In fact, this grain is highly nutritious and easily outshines European cereals. The seeds usually grow on inflorescences that can be up to a metre long.

1. Put the water into a large saucepan and bring to the boil. Add the jaggery, honey and lemon juice, bring back to the boil and cook until a thick syrup forms.

2. Remove from the heat, then add the amaranth to the syrup and mix to combine. Add the raisins and peanuts and mix again. Leave to cool slightly, then press into 10–15 small moulds or shape into pyramids. Turn out of the moulds and serve.

# Polvorones

## BISCUITS

2.

MAKES 20–25

PREP TIME: 15 minutes

COOKING TIME: 10 minutes

Polvorones comes from the Spanish word for 'dust': these heavy, crumbly biscuits are eaten in various forms in Latin America and Spain and are particularly popular during the Christmas season. The cinnamon and vanilla flavour is also appropriate for the festive season.

## INGREDIENTS

*225 g/8 oz butter,*
*plus extra for greasing*

*225 g/8 oz granulated sugar*

*40 g/1½ oz icing sugar*

*2 eggs*

*1 tsp vanilla extract or 1 vanilla pod,*
*scraped*

*550 g/1 lb 4 oz plain flour, sifted,*
*plus extra for dusting*

*1 tsp baking powder*

*½ tsp salt*

*100 g/3½ oz cinnamon sugar*
*(available online)*

1. Preheat the oven to 190°C/375°F/Gas Mark 5. Line a baking tray with greased baking paper. Put the butter, granulated sugar and icing sugar into a large bowl and whisk with an electric whisk until light and fluffy. Add the eggs, one at a time, gently stirring after each addition, then stir in the vanilla extract. Add the flour, baking powder and salt and stir to combine.

2. Turn out the dough on to a lightly floured work surface and roll out to a thickness of 5 mm/¼ inch. Use a 5-cm/2-inch fluted cutter to cut out 20–25 biscuits, re-rolling the trimmings, if necessary. Place on the prepared baking tray and bake in the preheated oven for about 8–10 minutes until golden brown.

3. Remove the polvorones from the oven and sprinkle over the cinnamon sugar while they are still hot. Transfer to a wire rack to cool. The polvorones will keep for up to 1 week in an airtight container.

# Alfajores

## CARAMEL BISCUITS

MAKES 24

PREP TIME: 20 minutes,
plus 30 minutes to chill

COOKING TIME: 15 minutes

### INGREDIENTS

250 g/9 oz plain flour, sifted,
plus extra for dusting

25 g/1 oz icing sugar, sifted,
plus extra for sprinkling

½ tsp salt

225 g/8 oz butter, softened, diced

175 ml/6 fl oz dulce de leche
(caramel sauce)

¼ tsp ground cinnamon

¼ tsp ground cloves

¼ tsp grated nutmeg

Alfajores consist of two (or even three!) filled layers of very fine pastry. This sweet pastry has its origins in Arabia and then spread via Spain to South America as early as 1870. Nowadays it is particularly popular in Argentina. This recipe with dulce de leche, in which the biscuits are sprinkled with sugar, is only one of many versions.

1. Preheat the oven to 180°C/350°F/Gas Mark 4. Line a large baking tray with baking paper. Put the flour, sugar, salt and butter into the bowl of an electric whisk and mix until a smooth dough forms. Wrap in clingfilm and chill in the refrigerator for 30 minutes.

2. Turn out the dough on to a lightly floured work surface and roll out to a thickness of 5 mm/¼ inch. Use a 5-cm/2-inch cutter to cut out 48 rounds, re-rolling the trimmings, if necessary. Place the rounds on the prepared baking tray. Use a skewer to make 3 holes in 24 of the rounds. Bake in the preheated oven for about 15 minutes until golden brown.

3. Meanwhile, put the dulce de leche, cinnamon, cloves and nutmeg into a bowl and mix to combine.

4. Spread 1 teaspoon of this mixture on the flat side of the 24 solid biscuits, then top with the remaining biscuits. Sprinkle with icing sugar and serve.

4.

# Coconut Kisses

2.

3.

There is a huge variety of recipes for coconut macaroons throughout the world. But this sweet biscuit in combination with coconut always provides a tropical thrill. Crispy on the outside and slightly sticky on the inside, these kisses are irresistible!

1. Preheat the oven to 180°C/350°F/Gas Mark 4. Line a baking tray with baking paper and grease the paper.

2. Put all the ingredients into a large bowl and mix to a firm dough. Divide the dough into 24 pieces and roll each piece into a ball.

3. Place the balls on the prepared baking tray, brush with egg white and bake in the preheated oven for 15 minutes until the tops are golden brown. Remove from the oven and transfer to a wire rack to cool. Decorate with the cherries and serve.

MAKES 24

PREP TIME: 10 minutes

COOKING TIME: 15 minutes

## INGREDIENTS

*butter, for greasing*

*200 g/7 oz desiccated coconut*

*60 g/2¼ oz plain flour*

*4 egg yolks*

*1 egg white,*
*plus extra for brushing*

*2 tbsp coconut milk*

*225 g/8 oz soft light brown sugar*

*1 tsp vanilla extract or 1 vanilla pod,*
*scraped*

*glacé cherries, to decorate*

3.

1.

2.

3.

# MEXICAN
# *Corncake*

SERVES 6

PREP TIME: 15 minutes

COOKING TIME: 40 minutes

INGREDIENTS

*60 g/2¼ oz butter,*
*plus extra for greasing*
*2 tbsp vegetable fat*
*50 g/1¾ oz polenta*
*5 tbsp cold water, plus extra if needed*
*280 g/10 oz fresh sweetcorn kernels*
*3 tbsp whipping cream*
*3 tbsp cornflour*
*50 g/1¾ oz caster sugar*
*¼ tsp baking powder*
*¼ tsp salt*

Maize, or corn as we call it, has been cultivated for thousands of years in Mexico and the work involved has made it one of the outstanding achievements of prehistoric times. In Latin America (and Africa), maize is still the most important staple food. Of course, it also makes a versatile cake all year round: the fresh, juicy maize gives it a coarse and pleasing texture.

1. Preheat the oven to 180 °C/350 °F/Gas Mark 4. Grease a 35-cm/14-inch loaf tin. Cream the butter with the vegetable fat until light and fluffy. Fold in the polenta. Add the water, a little at a time, mixing after each addition until a firm but pliable dough forms. Add the sweetcorn and mix well.

2. Mix together the cream, cornflour, sugar, baking powder and salt in a large bowl. Add the corn and butter mixture and mix together until combined.

3. Transfer the mixture to the prepared tin and bake in the preheated oven for 40 minutes. If the cake is browning too quickly, cover it with foil. Remove from the oven and leave to cool in the tin for 1–2 minutes, then remove from the tin and transfer to a wire rack to cool completely. Serve cut into slices or squares.

1.

2.

3.

# Arepas
## FLATBREADS

MAKES 16

PREP TIME: 20 minutes,
plus 30 minutes to rest

COOKING TIME: 15–20 minutes

In Colombia and Venezuela, this round, flat corn bread is traditionally eaten for almost every meal. In the Andes, large, flat arepas are baked, while on the coast thick, small ones are fried. They are always freshly made and served hot. They sometimes have a filling. The thick ones are also cut open and filled with meat, fish, cheese and vegetables.

1. Mix together the flour and salt in a large bowl and pour over the hot water to cover. Add the butter and mix well until a firm dough forms, then wrap in clingfilm and leave to rest for 30 minutes.

2. Divide the dough into 16 equal sized pieces and shape each piece into a 10-cm/4-inch round, about 1.5 cm/½ inch thick. Place on a sheet of baking paper and cover with clingfilm.

3. Heat some oil in a frying pan, add the arepas in small batches and fry over a medium heat on both sides until golden brown. If the arepas are browning too quickly, reduce the heat. The arepas are cooked when they are crisp outside but soft in the middle.

4. Serve straight from the pan with salad leaves, cheese and ham.

## INGREDIENTS

280 g/10 oz arepa flour or quick-cook polenta
1 tsp salt
700 ml/1¼ pints hot water
25 g/1 oz butter, melted
vegetable oil, for frying

**to serve**
salad leaves
grated Cheddar cheese
sliced cooked ham

# Spicy Jalapeño

## CORNBREAD

Jalapeños are small, hot peppers named after the Mexican city of Xalapa (formerly Jalapa). Today this type of chilli is still mainly grown in that region as well as in the neighbouring state of Texas. It gives this hearty, tasty corn pancake its characteristic flavour.

**SERVES 6**

**PREP TIME:** 20 minutes

**COOKING TIME:** 35 minutes

### INGREDIENTS

*1 tbsp vegetable oil*

*4 fresh jalapeño chillies, halved, deseeded and thinly sliced*

*1 spring onion, thinly sliced*

*1 tbsp parsley*

*275 g/9¾ oz polenta*

*185 g/6½ oz plain flour*

*2 tbsp sugar*

*1 tbsp baking powder*

*1 tsp salt*

*3 eggs*

*450 ml/16 fl oz single cream*

*100 g/3½ oz butter, melted, plus extra for greasing*

1. Heat the oil in a small frying pan, then add the chillies, the spring onion and the parsley and sauté for 2 minutes until translucent. Remove from the heat and set aside.

2. Preheat the oven to 190 °C/375 °F/Gas Mark 5. Grease or line a 25-cm/ 10-inch square cake tin with baking paper. Mix together the polenta, flour, sugar, baking powder and salt in a large bowl. Put the eggs, cream, butter and chilli mixture into a separate large bowl and stir to combine. Add the polenta mixture and mix to a firm batter.

3. Pour the batter into the prepared tin and bake in the preheated oven for 30 minutes, or until a cocktail stick inserted into the centre comes out clean. Remove from the oven and leave to cool in the tin for 5 minutes. Turn out of the tin and carefully remove the baking paper, brushing it with water if it sticks to the bread. Place the bread on a wire rack to cool completely, then cut into small rectangles and serve.

1.

2.

3.

3.

# Out of AFRICA

It is a little known fact that the art of bread baking had its origins in Africa. About 5,000 years ago, the Egyptians discovered the effects of yeast and made the first leavened breads. In fact, there were over 30 different types of bread in Egypt. So it is hardly suprising that the Egyptians were known to the Romans as 'bread eaters'. However, very early on, people in other parts of Africa had also started experimenting with bread making. The Bedouin, for example, invented an earth oven where dough could be baked into bread using the hot Sahara sand and heated coals. Africans mainly used cassava, millet and maize to make their early breads.

*If you want to learn about how ovens worked 5,000 years ago when baking was invented by Egyptians, then watch some African tribes. They still bake bread in holes in the ground, naturally heated by the sun.*

# AFRICAN
# Ginger Biscuits

MAKES 25

PREP TIME: 10 minutes

COOKING TIME: 20 minutes

### INGREDIENTS

*265 g/9½ oz plain flour,*
*plus extra for dusting*
*85 g/3 oz caster sugar*
*3 tsp ground ginger*
*½ tsp freshly ground cayenne pepper*
*125 g/4¼ oz butter, softened,*
*plus extra for greasing*
*125 ml/4 fl oz water*

Originating from South Asia, ginger was initially mainly valued by Europeans for its positive effects on health. However, from the Middle Ages onwards, they also began to use it as a spice in foods. It was then introduced to the African colonies. These delicious spicy biscuits are still popular in Africa today.

1.  Preheat the oven to 180 °C/350 °F/Gas Mark 4. Line a baking tray with baking paper, then grease the paper. Sift together the flour, sugar, ginger and cayenne pepper into a large bowl.

2.  Thoroughly rub in the butter until the mixture resembles coarse crumbs. Add the water and mix to a firm dough.

3.  Roll out the dough on a floured work surface to a thickness of about 1 cm/½ inch. Use a 5-cm/2-inch round cutter to cut out 25 rounds. Place the rounds on the prepared tray and bake in the preheated oven for 15–20 minutes or until pale golden. Remove from the oven, transfer to a wire rack and leave to cool. The biscuits can be stored in an airtight container for up to 1 week.

2.

3.

2.

3.

3.

3.

# SOUTH AFRICAN
# *Milk* Tarts

MAKES 12

PREP TIME: 45 minutes,
plus 1 hour to chill

COOKING TIME: 25 minutes

## INGREDIENTS

*40 g/1½ oz butter, melted*
*225 g/8 oz caster sugar*
*3 egg yolks*
*140 g/5 oz plain flour*
*1 tsp baking powder*
*¼ tsp salt*
*1 tsp vanilla extract*
*or 1 vanilla pod, scraped*
*1 litre/1¾ pints milk*
*3 egg whites*
*1 tbsp cinnamon sugar (available online)*
*halved fresh strawberries and*
*icing sugar, to decorate*

## pastry
*225 g/8 oz butter, plus extra for greasing*
*55 g/2 oz caster sugar*
*2 egg yolks*
*2 tbsp whipping cream*
*300 g/10½ oz plain flour,*
*plus extra for dusting*

In contrast to the traditional English custard tart, the milk tart has a higher proportion of milk and egg. This creates a lighter texture and stronger milk flavour. These tarts are one of the most popular pastries in South Africa.

1.  Preheat the oven to 180 °C/350 °F/Gas Mark 4. Lightly grease the holes in a 12-hole bun tin and dust with flour. To make the pastry, put the butter and sugar into a bowl and cream together. Add the egg yolks and mix to incorporate, then add the cream and mix until combined. Using a palette knife, carefully fold in the flour to form a dough. Leave to chill for 1 hour.

2.  Roll out the pastry on a floured work surface, then use a 5-cm/2-inch round cutter to cut out 12 rounds. Use the rounds to line the holes in the prepared tin, then line with baking paper, fill with baking beans and bake in the preheated oven for 10 minutes. Remove from the oven and increase the oven temperature to 190 °C/375 °F/Gas Mark 5. Remove the paper and beans.

3.  Put the butter and sugar into a large bowl and beat together until smooth. Add the egg yolks, one at a time, and beat until smooth. Sift in the flour, baking powder and salt and stir until well mixed. Add the vanilla extract and milk and stir. Put the egg whites into a separate bowl and whisk until they hold stiff peaks. Carefully fold into the butter and sugar mixture, then pour into the pastry cases and sprinkle over the cinnamon sugar.

4.  Bake for 25 minutes, then remove from oven and leave to cool. Place a halved strawberry on each tart, dust with icing sugar and serve.

# Moroccan
## COUNTRY BREAD

MAKES 3 LOAVES

PREP TIME: 25 minutes,
plus 1 hour to rise

COOKING TIME: 30 minutes

### INGREDIENTS

*1 tbsp easy-blend dried yeast*
*500 ml/18 fl oz lukewarm water*
*2 tsp salt*
*850 g/1 lb 14 oz plain flour,*
*plus extra for dusting*
*1 tbsp olive oil*

1.

1.

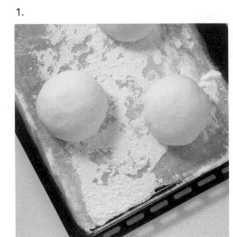

Many Moroccans still bake their own bread. To this end, families in rural areas use small dome-shaped wood-burning ovens, adding different ingredients to give their bread its own unique character. This rustic bread is a great accompaniment to stews or even with a salad. They deliberately avoid kneading the dough to give the bread its characteristic coarse texture.

1.  Preheat the oven to 180 °C/350 °F/Gas Mark 4. Lightly dust a baking sheet with flour. Put the yeast into a large bowl with the water and stir until dissolved. Add the salt and gradually stir in the flour, about 125 g/4½ oz at a time. Knead until the dough forms a ball. Turn out the dough on to a lightly floured work surface and shape it into a 25-cm/10-inch log. Divide the dough into 3 equal-sized pieces and shape each piece into a 10-cm/ 4-inch dome-shaped loaf.

2.  Place the loaves on the prepared baking sheet. Cover with a tea towel and leave to rise in a warm place for 1 hour, or until doubled in size.

3.  Brush each loaf with 1 teaspoon of the oil. Bake in the bottom of the preheated oven for 30 minutes. Remove from the oven and transfer to wire racks to cool.

# The Home
## of Afternoon Tea

Afternoon tea is as important to the British as spaghetti to the Italians or baguettes to the French. In the UK, the importance of cakes and pastries is especially apparent during the afternoon ritual. Of course, the visual effect must not be neglected at such an important time of the day. Whether it's home bakers having a go at making elaborate fondant decorations or creating seasonal specialities, such as Christmas Cakes, the British love show-stopping baking. But there are also the simpler bakes of Chelsea buns, crumpets, sausage rolls and muffins. These and similar plain and savoury goodies can be found in bakeries on almost every street in the UK. But, when possible, the British love to bake at home and to serve their own home-made cakes and biscuits at tea time just like their mothers and grandmothers before them.

*Queen Elizabeth II entertains those of her subjects who have contributed to society by holding large garden tea parties in the summer, at Buckingham Palace and in Edinburgh at Holyrood House.*

# DORSET
# Apple Cake

SERVES 12

PREP TIME: 25–30 minutes

COOKING TIME: 40 minutes

## INGREDIENTS

*250 g/9 oz apples*
*225 g/8 oz plain flour*
*1 tsp baking powder*
*125 g/4½ oz chilled butter, diced,*
*plus extra for greasing*
*125 g/4½ oz caster sugar,*
*plus extra for sprinkling*
*finely grated zest of 1 lemon*
*2 eggs, beaten*
*whipped cream, to serve (optional)*

The Romans originally brought the apple from Turkey to Central Europe. Dozens of new varieties were produced. Apple trees flourished in the mild, slightly damp south of England, like the county of Dorset.

1.  Preheat the oven to 190 °C/375 °F/Gas Mark 5. Lightly grease a 20-cm/ 8-inch round springform cake tin. Peel and core the apples, cut 1 apple into quarters lengthways, then thinly slice the quarters vertically and set aside. Dice the remaining apple and set aside.

2.  Sift together the flour and baking powder into a large bowl. Add the butter and rub it in with your fingertips until the mixture resembles bread crumbs.

3.  Add the sugar, diced apple, lemon zest and eggs to the flour mixture and mix to a firm dough. Pour the batter into the prepared tin and prick several times with a fork. Decorate the top of the cake with the apple slices.

4.  Bake the cake in the preheated oven for 40 minutes. Remove from the oven and leave to cool for 1–2 minutes. Unclip and remove the spring-form, leaving the cake on the base of the tin, then transfer to a wire rack to cool completely. Sprinkle with caster sugar and serve with whipped cream, if using.

1.

3.

3.

1.

2.

3.

# Strawberry & Cream *Cheesecake*

SERVES 12

PREP TIME: 45 minutes,
plus time to cool

COOKING TIME: 1 hour

This British cheesecake is made with a base of crushed biscuits and the layer of fruit provides a sharp, fresh contrast to the rich, creamy cheese filling. It makes a very colourful and mouth-watering dessert.

1. Preheat the oven to 180 °C/350 °F/Gas Mark 4. Grease a 25-cm/10-inch round springform cake tin and chill in the refrigerator. Put the biscuits into a food processor and pulse until reduced to fine crumbs. Mix in the butter, then press the mixture into the base of the prepared tin. Bake in the middle of the preheated oven for 10 minutes. Remove from the oven and leave to cool. Do not turn off the oven.

2. Meanwhile, put the cream cheese and mascarpone cheese into a large bowl and whisk until combined. Whip together the cream, sugar and vanilla extract until frothy, then pour into the cheese mixture. Add the eggs and the egg yolks, one at a time, whisking after each addition until combined.

3. Pour the cheesecake mixture on to the base, then bake for 50 minutes. Remove from the oven and leave to cool.

4. Unclip and release the springform, leaving the cheesecake on the base. Arrange the strawberry slices decoratively on top of the cooled cheesecake, then chill in the refrigerator until ready to serve.

## INGREDIENTS

*250 g/9 oz digestive biscuits
or butter biscuits*

*100 g/3½ oz butter,
plus extra for greasing*

*300 g/10½ oz cream cheese*

*250 g/9 oz mascarpone cheese*

*250 ml/9 fl oz whipping cream*

*200 g/7 oz sugar*

*1 tsp vanilla extract or 1 vanilla pod,
scraped*

*4 eggs*

*2 egg yolks*

*fresh strawberries, sliced, to decorate*

# Sally Lunn
# *Bun*

SERVES 10–12

PREP TIME: 35 minutes,
plus 2 hours to rise

COOKING TIME: 20 minutes

### INGREDIENTS

*175 g/6 oz butter,
plus extra for greasing*

*4 eggs*

*225 ml/8 fl oz milk*

*40 g/1½ oz fresh yeast (available in
bakeries or online)*

*500 g/1 lb 2 oz plain flour,
plus extra for dusting*

*50 g/1¾ oz caster sugar*

*2 tsp salt*

*1 egg yolk, beaten, for brushing*

This recipe for large, round, very soft buns is said to have been first brought to the English city of Bath by the Huguenot Sally Lunn on her flight from France in 1680. Since then, this sweet bun has been closely associated with this spa town in the West of England. The yeast dough for the bun is unusually rich in egg and butter.

1.  Melt the butter in a small saucepan. Whisk the eggs in a large bowl, then gradually add the melted butter, whisking constantly.

2.  Heat the milk in a small saucepan, then remove from the heat and crumble in the yeast. Sift together the flour, sugar and salt into a separate bowl, then whisk in the egg and butter mixture. Add the yeast mixture and mix to a smooth dough.

3.  Put the dough into a bowl, cover with clingfilm and leave to rise in a warm place for about 90 minutes, until doubled in size.

4.  Grease a 20-cm/8-inch round springform cake tin and dust with flour, shaking off any excess. Knock back the dough, knead for 1–2 minutes, then place in the prepared tin. Cover with a damp dish towel and leave to rise for 30 minutes. Preheat the oven to 190 °C/375 °F/Gas Mark 5.

5.  Brush the top of the dough with the egg yolk. Bake in the preheated oven for 15–20 minutes until golden brown. Leave to cool slightly, then slice and serve.

1 2 3

1.

2.

3.

# *Teatime*

## A SWEET TEMPTATION IN THE AFTERNOON

The baking world owes a debt of gratitude to Anna Maria Russell, Duchess of Bedford, for such delights as scones with clotted cream and little tartlets so sweet and colourful they make your stomach rumble just looking at them.

*Fancy individual little cakes that are painstakingly decorated with fondant icing, sweeties and even ribbons make any afternoon tea a special occasion.*

In the middle of the 19th century, tea time was invented as a late afternoon repast for the Duchess of Bedford, who found the time between lunch and dinner too long. The story goes that all she asked for was a little cup of tea. Actually the duchess was just glad to have a little something to eat and a way of entertaining the constant stream of visitors and 'hangers on'. The custom of afternoon tea has never really disappeared but has developed a variety of styles over the years. At one time, it offered a respectable opportunity for ladies to enter hotels unaccompanied by a male relative to meet with their friends to gossip over tea and cakes. In recent years the pastry chefs in the best London hotels started to vie with each other to produce the most attractive and exquisite little cakes and 'fancies' for afternoon tea. This was soon noticed and reported in the press. It quickly caught on with the public and nowadays with certain hotels it is sensible to book in advance, especially if it is for a special occasion. These little afternoon intervals are not inexpensive and, like the Duchess, the hotels realized this was a way of filling in vacant time, but for them at a profit.

Whether the Duchess is truly the creator of this tradition is doubtful from a historical perspective. In reality, Charles II and his wife, Catherine of Braganza, were the ones who brought the tea ceremony to the court when they returned from exile in 1662. As a new-fangled drink from China, tea was all the rage in London and it was only polite to offer a dainty biscuit to nibble on while one sipped tea and gossipped.

But the concept of an afternoon meal was by no means restricted to the privileged - it served a very practical purpose for the entire population. With the advent of the Industrial Revolution, people would go off to work in factories for long days with minimal breaks and would need a quick meal immediately upon their return home. 'High tea', not to be confused with 'afternoon tea', was more of a meal for the working classes that happened late in the afternoon. Before the Industrial Revolution, most of the population had their main meal at midday but this was now delayed until the workers arrived home late in the afternoon. Once home, a substantial meal was dished up as soon as possible. The first reference to 'high tea' was in 1825.

Restaurant staff around the world owe the tip or gratuity to the tradition of drinking a cup of tea in the afternoon. The gentry relied upon quick service to ensure properly hot tea. To encourage this, there was a box on each table for a 'voluntary' contribution to speed up service, which evolved into what we know as tipping today.

1.

2.

4.

4.

7.

8.

# Lemon Meringue Pie

The crucial ingredient of lemon meringue pie is lemon curd. The intensely aromatic lemon cream, made with egg yolks and sugar, as well as lemon juice and zest, is a classic of English cuisine that can also be spread on bread. For the right consistency of the meringue topping, only the peaks should be allowed to brown. Underneath, the meringue should still retain its creamy consistency.

1. To make the pastry, sift the flour into a bowl. Rub in the butter with your fingertips until the mixture resembles fine bread crumbs.

2. Mix in the remaining pastry ingredients. Turn out on to a lightly floured board and knead briefly. Wrap in clingfilm and chill in the refrigerator for 30 minutes.

3. Preheat the oven to 180°C/350°F/Gas Mark 4. Grease a 20-cm/8-inch round tart tin. Roll out the pastry on a lightly floured work surface to a thickness of 5 mm/¼ inch, then use it to line the tin.

4. Prick all over with a fork, line with baking paper and fill with baking beans. Bake blind in the preheated oven for 15 minutes.

5. Remove from the oven and take out the paper and beans. Reduce the oven temperature to 150°C/300°F/Gas Mark 2.

6. Mix the cornflour with a little of the water to form a paste. Put the remaining water into a saucepan. Stir in the lemon juice and rind and the cornflour paste.

7. Bring to the boil, stirring, and cook for a further 2 minutes. Leave to cool slightly. Stir in 60 g/2½ oz of the sugar and the egg yolks. Pour into the pastry case.

8. Whisk the egg whites until stiff. Gradually whisk in the remaining sugar and spread over the pie. Return to the oven and bake for a further 40 minutes. Remove from the oven and leave to cool before serving.

SERVES 6–8

PREP TIME: 45 minutes, plus 30 minutes to chill

COOKING TIME: 1 hour

## INGREDIENTS

3 tbsp cornflour

300 ml/10 fl oz water

juice and grated rind of 2 lemons

175 g/6 oz caster sugar

2 egg yolks, beaten

2 egg whites

### pastry

150 g/5½ oz plain flour, plus extra for dusting

85 g/3 oz butter, cut into small pieces, plus extra for greasing

35 g/1¼ oz icing sugar, sifted

finely grated rind of ½ lemon

½ egg yolk, beaten

1½ tbsp milk

# Victoria

## SPONGE CAKE

SERVES 8

PREP TIME: 30 minutes,
plus time to cool

COOKING TIME: 25–30 minutes

### INGREDIENTS

*175 g/6 oz self-raising flour*
*1 tsp baking powder*
*175 g/6 oz butter, softened,*
*plus extra for greasing*
*175 g/6 oz golden caster sugar*
*3 eggs*
*icing sugar, for dusting*

### filling

*3 tbsp raspberry jam*
*300 ml/10 fl oz double cream, whipped*
*16 fresh strawberries, halved*

This traditional sponge cake owes its name to Queen Victoria (1819–1901). She liked to enjoy a slice for afternoon tea. As its light batter is sensitive to cooking times and temperatures, oven manufacturers use this recipe to test their ovens.

1. Preheat the oven to 180 °C/350 °F/Gas Mark 4. Grease two 20-cm/8-inch sandwich tins and line with baking paper.

2. Sift the flour and baking powder into a bowl and add the butter, sugar and eggs. Mix together, then whisk well until smooth.

3. Divide the mixture evenly between the prepared tins and smooth the surfaces. Bake in the preheated oven for 25–30 minutes, or until well risen and golden brown and the cakes feel springy when lightly pressed.

4. Leave to cool in the tins for 5 minutes, then turn out and peel off the baking paper. Transfer to wire racks to cool completely. Sandwich the cakes together with the raspberry jam, cream and strawberry halves. Dust with icing sugar and serve.

2.

3.

4.

2.

3.

5.

# White Chocolate & Rose Cupcakes

**MAKES 12**

**PREP TIME:** 25 minut
plus 30 minutes to
and 1 hour to chill

**COOKING TIM** –20 minutes

**INGREDIE**

115 g/4 o alted butter, softened
115 g/4 ster sugar
1 tsp ater
2 e eaten
 oz self-raising flour
 2 oz white chocolate, grated

cing
115 g/4 oz white chocolate,
broken into pieces
2 tbsp milk
175 g/6 oz full-fat soft cheese
25 g/1 oz icing sugar, sifted

**to decorate**
100 g/3½ oz caster sugar
24 pink rose petals
1 egg white, beaten

These pretty, delicate cupcakes are ideal for a young girl's birthday party. This cupcake, with its white, artistically swirled icing, is easy to decorate, for example, with coloured fondant icing shapes or edible rose petals. They can be served at wedding receptions or on Valentine's Day.

1. Preheat the oven to 180 °C/350 °F/Gas Mark 4. Place 12 paper cases in a bun tin.

2. Put the butter, sugar and rosewater into a bowl and whisk until pale and creamy. Gradually whisk in the eggs. Sift in the flour and fold in gently. Fold in the white chocolate. Divide the mixture between the paper cases.

3. Bake the cupcakes in the preheated oven for 15–20 minutes, or until golden and firm to the touch. Transfer to a wire rack and leave to

4. To make the icing, put the chocolate and milk into a heatproof over a saucepan of barely simmering water and heat until the choc melted. Remove from the heat and stir until smooth. Leave to co minutes. Put the soft cheese and icing sugar into a bowl and whi smooth and creamy. Fold in the chocolate. Chill in the refrigerator ur.

5. Meanwhile, make the decoration. Put the a shallow bowl. Gently brush each side of the rose petals w ite. Dip in the sugar, gently turning to coat, then place on a s ing paper to dry.

6. Swirl the icing over the top of th es. Decorate with the sugar-frosted rose petals and serve.

# Cherry Bakewell
## TARTLETS

4.

**MAKES 10**

**PREP TIME: 40 minutes,**
**plus 1 hour 15 minutes to chill**

**COOKING TIME: 30 minutes**

### INGREDIENTS

*125 g/4½ oz unsalted butter, softened,*
*plus extra for greasing*
*125 g/4½ oz icing sugar*
*3 eggs*
*125 g/4½ oz ground almonds*
*30 g/1 oz self-raising flour*
*1 tbsp rum*
*225 g/8 oz cherry jam*

### pastry

*300 g/10½ oz plain flour,*
*plus extra for dusting*
*50 g/1¾ oz caster sugar*
*pinch of salt*
*1 egg yolk*
*150 g/5½ oz chilled unsalted butter, diced*
*2–3 tbsp cold water*

In the hills of the central English county of Derbyshire, in the little town of Bakewell, there are several shops selling the 'original' pastry that bears its name. And yet, although it has spread throughout Britain, the origin of the Bakewell tart with cherry jam is uncertain. Recipes for it have been found in different areas since the 19th century.

1.  To make the pastry, sift together the flour, sugar and salt into a large bowl. Add the egg yolk, butter and water and mix using the dough hook of a food processor. Turn out on to a lightly floured work surface and knead to a smooth dough. Wrap in clingfilm and chill in the refrigerator for 1 hour.

2.  Meanwhile, put the butter and the icing sugar into a bowl and whisk with an electric whisk until pale and fluffy. Add the eggs, one at a time, whisking after each addition until combined. Add the ground almonds and the flour. Mix to combine, then stir in the rum.

3.  Grease ten 7.5-cm/3-inch tartlet tins. Remove the pastry from the refrigerator and roll out to a thickness of 3 mm/⅛ inch. Cut out 10 rounds and press them into the tins, re-rolling the trimmings if necessary. Chill the tartlet cases in the refrigerator for 15 minutes.

4.  Meanwhile, preheat the oven to 200 °C/400 °F/Gas Mark 6. Spread a thin layer of cherry jam in the base of the tartlet cases, then spread the almond mixture evenly over the top. Bake in the middle of the preheated oven for 30 minutes, or until golden brown. Remove from the oven and transfer to a wire rack to cool completely. Carefully turn out of the tins and serve.

# Hot Cross Buns

4.

MAKES 14

PREP TIME: 30 minutes,
plus 2 hours to rise

COOKING TIME: 15–20 minutes

## INGREDIENTS

*125 ml/4 fl oz lukewarm water*

*40 g/1½ oz fresh yeast (available in bakeries or online)*

*500 g/1 lb 2 oz strong white flour, plus extra for dusting*

*2 tsp milk, plus extra for brushing*

*2 eggs*

*60 g/2¼ oz sugar*

*⅓ tbsp salt*

*85 g/3 oz butter, softened, plus extra for greasing*

*100 g/3½ oz sultanas*

*½ tsp cinnamon*

*½ tsp mixed spice*

*pinch of nutmeg*

*butter and marmalade, to serve*

### to decorate

*60 g/2¼ oz plain flour*

*1 tsp icing sugar*

*4 tbsp water*

Traditionally, Christians eat this spicy-sweet bun on Good Friday. The cross with which it is marked is seen as a symbol of the Crucifixion of Christ. In Britain, many superstitions surround these buns. Healing effects are attributed to them as well as protection from shipwreck. If a bun is hung in the kitchen, it is supposed to protect the house from fire and ensure successful bread baking.

1. Pour the water into a large bowl, crumble in the yeast, stir in 100 g/3½ oz of the flour, then cover the bowl with a dish towel and leave to stand for 20 minutes.

2. Add the milk, eggs, sugar, salt and the remaining flour and knead using the dough hook of a food processor or electric whisk until smooth. Stir in the butter, sultanas, cinnamon, mixed spice and nutmeg. Cover with a damp tea towel and leave to rise for about 1 hour, until doubled in size.

3. Meanwhile, to make the decoration, mix together the flour, sugar and water in a small bowl.

4. Grease two large baking trays. Turn out the dough on to a lightly floured work surface, knock back, then divide into 14 pieces. Roll each piece into a ball and place the balls on the prepared trays. Fill a disposable piping bag with the flour mixture, cut off the tip and pipe a cross on to each ball, then gently brush some milk over the tops of the buns. Leave the buns to rise for 40 minutes, then brush with milk again.

5. Meanwhile, preheat the oven to 190 °C/375 °F/Gas Mark 5. Bake the buns in the preheated oven for 15–20 minutes until golden. Serve warm with butter and marmalade.

# Brandy Snaps

MAKES 20

PREP TIME: 30–35 minutes

COOKING TIME: 20 minutes

## INGREDIENTS

*85 g/3 oz unsalted butter*
*85 g/3 oz golden caster sugar*
*3 tbsp golden syrup*
*85 g/3 oz plain flour*
*1 tsp ground ginger*
*1 tbsp brandy*
*finely grated rind of ½ lemon*

### filling
*150 ml/5 fl oz double cream*
*1 tbsp brandy (optional)*
*1 tbsp icing sugar*

In the Middle Ages, the Belgians and the French used to eat small waffles, especially on market days. The recipe reached England and there it evolved into brandy snaps. The waffles are rolled and filled with whipped cream (and brandy). But other fillings – chocolate chips or buttercream – can also be used.

1. Preheat the oven to 160 °C/325 °F/Gas Mark 3. Line 3 large baking trays with baking paper.

2. Put the butter, sugar and golden syrup into a saucepan and heat gently over a low heat, stirring occasionally, until smooth. Remove from the heat and leave to cool slightly.

3. Sift the flour and ginger into the pan and whisk until smooth, then stir in the brandy and lemon rind. Drop 20 small spoonfuls of the mixture on to the prepared baking trays, spaced well apart.

4. Bake in the preheated oven, one sheet at a time, for 10–12 minutes, or until the snaps are golden brown. Remove from the oven, leave to cool for about 30 seconds, then lift each snap with a palette knife and wrap around the handle of a wooden spoon. If the snaps become too firm to wrap, return to the oven for about 30 seconds to soften.

5. When firm, remove the snaps from the spoon handles and transfer to a wire rack to cool completely.

6. To make the filling, whip the cream with the icing sugar and the brandy, if using, until thick. Chill in the refrigerator until required.

7. Just before serving, pipe the cream mixture into both ends of each snap.

4.

5.

6.

2.

3.

4.

# Iced
# *Madeira Cake*

This traditional Madeira cake has a firm yet light texture due to the sponge mixture. The lemon flavour and sugar icing are an integral part of this recipe. The cake originally derives its name from the wine that was imported from the Portuguese island of Madeira and was popular in Britain in around 1800. A slice often accompanied a glass of the wine as a dessert. Nowadays, it is served with tea or liqueur instead of the wine from this Portuguese island.

1.  Preheat the oven to 160 °C/325 °F/Gas Mark 3. Grease a 900-g/2-lb loaf tin and line with baking paper.

2.  Put the butter and caster sugar into a large bowl and whisk together until very pale and creamy. Whisk in the lemon rind, then gradually whisk in the eggs. Sift the self-raising and plain flours into the mixture and fold in gently until thoroughly incorporated. Fold in the milk and lemon juice.

3.  Spoon the mixture into the prepared tin and bake in the preheated oven for 1–1¼ hours, or until well risen, golden brown and a skewer inserted into the centre comes out clean. Leave to cool in the tin for 15 minutes, then turn out on to a wire rack to cool completely.

4.  To make the icing, sift the icing sugar into a bowl. Add the lemon juice and stir to make a smooth, thick icing. Gently spread over the top of the cake. Drizzle the warmed lemon curd over the icing and drag a skewer through the icing to create a swirled effect.

SERVES 10

PREP TIME: 30 minutes, plus cooling

COOKING TIME: 1–1¼ hours

## INGREDIENTS

*175 g/6 oz unsalted butter, softened, plus extra for greasing*
*175 g/6 oz caster sugar*
*finely grated rind of 1 lemon*
*3 eggs, lightly beaten*
*140 g/5 oz self-raising flour*
*115 g/4 oz plain flour*
*2 tbsp milk*
*1 tbsp lemon juice*

### icing
*175 g/6 oz icing sugar*
*2–3 tbsp lemon juice*
*2 tsp lemon curd, warmed*

# Strawberry
## SHORTCAKE

SERVES 6–8

PREP TIME: 25 minutes

COOKING TIME: 15–20 minutes

### INGREDIENTS

*250 g/9 oz self-raising flour*
*50 g/1¾ oz butter, diced,*
*plus extra for greasing*
*50 g/1¾ oz caster sugar*
*125–150 ml/4–5 fl oz milk*

#### topping
*4 tbsp milk*
*500 g/1 lb 2 oz mascarpone cheese*
*5 tbsp caster sugar*
*500 g/1 lb 2 oz strawberries,*
*hulled and quartered*
*finely grated rind of 1 orange*
*fresh mint leaves, to decorate*

The shortbread-like base is covered with a tasty cream-cheese layer with lovely fresh strawberries. Strawberries and cream are the epitome of summer for many people. In Britain, the heart-shaped fruits have been enjoyed since the Middle Ages and have long been a symbol of purity, passion and healing.

1. Preheat the oven to 200 °C/400 °F/Gas Mark 6. Lightly grease a 20-cm/ 8-inch loose-based round cake tin.

2. Sift the flour into a large bowl, add the butter and rub in with your fingertips until the mixture resembles fine bread crumbs. Add the sugar. Stir in enough of the milk to form a soft but smooth dough. Gently press the dough evenly into the prepared tin. Bake in the preheated oven for 15–20 minutes until risen, firm to the touch and golden brown. Leave to cool for 5 minutes in the tin, then turn out on to a wire rack and leave to cool completely.

3. To make the topping, put the milk, mascarpone cheese and 3 tablespoons of the sugar into a bowl and whisk until smooth and fluffy. Put the strawberries into a separate bowl and sprinkle with the remaining sugar and the orange rind.

4. Spread the mascarpone mixture over the cake and pile the strawberries on top. Spoon over any juices left over from the strawberries in the bowl, scatter with mint leaves and serve.

# RASPBERRY CRUMBLE
# *Muffins*

MAKES 12

PREP TIME: 20 minutes,
plus 5 minutes to cool

COOKING TIME: 20 minutes

Their pinkish colour makes these muffins very attractive. Raspberry pieces peek out from the delicious cake, giving it a fresh fruity aroma. These summer berries grow even in the relatively cool country of Scotland.

1. Preheat the oven to 200 °C/400 °F/Gas Mark 6. Grease a 12-hole muffin tin or line with 12 paper cases.

2. To make the crumble topping, sift the flour into a bowl. Cut the butter into small pieces, add to the bowl with the flour and rub it in with your fingertips until the mixture resembles fine breadcrumbs. Stir in the sugar and set aside.

3. To make the muffins, sift together the flour, baking powder, bicarbonate of soda and salt into a large bowl. Stir in the sugar.

4. Lightly whisk the eggs in a large bowl, then whisk in the yogurt, butter and vanilla extract. Make a well in the centre of the dry ingredients, pour in the beaten liquid ingredients and add the raspberries. Stir gently until just combined. Do not over-mix.

5. Spoon the mixture into the prepared tin. Scatter the crumble topping over each muffin and press down lightly. Bake in the preheated oven for about 20 minutes until well risen, golden brown and firm to the touch.

6. Leave the muffins to cool in the tin for 5 minutes, then serve warm or transfer to a wire rack to cool completely.

## INGREDIENTS

*280 g/10 oz plain flour*
*1 tbsp baking powder*
*½ tsp bicarbonate of soda*
*pinch of salt*
*115 g/4 oz caster sugar*
*2 eggs*
*250 ml/9 fl oz natural yogurt*
*85 g/3 oz butter, melted and cooled, plus extra for greasing*
*1 tsp vanilla extract*
*150 g/5½ oz frozen raspberries*

### crumble topping
*50 g/1¾ oz plain flour*
*35 g/1¼ oz butter*
*25 g/1 oz caster sugar*

# Gingernuts

In the Middle Ages it was hard to find pepper in Europe, so ginger was used for seasoning instead. The spice gives these hard biscuits with the rich syrupy flavour a faintly pungent touch.

**MAKES 30**

**PREP TIME:** 25 minutes

**COOKING TIME:** 15–20 minutes

## INGREDIENTS

*350 g/12 oz self-raising flour*
*pinch of salt*
*200 g/7 oz caster sugar*
*1 tbsp ground ginger*
*1 tsp bicarbonate of soda*
*125 g/4½ oz butter,*
*plus extra for greasing*
*70 g/2½ oz golden syrup*
*1 egg, beaten*
*1 tsp grated orange rind*

1. Preheat the oven to 160 °C/325 °F/Gas Mark 3. Lightly grease several baking trays.

2. Sift together the flour, salt, sugar, ginger and bicarbonate of soda into a large mixing bowl.

3. Heat the butter and golden syrup together in a saucepan over a very low heat until the butter has melted. Remove the pan from the heat and leave to cool slightly, then pour the contents on to the dry ingredients.

4. Add the egg and orange rind and mix thoroughly with a wooden spoon to form a dough. Using your hands, carefully shape the dough into 30 even-sized balls. Place the balls on the prepared baking trays, spaced well apart, then flatten them slightly with your fingers.

5. Bake in the preheated oven for 15–20 minutes, then carefully transfer to a wire rack to cool completely.

3.

4.

# MILLIONAIRE'S
# *Shortbread*

3.

4.

These pieces of confectionery, very popular in the UK with a cup of tea or coffee, are probably found in over a hundred varieties (including with peanut butter and raisins). But they all are made of a biscuit base with a layer of caramel and a chocolate coating. They taste a bit like a chocolate bar – only much better! A touch of sea salt gives the caramel layer a modern tinge.

1. Preheat the oven to 180°C/350°F/Gas Mark 4. Grease a shallow 20-cm/8-inch square cake tin.

2. Put the butter and sugar into a bowl and whisk together until pale and creamy. Sift in the flour and add the ground almonds. Use clean hands to mix and knead to a crumbly dough. Press into the base of the prepared tin and prick the surface all over with a fork. Bake in the preheated oven for 15 minutes, or until pale golden. Leave to cool.

3. To make the topping, put the butter, sugar, golden syrup and condensed milk into a saucepan over a low heat and heat gently until the sugar has dissolved. Increase the heat to medium, bring to the boil, then simmer for 6–8 minutes, stirring constantly, until the mixture becomes very thick. Stir in half the salt, then quickly pour the caramel over the shortbread base. Sprinkle over the remaining salt.

4. Spoon the chocolate into a paper piping bag and snip off the end. Pipe the chocolate over the caramel and swirl with the tip of a knife. Leave to cool, then chill for 2 hours, or until firm. Cut into 16 squares.

MAKES 16

PREP TIME: 30 minutes, plus 2 hours to chill

COOKING TIME: 15 minutes

## INGREDIENTS

*115 g/4 oz butter, softened, plus extra for greasing*
*55 g/2 oz caster sugar*
*175 g/6 oz plain flour*
*55 g/2 oz ground almonds*

### topping
*175 g/6 oz butter*
*115 g/4 oz caster sugar*
*3 tbsp golden syrup*
*400 ml/14 fl oz canned condensed milk*
*¼ tsp sea salt crystals*
*85 g/3 oz plain chocolate, melted*

# Scones

1.

2.

MAKES 9

PREP TIME: 15 minutes

COOKING TIME: 10–12 minutes

## INGREDIENTS

450 g/1 lb plain flour,
plus extra for dusting

½ tsp salt

2 tsp baking powder

55 g/2 oz butter

2 tbsp caster sugar

250 ml/9 fl oz milk, plus extra
for glazing

strawberry jam and
clotted cream, to serve

Rich, salty-sweet scones are widely popular in the British Isles – but they originate in Scotland. Here, before baking powder was invented, they were prepared in a frying pan, like pancakes. Baking powder and a careful mixing of ingredients ensure the unusual consistency of this soft, crustless pastry that is eaten for tea.

1.  Preheat the oven to 220 °C/425 °F/Gas Mark 7. Sift together the flour, salt and baking powder into a bowl. Rub in the butter using your fingertips until the mixture resembles fine breadcrumbs.

2.  Stir in the sugar. Make a well in the centre and pour in the milk. Stir in using a palette knife and bring together to make a soft dough.

3.  Turn out the dough on to a floured surface and very lightly flatten it until it is 1 cm/½ inch thick. Cut out scones using a 6-cm/2½-inch biscuit cutter and place on a lined baking tray.

4.  Brush with a little milk and bake in the preheated oven for 10–12 minutes until golden and well risen. Leave to cool on a wire rack. Serve freshly baked with strawberry jam and clotted cream.

3.

4.

3.

3.

# Chelsea Buns

An English baker created these sweet buns in Chelsea, London, in the early 18th century. The Bun House there was so popular that even English kings used to shop there. According to legend, in 1829, more than 50,000 people waited outside the shop on Good Friday – and 240,000 warm buns were sold over the counter.

1. Preheat the oven to 200 °C/400 °F/Gas Mark 6. Lightly grease a baking tray. Combine the yeast in a bowl with the milk and a small amount of the granulated sugar and set aside for 10 minutes

2. Meanwhile, sift together the flour and salt into a mixing bowl, add the butter and rub in, then add the yeast mixture and beat well. Cover and set aside until the mixture doubles in size.

3. Turn out the dough on to a lightly floured work surface, lightly knead and roll out to a 25-cm/10-inch square. Sprinkle with the remaining granulated sugar, the mixed spice, sultanas and mixed peel and roll into a sausage shape. Cut into 6 slices and lay the slices flat on the prepared tray. Leave to stand until doubled in size. Brush with the beaten egg, then bake in the preheated oven for 20 minutes, or until golden.

4. Sprinkle with the caster sugar and serve.

**MAKES 6**

PREP TIME: 40 minutes, plus about 35 minutes to rise

COOKING TIME: 20 minutes

## INGREDIENTS

*½ tsp easy-blend dried yeast*
*150 ml/5 fl oz lukewarm milk*
*30 g/1 oz granulated sugar*
*280 g/10 oz plain flour, plus extra for dusting*
*¼ tsp salt*
*30 g/1 oz butter, 25 extra for greasing*
*½ tsp mixed spice*
*30 g/1 oz sultanas*
*30 g/1 oz mixed peel*
*1 egg, beaten*
*30 g/1 oz caster sugar, for sprinkling*

# CHOCOLATE
# Shortbread

MAKES 22

PREP TIME: 25 minutes,
plus 20–25 minutes to chill

COOKING TIME: 15–20 minutes

Shortbread is a sweet pastry from Scotland. The large, firm but brittle biscuits, which – due to the high butter content – crumble easily when bitten into, are an afternoon tea classic. The biscuits are baked at a low temperature so that they keep their light colour and the delicious chocolate pieces can stand out.

## INGREDIENTS

*225 g/8 oz plain flour*

*85 g/3 oz cornflour,
plus extra for dusting*

*225 g/8 oz butter, softened,
plus extra for greasing*

*115 g/4 oz caster sugar*

*115 g/4 oz milk chocolate
or plain chocolate, chopped into
small chunks*

1. Preheat the oven to 180 °C/350 °F/Gas Mark 4. Lightly grease 2 baking trays. Sift together the flour and cornflour into a bowl and set aside.

2. Put the butter and sugar into a bowl and beat with a wooden spoon until pale and creamy. Gradually stir in the flour and cornflour and three quarters of the chocolate chunks and mix to a soft dough. Divide the dough into 2 pieces, then shape each piece into a ball and wrap in clingfilm. Chill in the refrigerator for 20–25 minutes.

3. Lightly dust a work surface with a little cornflour and gently roll out the dough to a thickness of 1 cm/½ inch. Using a 5.5-cm/2¼-inch round cutter, stamp out 22 rounds, re-rolling the trimmings, if necessary. Place the rounds on the prepared baking trays and top with the remaining chocolate chunks, lightly pressing them into the dough. Bake in the preheated oven for 15–20 minutes, or until pale golden. Leave to cool on the baking trays for 10 minutes, then transfer to a wire rack to cool completely.

1.

2.

3.

1.

4.

4.

# Fruit Cake

The Romans were already using candied and dried fruits for their cakes. With the fall of the price of sugar in the 16th century, a rich range of candied fruit became available. Since then, many different versions of fruit cakes have been popular, especially in the UK, where this rich, juicy cake is baked especially for weddings and Christmas.

1. Place the sultanas, raisins, apricots and dates in a large bowl and stir in the rum, if using, orange rind and orange juice. Cover and leave to soak for several hours or overnight.

2. Preheat the oven to 150°C/300°F/Gas Mark 2. Grease a 20-cm/8-inch round springform cake tin and line with baking paper.

3. Whisk the butter and sugar together until pale and creamy. Gradually whisk in the eggs, whisking hard after each addition. Stir in the soaked fruits, mixed peel, glacé cherries, glacé ginger and blanched almonds.

4. Sift together the flour and mixed spice, then fold lightly and evenly into the mixture. Spoon into the prepared tin and smooth the surface, making a slight depression in the centre with the back of the spoon.

5. Bake in the preheated oven for 2¼–2¾ hours, or until the cake is beginning to shrink away from the sides and a skewer inserted into the centre comes out clean. Leave to cool completely in the tin.

6. Unclip and release the springform, turn out the cake and remove the baking paper. Wrap in some greaseproof paper and foil, and store for at least 2 months. To add a richer flavour, prick the cake with a skewer and spoon over 1–2 tablespoons of rum or brandy, if using, before storing.

SERVES 16

PREP TIME: 30 minutes, plus several hours or overnight to soak and 2 months to store

COOKING TIME: 2¼–2¾ hours

## INGREDIENTS

*350 g/12 oz sultanas*

*225 g/8 oz raisins*

*115 g/4 oz ready-to-eat dried apricots, chopped*

*85 g/3 oz stoned dates, chopped*

*4 tbsp dark rum or brandy, plus extra for flavouring (optional)*

*finely grated rind and juice of 1 orange*

*225 g/8 oz unsalted butter, softened, plus extra for greasing*

*225 g/8 oz light muscovado sugar*

*4 eggs, beaten*

*70 g/2½ oz chopped mixed peel*

*85 g/3 oz glacé cherries, quartered*

*25 g/1 oz chopped glacé ginger or stem ginger*

*40 g/1½ oz blanched almonds, chopped*

*200 g/7 oz plain flour*

*1 tsp mixed spice*

# Cherry Cake

SERVES 8

PREP TIME: 20 minutes

COOKING TIME: 1–1¼ hours

### INGREDIENTS

*250 g/9 oz glacé cherries, quartered*
*85 g/3 oz ground almonds*
*200 g/7 oz plain flour*
*1 tsp baking powder*
*200 g/7 oz unsalted butter,*
*plus extra for greasing*
*200 g/7 oz caster sugar*
*3 large eggs*
*finely grated rind and juice*
*of 1 lemon*
*6 sugar cubes, crushed*

King Henry VIII brought the cherry to England in the 16th century, assisted by his gardener Richard Harrys. He had previously tasted cherries in Flanders. The first cherry trees were planted in Teynham. This village in the county of Kent became a centre for cherry cultivation. Since then, cherry cake has become a classic – with a good portion of sugar and almonds.

1. Preheat the oven to 180 °C/350 °F/Gas Mark 4. Grease a 20-cm/8-inch round cake tin and line with baking paper.

2. Stir together the cherries, almonds and 1 tablespoon of the flour. Sift together the remaining flour and the baking powder into a separate bowl.

3. Cream together the butter and sugar until light and fluffy. Gradually add the eggs, whisking hard, until evenly mixed.

4. Add the flour mixture and fold lightly and evenly into the creamed mixture with a metal spoon. Add the cherry mixture, fold in evenly, then fold in the lemon rind and juice.

5. Spoon the mixture into the prepared tin and sprinkle with the crushed sugar cubes. Bake in the preheated oven for 1–1¼ hours or until risen and golden brown and shrinking from the sides of the tin.

6. Leave to cool in the tin for about 15 minutes, then turn out on to a wire rack to cool completely.

1.
2.
3.

4.
5.
6.

# British Pies

## LIVE AND LET PIE

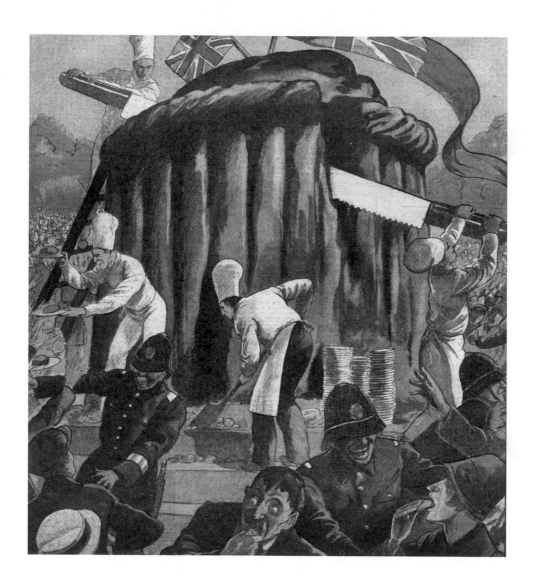

In terms of their pies, when it comes to this culinary feat, there is no joking with the British. There is a long tradition of pie making in Britain and there are many variations on recipes for both pastries and fillings.

Denby Dale, a modest town in the English county of Yorkshire, has only rarely been a talking point during its unremarkable history. The first time was in 1788, at the celebration of the recovery of King George III from a mental breakdown. In honour of this special event, the owners of the White Hart pub baked an over-sized pie, which they themselves demolished – and washed down with decent ale, of course. If you believe the chroniclers, the pie filling was as large as two sheep. With Wellington's victory over Napoleon in 1815, the time had finally come for the name of the town to be carved in stone as the ultimate Pie Village. A certain George Wilby, who had been at the battle, celebrated it accordingly. The Golden Jubilee of Queen Victoria in 1887 and the end of World War I in 1918 also justified the continuation of the giant pie tradition in Denby, as did the anticipated four Royal births in 1964. The 6-metre-long, 2-metre-wide and 50-centimetre-high pie provided 30,000 servings. However, this was surpassed in 1988 when Denby Dale duly celebrated its two hundred year pie-baking tradition anniversary. The most recent pie in 2000 holds the current record: 13 metres long, nearly 3 metres wide and filled with 5 tons of beef mince.

Pies are integral to British food culture, even if they weren't actually invented there. Evidence of pie-baking goes back to the time of the Egyptian pharaohs, where the pastries were so popular that they were included in grave goods to provide the deceased with sustenance 'for the long journey to eternity'. Dried flatbreads filled with honey were found in the tomb of Ramses II. In fact, we still think of pies as being perfect to take on long journeys. It was for this reason that they were so popular with the Royal Navy and in the mining industry. After all, they combine several practical features, but most importantly are nutritious and durable. In the days of the Cornish mining industry, miners would take a special version of the treat with them as they descended into the darkness below: a single pie, one half sweet, one half savoury. It was a main course and dessert rolled into one piece of dough.

The first time 'pye' made its official debut with the English public was at the luncheon following the coronation of King Henry VI (1422–61). The 'Partryche and Pecock enhackyll' pie contained whole peacocks that had been cooked and then baked in the crust. This later developed into the tradition of decorating pie crusts with pastry chickens or pheasants to indicate the meat contained within. This eventually evolved into the pre-Victorian practice of putting a porcelain bird under the pastry lid of every pie to 'let the steam escape and to draw attention to the quality of the content'.

For Denby Dale, such adaptations are probably rather superfluous given the size of its pies. All that remains to be seen is just what happy event will soon be found in Yorkshire to be worthy of honouring with an even bigger pie.

*A good pie is a magnificent dish – sweet or savoury, it may have very different ingredients. For centuries pies have been known for being nutritious and durable. Today fruit pies have made their triumphal procession in the baking world.*

## DATE & WALNUT
# LOAF

MAKES 1 LOAF

PREP TIME: 20 minutes

COOKING TIME: 35–40 minutes

### INGREDIENTS

*100 g/3½ oz dried dates,
stoned and chopped*
*½ tsp bicarbonate of soda*
*finely grated rind of ½ lemon*
*100 ml/3½ fl oz hot tea*
*40 g/1½ oz unsalted butter,
plus extra for greasing*
*70 g/2½ oz light muscovado sugar*
*1 small egg*
*125 g/4½ oz self-raising flour*
*25 g/1 oz walnuts, chopped*
*walnut halves, to decorate*

When it's raining or snowing outside, and warm and cosy inside – that's just the right time for some rich date and walnut loaf. The nuts give it a touch of winter and the sticky fruit of the date palm ensure a high sugar concentration. And even though this is really a cake – the cut slices may be spread with butter, like bread.

1. Preheat the oven to 180 °C/350 °F/Gas Mark 4. Grease a 450-g/1-lb loaf tin and line with baking paper.

2. Put the dates, bicarbonate of soda and lemon rind into a bowl and add the hot tea. Leave to soak for 10 minutes until soft.

3. Cream together the butter and sugar until light and fluffy, then whisk in the egg. Stir in the date mixture.

4. Fold in the flour using a large metal spoon, then fold in the walnuts. Spoon the mixture into the prepared tin and smooth the surface. Top with the walnut halves.

5. Bake in the preheated oven for 35–40 minutes or until risen, firm and golden brown. Leave to cool in the tin for 10 minutes, then turn out on to a wire rack to cool completely.

2.

3.

4.

1.

2.

3.

# Crumpets

MAKES 10

PREP TIME: 20 minutes,
plus 1 hour to rest

COOKING TIME: 6 minutes

The English crumpet has a chewy, spongy texture – crispy on the outside and juicy inside – and is typically eaten hot: with butter, cheese, or egg, but also with jam. It probably evolved in the 19th century from the Scottish crumpet, which looks like a pancake and is made with baking powder.

1. Sift together the flour, baking powder and salt into a large bowl. Gradually add the milk and water, adding the yeast halfway through. Whisk vigorously until the mixture is the consistency of double cream.

2. Cover the bowl with clingfilm and leave to rest for 1 hour at room temperature, until the mixture has expanded and bubbles have formed in it.

3. Oil 4 individual 8-cm/3¼-inch pastry rings and heat some oil in a heavy-based frying pan. Place the rings in the pan and pour 2–3 tablespoons of mixture into each ring. Gently fry until the tops are dry or have developed small holes.

4. Turn out the crumpets using a knife and transfer to a warmed plate. Repeat until all the mixture has been used, oiling the rings and pan when necessary.

## INGREDIENTS

230 g/8¼ oz strong white flour
1 tsp baking powder
½ tsp salt
230 ml/8¼ fl oz lukewarm milk
150 ml/5 fl oz lukewarm water
1 tsp easy-blend dried yeast
oil, for oiling and frying

# CRUSTY
# *White Loaf*

MAKES 1 LOAF

PREP TIME: 20 minutes,
plus 1 hour 30 minutes to rise

COOKING TIME: 30 minutes

## INGREDIENTS

*1 egg*
*1 egg yolk*
*150–200 ml/5–7 fl oz lukewarm water*
*500 g/1 lb 2 oz strong white flour,*
*plus extra for dusting*
*1½ tsp salt*
*2 tsp sugar*
*1 tsp easy-blend dried yeast*
*25 g/1 oz butter, diced*
*sunflower oil, for greasing*

This loaf is easy to make with just a few ingredients. This good old-fashioned bread, tender on the inside and crisp on the outside, is a wonderful choice for divine toast or a sandwich. This bread keeps well, due to the white flour, and can be found almost everywhere in Britain.

1. Brush a bowl with oil. Put the egg and egg yolk into a jug and lightly whisk to mix. Add enough lukewarm water to make up to 300 ml/10 fl oz. Stir well.

2. Put the flour, salt, sugar and yeast into a large bowl. Add the butter and rub it in with your fingertips until the mixture resembles bread crumbs. Make a well in the centre, add the egg mixture and work to a smooth dough.

3. Turn out on to a lightly floured work surface and knead well for about 10 minutes, or until smooth. Shape the dough into a ball, place it in the prepared bowl and cover with a damp tea towel. Leave to rise in a warm place for 1 hour, or until the dough has doubled in size.

4. Oil a 900-g/2-lb loaf tin. Turn out the dough on to a lightly floured work surface and knead for 1 minute, or until smooth. Shape the dough the length of the tin and 3 times the width. Fold the dough in 3 lengthways and place it in the tin with the join underneath. Cover and leave in a warm place for 30 minutes, or until it has risen above the tin. Preheat the oven to 220 °C/425 °F/Gas Mark 7.

5. Bake in the preheated oven for 30 minutes, or until firm and golden brown. Test that the loaf is cooked by tapping on the base with your knuckles – it should sound hollow. Transfer to a wire rack to cool.

2.

3.

4.

1.

2.

3.

# ENGLISH Muffins

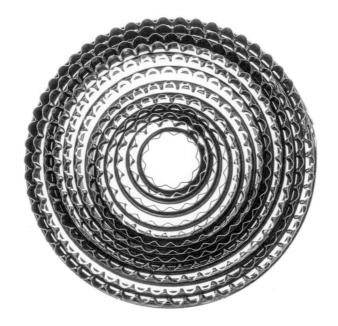

MAKES 8–10

PREP TIME: 15 minutes, plus
2 hours to rise and 1 hour to rest

COOKING TIME: 8–10 minutes

English muffins are nourishing, savoury buns. They are flat and are freshly toasted just before eating. In Central Europe, they are also called 'toasties'. In the 19th century, they were very popular at tea time and were sold on the street by loud yelling 'muffin men'.

1. Mix together the wholemeal flour, plain flour, yeast, salt and bicarbonate of soda in a large bowl. Add the buttermilk and water and mix to combine. Turn out on to a floured work surface and knead until a smooth dough forms. If it is too wet, add a little flour. Transfer to a clean bowl, cover with a damp tea towel and leave to rise for about 2 hours.

2. Turn out the dough on to a lightly floured work surface and roll out to thickness of 1 cm/½ inch. Use a 7.5-cm/3-inch round cutter to cut out 8–10 rounds, re-rolling the trimmings if necessary. Do not overwork the dough. Sprinkle the rounds with polenta and leave to rest for 1 hour.

3. Put some oil into a large frying pan and heat over a medium heat. Add the muffins to the pan in batches and cook on one side for 4–5 minutes until golden brown. Turn and cook on the other side for 4–5 minutes until golden brown. Place the cooked muffins on some kitchen paper and leave to cool before serving.

## INGREDIENTS

*120 g/4¼ oz wholemeal flour*
*120 g/4¼ oz plain flour,*
*plus extra for dusting*
*2 tsp easy-blend dried yeast*
*1 tsp salt*
*¾ tsp bicarbonate of soda*
*175 ml/6 fl oz low-fat buttermilk*
*1–2 tbsp water*
*polenta, for dusting*
*vegetable oil, for frying*

1.

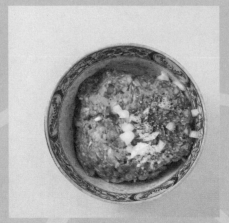

2.

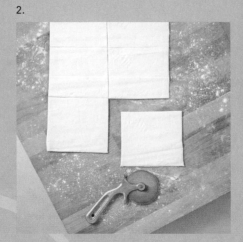

2.

# Sausage Rolls

MAKES 12

PREP TIME: 20 minutes

COOKING TIME: 20–25 minutes

## INGREDIENTS

*2 tsp milk, plus extra for brushing*
*20 g/¾ oz white bread, crusts removed and diced*
*400 g/14 oz sausage meat*
*1 onion, finely chopped*
*1 egg*
*1 egg yolk*
*½ tbsp ground cumin*
*1 tsp paprika*
*flour, for dusting*
*450 g/1 lb ready-made puff pastry*
*beaten egg white, for brushing*
*salt and pepper*

These puff pastry rolls with a sausage filling are a typically British pastry and a popular savoury party snack. You can enjoy them hot or cold, but they must be fresh! For this reason, sausage rolls are best made at home and eaten with friends and family.

1. Preheat the oven to 180 °C/350 °F/Gas Mark 4. Line a baking tray with baking paper. Put the milk into a large bowl, add the bread and leave to soak until soft. Add the sausage meat, onions, egg, egg yolk, cumin and paprika, season to taste with salt and pepper, and mix to combine.

2. Roll out the pastry on a lightly floured work surface and cut out twelve 13-cm/5-inch squares, reserving the trimmings. Brush the pastry squares with the egg white. Spread the sausage meat mixture evenly down the centre of each square, then roll up the pastry to enclose the filling.

3. Transfer the sausage rolls to the prepared tray with the join underneath. Re-roll the pastry trimmings and use a shaped cutter to cut out 12 decorative shapes.

4. Brush the sausage rolls with milk and decorate each one with a pastry shape. Brush the shapes with milk, then bake the sausage rolls in the middle of the preheated oven for 20–25 minutes until golden.

# MIXED SEED

# *Bread*
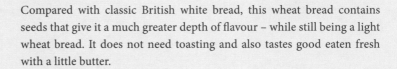

MAKES 1 LOAF

PREP TIME: 25–30 minutes,
plus 1 hour 30 minutes to rise

COOKING TIME: 30 minutes

## INGREDIENTS

*375 g/13 oz strong white flour,
plus extra for dusting*
*125 g/4½ oz rye flour*
*1½ tbsp skimmed milk powder*
*1½ tsp salt*
*1 tbsp soft light brown sugar*
*1 tsp easy-blend dried yeast*
*1½ tbsp sunflower oil, plus extra
for greasing and brushing*
*2 tsp lemon juice*
*300 ml/10 fl oz lukewarm water*
*1 tsp caraway seeds*
*½ tsp poppy seeds*
*½ tsp sesame seeds*

### topping
*1 egg, beaten with 1 tbsp water*
*1 tbsp sunflower seeds*

Compared with classic British white bread, this wheat bread contains seeds that give it a much greater depth of flavour – while still being a light wheat bread. It does not need toasting and also tastes good eaten fresh with a little butter.

1.  Put the white flour, rye flour, milk powder, salt, sugar and yeast into a large bowl. Pour in the oil and add the lemon juice and water.

2.  Stir in the seeds and mix well until smooth. Turn out on to a lightly floured surface and knead well for about 10 minutes.

3.  Brush a bowl with oil. Shape the dough into a ball, place in the bowl and cover with a damp tea towel. Leave to rise in a warm place for 1 hour, until the dough has doubled in volume.

4.  Oil a 900-g/2-lb loaf tin. Turn out the dough on to a lightly floured surface and knead for 1 minute until smooth. Shape into a loaf the length of the tin and 3 times the width. Fold the dough in 3 lengthways and place in the tin with the join underneath. Cover and leave in a warm place for 30 minutes until it has risen above the tin.

5.  Preheat the oven to 220 °C/425 °F/Gas Mark 7. Brush the egg and water glaze over the loaf, then gently press the sunflower seeds all over the top.

6.  Bake in the preheated oven for 30 minutes, or until golden brown and hollow on the base when tapped. Transfer to a wire rack to cool.

1.

2.

4.

4.

4.

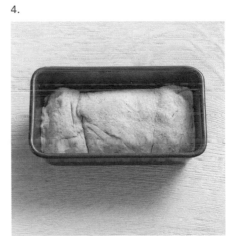

6.

# A Long &
## Rich Tradition

It is completely wrong to think that cooking on the Green Island of Europe is limited to just Irish stew or some substantial pies and cakes. For example, sourdough bread has long belonged to the Irish classics, and with the current trend for natural ingredients, sourdough bread has recently gained in popularity. Over the last few years the gourmet scene in Ireland has developed considerably, but without forgetting old traditions like 'blaa', a white and soft bread that is famous in the south of Ireland. Or 'boxty', the famous potato pancake that's often been served for Irish breakfast. And at any time of the day, a fruity tea cake is an absolute must.

# IRISH SODA *Bread*

4.

This bread is made with bicarbonate of soda and is popular throughout Ireland. It's quick and easy to make and works every time – its consistency just can't go wrong. On the Emerald Isle, several versions of this light and tasty bread are served at every possible occasion: in the morning with scrambled eggs, at lunchtime with Irish cheeses or with an Irish Stew in the evening for dinner.

1. Preheat the oven to 220 °C/425 °F/Gas Mark 7. Lightly grease a baking tray.

2. Sift the dry ingredients into a mixing bowl. Make a well in the centre, pour in most of the buttermilk and mix well, using your hands. The dough should be very soft but not too wet. If necessary, add the remaining buttermilk.

3. Turn out the dough onto a floured work surface and knead for about 10 minutes. Shape into a 20-cm/8-inch round.

4. Place the bread on the prepared baking tray, cut a cross in the top and bake in the preheated oven for 25–30 minutes.

5. Serve sliced with butter and a sweet or savoury topping.

MAKES 1 LOAF

PREP TIME: 10–15 minutes

COOKING TIME: 25–30 minutes

## INGREDIENTS

*40 g/1½ oz butter, melted, for greasing*
*450 g/1 lb plain flour,*
*plus extra for dusting*
*1 tsp salt*
*1 tsp bicarbonate of soda*
*400 ml/14 fl oz buttermilk*

# Irish

## TEA CAKE

SERVES 8–10

PREP TIME: 25 minutes

COOKING TIME: 1 hour

### INGREDIENTS

*175 g/6 oz butter, softened,
plus extra for greasing*
*200 g/7 oz caster sugar*
*1 tsp vanilla extract or 1 vanilla pod,
scraped*
*2 eggs*
*85 g/3 oz cream cheese*
*225 g/8 oz plain flour,
plus extra for dusting*
*1 tsp baking powder*
*¼ tsp salt*
*125 g/4½ oz sultanas*
*150 ml/5 fl oz buttermilk*

### glaze
*50 g/1¾ oz icing sugar, sifted*
*2 tsp fresh lemon juice*

This cake is simple yet delicious, and it can be served with fresh fruit or whipped cream as a dessert or just enjoyed on its own with a cup of tea.

1. Preheat the oven to 160 °C/325 °F/Gas Mark 3. Grease a 900-g/2-lb loaf tin. Dust with flour and line the base with baking paper.

2. Put the butter, sugar and vanilla extract into a large mixing bowl and beat with an electric whisk until fluffy. Add the eggs, one at a time, beating after each addition until combined.

3. Add the cream cheese and beat until well combined. Sift together the flour, baking powder and salt into a separate bowl. Put the sultanas into a small bowl. Add 25 g/1 oz of the flour mixture to the sultanas and stir until they are well coated. Gradually add the remaining flour mixture to the butter mixture, alternating with the buttermilk, and mix until smooth. Add the sultanas and stir with a wooden spoon until well combined.

4. Transfer the mixture to the prepared tin, smoothing the surface with a palette knife. Bake in the middle of the preheated oven for about 1 hour until golden, and a skewer inserted into the centre comes out clean. Remove from the oven and leave to cool in the tin for 10 minutes. Using a palettte knife, separate the cake from the sides of the tin and transfer to a wire rack to cool.

5. Meanwhile, to make the glaze, combine the sugar and lemon juice in a small bowl and stir until smooth. Spread the icing over the warm cake and leave to cool completely. Cut into slices and serve.

2.

3.

4.

# THE WONDERS
### *of*
# FRENCH BAKING

Fine pastries are just as much a symbol of France as the Eiffel Tower or the Louvre museum in Paris. Consequently, whether you are in a big French city or a small village, one sight is common: the streets are peppered with people enjoying a nice cup of coffee with a crispy croissant, and a newspaper. Fruit tarts, petits fours and the lavishly colourful macaroons that are currently enjoying something of a revival are of the same cultural importance as the classy fashion and shoe boutiques. However, all those sweet treats are still overshadowed by the baguette, which is a staple part of the daily diet for all French people. A small piece of this bread greets the new day in France when served for breakfast with jam; later on in the day, it turns into a welcome companion during lunch and dinner. A meal without a baguette would be just as unthinkable for a French person as a meal that is not graced with an exquisite tart to round it off.

The baguette is a politically sensitive product. Any party who tried to change the price of this bread provoked major discussions. In France, as with coffee and milk, the price of bread is controlled by the Government.

# Croissants

MAKES 12

PREP TIME: 30 minutes,
plus rising and chilling

COOKING TIME: 15–20 minutes

## INGREDIENTS

*500 g/1 lb 2 oz strong white flour,
plus extra for dusting*

*40 g/1½ oz caster sugar*

*1 tsp salt*

*2¼ tsp easy-blend dried yeast*

*300 ml/10 fl oz lukewarm milk,
plus extra if needed*

*300 g/10½ oz butter, softened,
plus extra for greasing*

*1 egg, lightly beaten with
1 tbsp milk, for glazing*

Croissants are a classic breakfast item in France and are made with puff pastry. Cold butter is worked into a yeast dough in several folding and rolling operations. Croissants are a fairly recent recipe. The first one was baked in the 19th century. Its moon shape is mentioned for the first time in 1863. The French term *croissant de lune* means 'crescent moon' in English.

1. Stir the dry ingredients into a large bowl, make a well in the centre and add the milk. Mix to a soft dough, adding more milk if too dry. Knead on a lightly floured work surface for 5–10 minutes or until smooth and elastic. Leave to rise in a large greased bowl covered in clingfilm in a warm place until doubled in size. Meanwhile, flatten the butter with a rolling pin between two sheets of greaseproof paper to form a rectangle about 5 mm/¼ inch thick, then chill in the refrigerator.

2. Preheat the oven to 200°C/400°F/Gas Mark 6. Knead the dough for 1 minute. Remove the butter from the refrigerator and leave to soften slightly. Roll out the dough on a well-floured work surface to 46 x 15 cm/18 x 6 inches. Place the butter in the centre, fold up the sides and squeeze the edges together gently. With the short end of the dough towards you, fold the top third down towards the centre, then fold the bottom third up. Rotate 90° clockwise so that the fold is to your left and the top flap opens towards your right. Roll out to a rectangle and fold again. If the butter feels soft, wrap the dough in clingfilm and chill. Repeat the rolling process twice more. Cut the dough in half. Roll out one half into a triangle 5 mm/¼ inch thick (keep the other half refrigerated). Use a card triangular template with a base of 18 cm/7 inches and sides of 20 cm/ 8 inches to cut out the croissants. Repeat with the refrigerated dough.

3. Brush the triangles lightly with the egg glaze. Roll into croissant shapes, starting at the base and tucking the point under to prevent unrolling while cooking. Brush again with the glaze. Place on an ungreased baking tray and leave to double in size. Bake in the preheated oven for 15–20 minutes or until golden brown.

1.

1.

3.

3.

4.

5.

# VANILLA
# Macaroons

MAKES 16

PREP TIME: 20 minutes, plus cooling

COOKING TIME: 10–15 minutes

In France a pastry chef is only considered a real artist if he is able to make quality macaroons. The French patisserie Ladurée claims to have invented macaroons in 1791, but in fact they first appeared during a royal wedding in 1533, served with foie gras pâté.

1. Place the ground almonds and icing sugar in a food processor and process for 15 seconds. Sift the mixture into a bowl. Line two baking trays with baking paper.

2. Place the egg whites in a clean, grease-free bowl and whisk until holding soft peaks. Gradually whisk in the caster sugar to make a firm, glossy meringue. Whisk in the vanilla extract.

3. Using a palette knife, fold the almond mixture into the egg mixture, one third at a time. When all the dry ingredients are thoroughly incorporated, continue to cut and fold the mixture until it forms a shiny mixture with a thick, ribbon-like consistency.

4. Pour the mixture into a piping bag fitted with a 1-cm/½-inch plain nozzle. Pipe 32 small rounds on to the prepared baking trays. Tap the baking trays firmly on to a work surface to remove air bubbles. Leave at room temperature for 30 minutes. Preheat the oven to 160°C/325°F/Gas Mark 3.

5. Bake in the preheated oven for 10–15 minutes. Leave to cool for 10 minutes, then carefully peel the macaroons off the baking paper. Leave to cool completely.

6. To make the filling, beat the butter and vanilla extract in a bowl until pale and fluffy. Gradually beat in the icing sugar until smooth and creamy. Use to sandwich pairs of macaroons together.

## INGREDIENTS

*85 g/3 oz ground almonds*
*115 g/4 oz icing sugar*
*2 large egg whites*
*50 g/1¾ oz caster sugar*
*½ tsp vanilla extract*

### filling
*55 g/2 oz unsalted butter, softened*
*½ tsp vanilla extract*
*115 g/4 oz icing sugar, sifted*

# Tarte Tatin

SERVES 6

PREP TIME: 25–30 minutes,
plus resting

COOKING TIME: 45–50 minutes

## INGREDIENTS

*200 g/7 oz caster sugar*
*150 g/5½ oz unsalted butter*
*800 g/1 lb 12 oz Cox or Golden Delicious*
*apples, peeled, cored and sliced*
*350 g/12 oz ready-made puff pastry*
*plain flour, for dusting*
*vanilla ice cream, to serve (optional)*

The principal feature of this apple pie is the layer of caramel that covers the fruit when you turn the cake out. According to legend, the Tatin sisters invented the tart by accident. They ran a hotel in Lamotte-Beuvron in central France in 1900. Amidst the hustle and bustle of the establishment, a cake fell out of its baking tray. They put it back with the apples underneath, covered it with fresh pastry and baked it again.

1.  Put a 20-cm/8-inch ovenproof frying pan over a low heat and add the sugar. Melt the sugar until it starts to caramelize, but do not allow it to burn, then add the butter and stir it in to make a light toffee sauce. Remove from the heat.

2.  Place the apple slices in the pan on top of the toffee sauce. The apples should fill the pan. Put the pan over a medium heat and cover. Simmer, without stirring, for about 5–10 minutes or until the apples have soaked up some of the sauce, then remove from the heat.

3.  Preheat the oven to 190 °C/375 °F/Gas Mark 5. Roll out the pastry on a lightly floured surface until the pastry is large enough to thickly cover the pan, with extra space on the sides. Lay it on top of the apples and tuck the edges down inside between the fruit and the pan until it is sealed. Don't worry about making it look too neat – it will be turned over before eating.

4.  Put the pan into the preheated oven and bake for 25–35 minutes, checking to make sure the pastry doesn't burn. The pastry should be puffed and golden. Remove from the oven and leave to rest for 30–60 minutes.

5.  When you're ready to eat, make sure the tart is still a little warm (reheat it on the hob, if necessary) and place a plate on top. Carefully turn it over and lift the frying pan off. Serve with some vanilla ice cream, if using.

# VANILLA
# *Millefeuille*

**SERVES 6**

**PREP TIME:** 1½–1¾ hours

**COOKING TIME:** 45 minutes

## INGREDIENTS

*1 kg/2 lb 4 oz ready-made puff pastry*
*flour, for dusting*

### crème pâtissière
*2 tbsp cornflour*
*125 g/4½ oz caster sugar*
*1 tsp vanilla extract*
*500 ml/18 fl oz milk*
*2 egg yolks*

### icing
*2 egg whites*
*350 g/12 oz icing sugar*
*100 g/3½ oz plain chocolate,*
*broken into pieces*

Fans of puff pastry cannot pass over this classic from France. The millefeuille (thousand leaves) consists of layers of puff pastry with a vanilla cream in between. The confectioner adds a decorative icing to the top of the cake. Nowadays, there are also savoury millefeuilles, some filled with cheese and spinach.

1. Preheat the oven to 220 °C/425 °F/Gas Mark 7. Line a baking tray with baking paper. Divide the pastry into 3 pieces on a work surface lightly dusted with flour. Roll out 1 piece to a 5-mm/¼-inch-thick square. Transfer to the prepared tray, prick all over with a fork, then place another tray on top to prevent the pastry rising.

2. Bake in the preheated oven for 10 minutes. Remove the top tray, then return the pastry to the oven and bake for a further 5 minutes until golden brown. Repeat with the remaining pastry. Leave to cool, then cut each pastry square in half to make 2 rectangles.

3. To make the crème pâtissière, put the cornflour, caster sugar and vanilla extract into a saucepan over a medium heat. Add the milk and egg yolks and cook, stirring, until the mixture comes to the boil and thickens. Remove from the heat and leave to cool completely.

4. Place a piece of pastry on a wire rack, spread with one fifth of the crème pâtissière, then place another piece of pastry on top. Spread with another fifth of the crème pâtissière and top with another piece of pastry. Repeat until you have used all of the crème pâtissière, then top with the final piece of pastry.

5. To make the icing, put the egg whites and icing sugar into a bowl over a saucepan of gently simmering water and beat with an electric whisk for 5 minutes until thick. Reserve and pour over the top piece of pastry.

6. Put the chocolate into a bowl over a saucepan of gently simmering water and heat until melted, then pour into a piping bag fitted with a fine nozzle and use it to draw wavy lines on the icing.

7. Using the tip of a knife, draw perpendicular lines through the chocolate, from bottom to top and from top to bottom to make the pattern. Use a sharp knife to trim the edges of the millefeuille.

8. Cut the millefeuille into 6 rectangles, chill in the refrigerator and serve cold.

1.

3.

4.

1.

2.

3.

4.

5.

6.

7.

8.

# STRAWBERRY

# *Éclairs*

MAKES 16–18

PREP TIME: 25 minutes

COOKING TIME: 20–25 minutes

French éclairs are usually filled or topped with cream, cream cheese, strawberries, or even chocolate. This oblong pastry has been produced since about 1850. It is made from choux pastry, a classic French pastry.

1. Preheat the oven to 220 °C/425 °F/Gas Mark 7. Grease 2 baking trays. Heat the butter and water in a saucepan until boiling.

2. Remove from the heat, quickly tip in the flour and beat until smooth. Transfer to a bowl.

3. Gradually beat in the eggs with an electric hand-held whisk, until glossy.

4. Spoon into a piping bag with a large plain nozzle and pipe up to eighteen 9-cm/3½-inch fingers on the baking trays.

5. Bake in the preheated oven for 12–15 minutes until golden brown. Cut a slit down the side of each éclair to release steam. Bake for a further 2 minutes. Cool on a wire rack.

6. Purée half the strawberries with the icing sugar.

7. To make the filling, finely chop the remaining strawberries and stir into the mascarpone.

8. Pipe or spoon the mascarpone mixture into the éclairs. Serve the éclairs with the strawberry purée spooned over. The éclairs are best served within an hour of filling.

## INGREDIENTS

**pastry**
*55 g/2 oz unsalted butter,
plus extra for greasing*
*150 ml/5 fl oz water*
*60 g/2¼ oz plain flour, sifted*
*2 eggs, beaten*

**filling**
*200 g/7 oz hulled strawberries*
*2 tbsp icing sugar*
*140 g/5 oz mascarpone cheese*

# Crème Brûlée
## TARTLETS

MAKES 6

PREP TIME: 35 minutes,
plus 8 hours to chill

COOKING TIME: 20 minutes

### INGREDIENTS

#### pastry
*175 g/6 oz plain flour, plus extra
for dusting*
*40 g/1½ oz caster sugar*
*pinch of salt*
*140 g/5 oz butter, plus extra for greasing*
*1–2 tsp cold water*

*4 egg yolks*
*50 g/1¾ oz caster sugar*
*400 ml/14 fl oz single cream*
*1 tsp vanilla extract or 1 vanilla pod,
scraped*
*demerara sugar, for sprinkling*

Crème brûlée is a flavoured egg custard with a caramel crust created by using a blowtorch at the end. The 'burnt cream' is the queen of desserts because of its unique taste and crunch. It is often on the menu in French bistros and it has been adapted here so the brûlée is in a tartlet case.

1. To make the pastry, sift together the flour, sugar and salt into a bowl. Gradually add the butter, then add the water and mix to a smooth dough using the dough hook of an electric whisk. Wrap the pastry in clingfilm and chill in the refrigerator for at least 1 hour.

2. Preheat the oven to 180 °C/350 °F/Gas Mark 4. Grease six 10-cm/4-inch tartlet tins. Turn out the pastry on to a work surface lightly dusted with flour and roll out to a thickness of 5 mm/¼ inch, then use to line the prepared tins. Re-roll and cut out the trimmings if necessary.

3. Ease the pastry into the prepared tins, pressing it up the sides of the tins. Trim the excess, then prick the pastry several times with a fork.

4. Line the pastry cases with baking paper and fill them with baking beans. Bake in the middle of the preheated oven for 10 minutes, then remove the beans and paper and bake for a further 10 minutes until golden brown, taking care that they don't burn.

5. Meanwhile, put the egg yolks and the sugar into a bowl and whisk until foaming. Heat the cream with the vanilla extract in a saucepan over a medium heat, but do not allow it to boil. Whisk in the egg and sugar mixture and continue to cook without boiling until thickened.

6. Remove from the heat and leave to cool, then pour into the pastry cases. Leave to cool completely, then chill in the refrigerator overnight.

7. Sprinkle a generous layer of demerara sugar over the chilled tartlets and heat with a kitchen blowtorch until the surface has caramelized. Alternatively, place the tartlets under a hot grill until the surface has caramelized. Serve immediately.

4.

5.

7.

# THE PAINT BOX OF THE
# SUN KING

Macaroons are a little taste of sugary heaven! Unlike most other foods, the colourful meringue biscuits have attained cult status. Like foie gras from Gascony, oysters from Arcachon and wine from Provence, they are French culinary classics.

*Available in an array of colours, macaroons
have become not only an export trend, but
also an extremely expensive sweet. A dozen
of the colourful pastries could cost more than
a bottle of a good quality red wine.*

Macaroons, along with the Eiffel Tower and the Arc de Triomphe, are now thought of as a classic French icon. Although, depending on which historic source you consult, they have been turning the heads of people from all walks of life for many centuries, it is only in recent years that they have become really popular. At every major railway station or airport, these colourful biscuits appear like gems or fashion accessories, often at fantastic prices. And yet, they neither travel well, nor keep well. It seems that macaroons occupy a curious position in this age of short-lived pleasures. Within a few years, they have turned into a sweet export hit, which has made certain Parisian elite patisseries claim to be the 'true inventors' of the macaroon. But, although Ladurée and Pierre Hermé are luxury shops that sell a medium-sized box of macaroons at the price of perfume, they actually have nothing to do with the original recipe. According to the *Larousse Gastronomique* culinary encyclopedia, its origins can be traced back to the French monastery of Cormery. The monks there, who were fond of sweet things, are supposed to have invented this type of biscuit as early as 1791. However, Catherine de Medici was also served fine almond biscuits from Florence at her wedding to the Duke of Orleans in 1533. And the writer François Rabelais heaped such praise on the recipe in his day that even Louis XIV enjoyed macaroons at his various weddings. In the mid-17th century, these biscuits formed part of the standard repertoire of the 'Officiers de Bouche', the chefs at Versailles. The Benedictine Order of Nancy also boasts of having breathed eternal life into macaroons. As the nuns were forbidden to eat meat, they specialized in making different types of bakes. Since 1792, the 'macaroons of the holy sisters' have been popular creations by the nuns of Nancy.

2.

3.

4.

# Lemon TARTE

SERVES 8–10

PREP TIME: 35 minutes, plus chilling

COOKING TIME: 25 minutes

## INGREDIENTS

**pastry**
*3 tbsp water*
*1 tbsp caster sugar*
*⅛ tsp salt*
*1 tbsp vegetable oil*
*90 g/3¼ oz unsalted butter, diced*
*150 g/5½ oz plain flour,*
*plus extra for dusting*

*2 eggs*
*2 egg yolks*
*125 ml/4 fl oz freshly squeezed lemon juice*
*grated zest of 1 lemon*
*100 g/3½ oz sugar*
*85 g/3 oz unsalted butter, diced*

The lemon has been growing in France for several centuries. One of the strongholds of its cultivation is the town of Menton on the French Riviera: a Lemon Festival has been celebrated there since 1934.

1. Preheat the oven to 200 °C/400 °F/Gas Mark 6. To make the pastry, mix together the water, sugar, salt, oil and butter with the flour. Refrigerate for 20 minutes.

2. Roll the dough on a lightly floured surface to a thickness of 5 mm/¼ inch. Place in a 23-cm/9-inch round flan tin, trimming the edge. Prick with a fork and bake for 15 minutes until golden brown. Remove from the oven and leave to cool in the tin. Do not switch off the oven.

3. Meanwhile, beat together the eggs and egg yolks and set aside. Put the lemon juice, lemon zest, sugar and butter into a saucepan over a medium heat and heat until the butter has melted. Reduce the heat, add the beaten egg and cook, stirring constantly until the mixture has thickened and bubbles are beginning to form.

4. Pour the lemon and egg mixture through a sieve set over the pastry case, evenly spreading the mixture with the back of a spoon. Return to the oven for 5 minutes. Remove from the oven and leave to cool. Serve cold.

# CINNAMON SPICED
# Orange Beignets

4.

**MAKES 8**

**PREP TIME:** 20 minutes,
plus time to rise

**COOKING TIME:** 5–10 minutes

## INGREDIENTS

*250 g/9 oz plain flour*
*1 tsp easy-blend dried yeast*
*1½ tbsp caster sugar*
*125 ml/4 fl oz lukewarm milk*
*1 egg, beaten*
*finely grated rind of 1 small orange*
*1 tsp orange flower water (available online)*
*40 g/1½ oz butter, melted*
*sunflower oil, for deep frying*
*cinnamon sugar, for dusting (available online)*
*orange slices or segments,*
*to serve*

In France most types of pastries that are baked in fat are known as beignets. They can be filled with fruit, meat, vegetables or even not have a filling at all. With orange slices, they create an intense, sweet taste experience.

1.  Sift the flour into a bowl and stir in the yeast and sugar.

2.  Add the milk, egg, orange rind, flower water and butter and mix to a soft dough, kneading until smooth.

3.  Cover and leave in a warm place until doubled in volume. Roll out on a lightly floured surface to 1 cm/½ inch in thickness and cut into eight 7.5-cm/3-inch squares.

4.  Heat the oil to 180 °C/350 °F or until a cube of bread browns in 30 seconds. Fry the beignets in batches until golden brown. Remove with a slotted spoon and drain on kitchen paper.

5.  Sprinkle with cinnamon sugar and serve hot with orange slices or segments.

# APRICOT & ALMOND Tarte

Apricot and almond trees are botanical cousins and are found in the South of France. These trees have been cultivated in this region for a long time, and they provide the fruit for this aromatic, but not overly juicy tart. The kernels of apricots harvested in warm regions are often so sweet that they may be used instead of almonds.

1. Preheat the oven to 190 °C/375 °F/Gas Mark 5. To make the pastry, put the flour, butter and icing sugar into a food processor and process to fine crumbs. Mix together the egg yolk and orange juice and stir into the flour mixture to make a soft dough.

2. Turn out the pastry on to a lightly floured work surface and roll out to a round large enough to line a 23-cm/9-inch loose-based flan tin. Prick the base with a fork, cover with a piece of greaseproof paper and fill with baking beans. Bake the base in the preheated oven for 10 minutes. Remove from the oven and take out the greaseproof paper and beans.

3. Put the butter, sugar, egg, almonds, flour and almond extract into a food processor and process to a smooth paste.

4. Spread the almond filling over the base of the pastry case and arrange the apricots, cut-side up, on top.

5. Reduce the oven temperature to 180 °C/350 °F/Gas Mark 4 and bake the tart for 35–40 minutes until the filling is set and golden brown.

6. Put the apricot jam into a small saucepan with the water and heat gently until melted. Brush over the apricots and serve the tart.

SERVES 6–8

PREP TIME: 30 minutes

COOKING TIME: 45–50 minutes

## INGREDIENTS

*85 g/3 oz unsalted butter, softened*
*85 g/3 oz caster sugar*
*1 large egg, beaten*
*140 g/5 oz ground almonds*
*40 g/1½ oz plain flour*
*½ tsp almond extract*
*10–12 apricots, stoned and quartered*
*4 tbsp apricot jam*
*1 tbsp water*

### pastry
*175 g/6 oz plain flour,*
*plus extra for dusting*
*100 g/3½ oz cold unsalted butter*
*2 tbsp icing sugar*
*1 egg yolk*
*2 tbsp orange juice*

# Brioche

MAKES 1 LOAF

PREP TIME: 20 minutes,
plus rising and overnight chilling

COOKING TIME: 35–40 minutes

## INGREDIENTS

*350 g/12 oz strong white flour,
plus extra for dusting*

*2¼ tsp easy-blend dried yeast*

*1 tbsp caster sugar*

*½ tsp salt*

*2 eggs, beaten*

*3 tbsp milk mixed with
1 tbsp lukewarm water*

*85 g/3 oz butter, softened,
plus extra for greasing*

*1 egg yolk beaten with 1½ tsp milk,
for glazing*

Normandy in the North of France is very likely the home of brioche, which was first mentioned in the 15th century. High quality butter is important for this yeast dough, which is rich in egg and fat. Its ribbed neck and the smooth round dough head on top first appeared in Paris in the 19th century.

1. Begin this recipe the day before you want to serve the brioche. Mix 280 g/10 oz of the flour, the yeast, sugar and salt together in a large bowl and make a well in the centre. Add the eggs and the milk mixture and mix, then gradually stir in the remaining flour until a sticky, flaky dough forms. Add the butter and knead it into the dough. Continue kneading until all the butter is incorporated.

2. Lightly dust a work surface with flour. Turn out the dough and knead for 5–10 minutes or until all the flour is incorporated and the dough is smooth. Lightly grease a bowl with butter. Shape the dough into a ball and roll it around in the bowl. Cover with clingfilm and set aside in a warm place until the dough doubles in volume, which can take up to several hours. Knock back the dough and re-roll it into a ball. Cover the bowl with clingfilm and chill for at least 4 hours and up to 20 hours. Generously grease a 1-litre/1¾-pint brioche mould and set aside.

3. Lightly dust a work surface with flour. Turn out the dough and very lightly knead it. Cut off a piece of dough about the size of a large egg and set aside. Roll the remaining dough into a smooth ball and place it in the mould, pressing down lightly. Use floured fingers to make a wide hole in the centre of the dough to the mould's base. Shape the remaining dough into a rounded teardrop and drop it, pointed-end down, into the hole.

4. Very lightly glaze the dough by brushing with the egg-yolk mixture, taking care not to let it drip between the dough and the mould. Cover with a clean tea towel and leave to rise until the dough is puffy and risen.

5. Meanwhile, preheat the oven to 200 °C/400 °F/Gas Mark 6. Lightly glaze the brioche again. Use scissors dipped in water to make eight snips from the edge of the mould to the edge of the teardrop. Place the mould in the preheated oven and bake for 35–40 minutes or until well risen, golden brown and the brioche sounds hollow when tapped on the base. Transfer to a wire rack to cool. Serve warm or at room temperature.

1.

2.

3.

2.

3.

4.

# MOUSSE-AU-CHOCOLAT
# TARTLETS

MAKES 6

PREP TIME: 45 minutes,
plus 2½–3½ hours to chill

COOKING TIME: 45 minutes

## INGREDIENTS

**pastry**
250 g/9 oz plain flour,
plus extra for dusting
pinch of salt
50 g/1¾ oz caster sugar
140 g/5 oz butter
1 egg
finely grated rind of 1 lemon

**filling**
375 ml/13 fl oz single cream
350 g/12 oz plain chocolate, at least 70 per
cent cocoa solids, broken into pieces
5 egg yolks
55 g/2 oz caster sugar
2½ tbsp water
chocolate, to decorate

Chocolate mousse is the most popular dessert in France and is produced here in a tartlet version. Fine chocolate mousse is wonderfully creamy because plenty of air gets in when it is beaten. The flavour depends on the quality of the chocolate, so buy the best quality chocolate that you can.

1. Preheat the oven to 180 °C/350 °F/Gas Mark 4. To make the pastry, put all the ingredients into a bowl and mix together. Roll the pastry into into a ball, wrap in clingfilm and chill for 30 minutes in the refrigerator.

2. Roll out the pastry on a lightly floured surface and ease it into six 10-cm/4-inch tartlet tins, then line them with baking paper and fill with baking beans. Bake in the preheated oven for 15 minutes, then remove the beans and paper and bake for a further 10 minutes.

3. To make the filling, heat the cream in a heatproof bowl set over a saucepan of simmering water, then add the chocolate and heat until melted. Remove from the heat and leave to cool to room temperature. Put the egg yolks, sugar and water into a separate heatproof bowl set over a saucepan of simmering water and heat, whisking constantly, for 8–10 minutes until the mixture thickens. Remove from the heat, stir into the chocolate mixture and beat with an electric whisk for 5–6 minutes.

4. Pour the filling into the pastry cases. Carefully transfer to the refrigerator and chill for 2–3 hours, or until the filling is firm. Serve chilled, decorated with chocolate.

# RASPBERRY
# *Charlotte*

SERVES 8–10

PREP TIME: 40 minutes,
plus 4 hours to chill

COOKING TIME: 10 minutes

### INGREDIENTS

*800 g/1 lb 12 oz fresh raspberries,
plus extra to decorate*
*9 gelatine leaves*
*175 g/6 oz caster sugar*
*3–4 tbsp water, plus extra for soaking*
*grated rind of ½ unwaxed lemon*
*400 ml/14 fl oz whipping cream*
*25–30 sponge fingers*
*icing sugar, to decorate*
*whipped cream, to serve (optional)*

The colourful cake is rumoured to be named after Princess Charlotte of England – the only daughter of King George IV – who died while giving birth in 1817 when she was only 21. At the time, the French chef Marie-Antoine Carême was working for the king. Originally, stale bread was used for the case, but sponge fingers are a perfect replacement. Different fruit can be used for the filling.

1.  Purée the raspberries in a food processor, then pass them through a sieve to remove the seeds. Soak the gelatine in a bowl of cold water. Heat the sugar in a small saucepan with the water, stirring until the sugar crystals have dissolved. Remove the sugar syrup from the stove, squeeze the excess water out of the soaked gelatine, add to the syrup and stir to dissolve. Stir in the raspberry purée and lemon rind. Cover and chill in the refrigerator until the mixture begins to set.

2.  Place a 26-cm/10½-inch cake ring on a plate. Cover the plate completely with tightly packed sponge fingers. Completely line the ring with sponge fingers arranged vertically, leaving no gaps.

3.  Whip the cream until it holds stiff peaks, then fold it into the raspberry mixture. Carefully fill the cake ring with the raspberry mixture, making sure that the sponges do not slip out of place, then smooth the top. Leave to set slightly.

4.  Carefully remove the cake ring. Decorate with raspberries and dust with icing sugar. Serve chilled, with dollops of whipped cream, if liked.

1.

2.

3.

3.

2.

3.

5.

# CHOCOLATE
# Petits Fours

MAKES 18

PREP TIME: 40 minutes, plus 30 minutes to chill

COOKING TIME: 25 minutes

There are numerous varieties of petits fours. Literally, it means 'small oven', as, at one time, after completing their daily production, bakers took advantage of the residual heat of the wood or coal ovens to bake this French confection. The petits fours are cut out of cake mixture, filled with jam, glazed with icing, and elaborately decorated.

1. Preheat the oven to 180 °C/350 °F/Gas Mark 4. Line a baking tray with baking paper. Put the eggs and sugar into a large bowl and beat with an electric whisk until light and fluffy. Mix together the flour, cocoa powder and cornflour in a separate bowl, then fold into the egg mixture.

2. Spread the mixture evenly on the prepared baking tray and bake in the preheated oven for 20 minutes. Remove from the oven, then lay a clean tea towel over the cake and quickly invert. Remove the baking tray and carefully peel off the baking paper.

3. Heat the jam in a small saucepan and stir in the kirsch. Cut the chocolate cake in half horizontally. On one half, spread the prepared jam evenly over the entire surface. Stack the remaining half on top. Chill in the refrigerator for 30 minutes.

4. To make the icing, heat the cream in a saucepan with the icing sugar. Stir in the butter, then add the chocolate piece by piece. Remove from the heat and leave to cool until thick, but still liquid.

5. Meanwhile, cut the chilled cake into 18 equal-sized pieces and transfer to a wire rack set over a sheet of baking paper. Pour the icing over the cakes, then place a sour cherry on each petit four and serve.

## INGREDIENTS

4 eggs
50 g/1¾ oz caster sugar
85 g/3 oz plain flour
25 g/1 oz cocoa powder
20 g/¾ oz cornflour
200 g/7 oz cherry jam
3 tbsp kirsch

### icing
100 ml/3½ fl oz whipping cream
85 g/3 oz icing sugar
40 g/1½ oz butter
150 g/5½ oz plain chocolate, at least 70 per cent cocoa solids, broken into pieces
18 sour cherries or maraschino cherries, to decorate

## LEMON POPPY SEED

# Madeleines

MAKES 36

PREP TIME: 20 minutes

COOKING TIME: 10 minutes

### INGREDIENTS

*oil, for oiling*
*3 eggs*
*1 egg yolk*
*finely grated rind of*
*1 lemon*
*140 g/5 oz golden caster sugar*
*140 g/5 oz plain flour*
*1 tsp baking powder*
*140 g/5 oz unsalted butter,*
*melted and cooled*
*1 tbsp poppy seeds*

The madeleine is a pastry that originated in around 1750 in the kitchens of the Polish aristocrat Stanislas Leszczynski. After his death, one of his pastry chefs settled in the town of Commercy in the Lorraine region and offered madeleines for sale. In the 19th century several madeleine factories were built, but the cake has only been manufactured industrially since 1939.

1. Preheat the oven to 190 °C/375 °F/Gas Mark 5. Lightly oil three 12-hole madeleine tins.

2. Whisk the eggs, yolk, lemon rind and sugar in a large bowl until very pale and thick.

3. Sift the flour and baking powder over the mixture and fold in lightly using a metal spoon. Fold in the melted butter and poppy seeds.

4. Spoon the mixture into the tins and bake in the preheated oven for about 10 minutes until well risen.

5. Turn out the cakes and cool on a wire rack, then serve while the cakes are very fresh.

1.

2.

3.

4.

1.

3.

4.

# Summer Fruit *Tartlets*

MAKES 12

PREP TIME: 30 minutes,
plus 30 minutes chilling time

COOKING TIME: 20 minutes

The combination of fresh fruit and cream on a slightly crumbly shortcrust pastry base is a wonderful summer dessert, and there are countless variations. French patisseries also offer the tartlets with a lemon, strawberry or chocolate filling.

1.  Sift the flour and icing sugar into a bowl. Stir in the almonds. Add the butter, rubbing in until the mixture resembles breadcrumbs. Add the egg yolk and milk and work in until the dough binds together. Wrap in clingfilm and chill for 30 minutes. Meanwhile, preheat the oven to 200 °C/400 °F/ Gas Mark 6.

2.  Roll out the dough on a lightly floured surface and use it to line 12 deep tartlet tins. Prick the bases with a fork and press a piece of foil into each.

3.  Bake in the preheated oven for 10–15 minutes or until light golden brown. Remove the foil and bake for a further 2–3 minutes. Transfer to a wire rack to cool.

4.  To make the filling, place the cream cheese and icing sugar in a bowl and mix together. Place a spoonful of filling in each tartlet and arrange the berries on top.

5.  Dust with sifted icing sugar and serve.

## INGREDIENTS

*200 g/7 oz plain flour, plus extra for dusting*

*85 g/3 oz icing sugar, sifted*

*55 g/2 oz ground almonds*

*115 g/4 oz butter*

*1 egg yolk*

*1 tbsp milk*

### filling

*225 g/8 oz cream cheese*

*icing sugar, to taste, plus extra, sifted, for dusting*

*350 g/12 oz fresh summer berries, such as hulled and quartered strawberries, raspberries and blueberries*

3.

5.

7.

# Fraisier

SERVES 8

PREP TIME: 40 minutes, plus 1 hour to chill

COOKING TIME: 40 minutes

## INGREDIENTS

125 g/4½ oz unsalted butter, softened, plus extra for greasing

250 g/9 oz caster sugar

1 tsp vanilla extract or 1 vanilla pod, scraped

2 eggs

375 g/13 oz plain flour

2 tsp baking powder

pinch of salt

175 ml/6 fl oz milk

375 g/13 oz fresh strawberries, hulled

icing sugar, for dusting

100 g/3½ oz marzipan

### buttercream filling

250 g/9 oz unsalted butter, softened

250 g/9 oz icing sugar

1 tsp vanilla extract or 1 vanilla pod, scraped

*Fraisier* is the French word for strawberry cake made from sponge and cream, which really showcases this fruit. The French naval officer and botanist Amédée-François Frézier first brought a strawberry plant with large berries to Europe in 1714. He had discovered it on the Chilean coast.

1.  Preheat the oven to 180 °C/350 °F/Gas Mark 4. Grease and line a 20 x 10-cm/ 8 x 4-inch loaf tin. Put the butter, sugar and vanilla extract into a bowl and beat with an electric whisk until light and fluffy. Add the eggs, one at a time, beating after each addition until combined.

2.  Sift together the flour, baking powder and salt into a separate bowl. Gradually beat in the butter mixture, alternating with the milk.

3.  Pour the mixture into the prepared tin and bake in the middle of the preheated oven for about 40 minutes or until a skewer inserted into the centre of the cake comes out clean.

4.  Turn the cake out of the tin on to a wire rack and leave to cool. Trim the top of the cake to make it flat, if necessary, then cut in two horizontally.

5.  To make the buttercream, put the butter, sugar and vanilla extract into a large bowl and beat with an electric whisk until creamy. Spread half the buttercream on top of one cake half and cover with the strawberries, standing on their bases. Cover with the remaining buttercream, filling in any gaps. Place the other cake half on top, pressing down gently but firmly.

6.  Dust a work surface with icing sugar. Roll out the marzipan into a rectangle. Place on top of the cake, covering both the top and the sides.

7.  Use a sharp knife to trim the edges of the marzipan. Chill in the refrigerator for at least 1 hour before serving.

# Baguette

## PAIN DE PARIS

When thinking about France, the mind immediately conjures up images: Paris and the Eiffel Tower, of course, with a glass of red wine and the obligatory cheese alongside it, most certainly. Perhaps one or two automobile relics are also making their way along the coils of the memory as we cast our minds back to the days when we still had dreams. Our first car, rusty and old, on its last legs during that first holiday together on the Côte. It was still fun though. French cuisine and wines are highly praised, and rightly so. French culture, literature, art and architecture were turned into icons and placed on a pedestal long ago and now serve to reinforce all of the common clichés.

However, the humble baguette, one of the greatest of all French inventions, is not even worthy of a line in the Larousse Gastronomique, a classic work in the French gastronomic world. It doesn't even mention the baguette's history. Born as the illegitimate offshoot of a coarse, round bread, the baguette was invented in the mid-18th century, when the Parisian nobility ignored the famine that was plaguing their own people, abandoning themselves to increasingly decadent culinary delights. The slender, delicate bread made from wheat was just right for the noble palate as it did not offend with its coarseness. It is difficult to tell exactly when the supposed descent of the baguette from luxury gourmet item to staple food for all began, but the likelihood is that myth and reality came together at the end of the 19th century. The global triumph of the baguette could no longer be stopped; be it on the harbour wall in the Vieux Port of La Rochelle or in New York's Times Square – the baguette has now found its place in global cuisine.

Goose liver from Gascony, truffles from Périgord, ham from Bayonne. Or even sea salt from the Atlantic, oysters from Normandy, escargots from Burgundy – the list of regional French culinary delights goes and on. But where does the baguette actually come from? Where exactly is the home of the greatest national culinary treasure? A simple bread that has accomplished the enormous feat of being considered both a blueprint for all fast foods and an indispensable accompaniment to cultured dining. A simple loaf of bread that has long since attained iconic status and is mentioned in the same breath as the Eiffel Tower and Concorde: where does it come from? While those icons embody technique and myth, the baguette is undoubtedly the minimalist among other French icons,

*Every year in February the World Championship of Baguette Making is held in Paris. More than 250 bakers from all over the world try to win the crown of French baking. The baking result is always the same as the traditional baguette is 72 cm long and weighs 200 grams.*

which have long been confined to spending the autumn of their lives in museums or as tourist attractions.

The baguette, however, is still on everyone's lips. Baked using the minimum of ingredients, energy and activity, it represents a return to basics and the bare essentials in the form of bread. By remaining both pure and original, the baguette has gained a sacrosanct status for itself. The baguette is wholesome, unadulterated and simply a purist. Any attempt to find decorative elements in this icon will be in vain. The baguette is everywhere because it has made itself an indispensable part of everyday life. No one dares put a regional stamp on it; a baguette from Paris is as much of an original as its counterpart from Nice, Bordeaux or Lyon. Even its foreign siblings have been standardized, probably because they carry the same label; be it in Polish (bagetka), Italian (baguette), German (baguette) or Portuguese (baguete), the language always adapts itself to the bread. When the baguette first began its triumph in noble palaces around 300 years ago, its task was to protect the palates of connoisseurs and save them from coarse and sharp-edged crusts. Nowadays, for many, the baguette is the first taste of continental living that holidaymakers, especially the British, experience on their first visit across the Channel to France and it is thought of with fondness. The baguette's popularity in so many countries has created a bread-making industry that produces a vast range of bakes in all shapes, sizes, grains, textures and flavours. The current desire for locally produced fresh bread, free from artificial ingredients, has its roots in people's experience of buying daily baguettes from bakeries while in France.

Porteuse de pain                28/8/04
*Ce n'est pas un pain, comme celui-là*
*que vous mériteriez!*
                Na

# Baguettes

MAKES 4

PREP TIME: 20 minutes,
plus 1 hour to rise

COOKING TIME: 20–25 minutes

## INGREDIENTS

500 g/1 lb 2 oz strong white flour,
plus extra for dusting

2 tsp sugar

2 tsp salt

15 g/½ oz fresh yeast (available in bakeries
or online)

375 ml/13 fl oz lukewarm water

The baguette is the classic white bread from France. Gluten-rich flour, yeast and cool dough processing make for the typical rough, uneven pores. A high proportion of crust creates the strong flavour.

1. Mix together the flour, sugar and salt in a bowl. Make a well in the centre and crumble the yeast into it. Pour the water into the well and mix in the yeast and flour to make a smooth dough.

2. Divide the dough into 4 pieces, cover with clingfilm and leave to rise for 30 minutes.

3. Transfer the dough pieces to a work surface lightly dusted with flour, knock back and shape each piece into a 5-cm/2-inch-thick roll.

4. Place the uncooked baguettes on a tea towel dusted with flour. Make folds in the towel to separate each baguette from the next. It is important that the loaves are not too close together so that they have room to rise. Cover with clingfilm and leave to rise in a warm place for about 30 minutes.

5. Preheat the oven to 240 °C/475 °F/Gas Mark 9 and place a bowl of water in the bottom of the oven. Line a baking tray with baking paper. Place the baguettes on the prepared sheet and use a sharp knife to make 5 diagonal cuts in each.

6. Dust the baguettes with flour and bake in the middle of the preheated oven for 20–25 minutes until golden brown.

1.

3.

4.

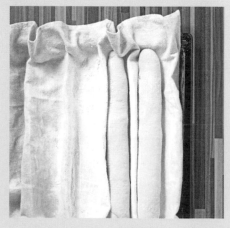

# Quiche

## LORRAINE

SERVES 4–6

PREP TIME: 30 minutes,
plus 30 minutes to chill

COOKING TIME: 45–50 minutes

This classic quiche from Alsace Lorraine is also known as bacon tart. Around 1850 the recipe spread throughout the rest of France. This savoury tart, baked in a flan tin, is eaten warm as a starter or as a main dish. Originally it was made from bread dough, but today shortcrust pastry is used. Onions, bacon or lardons, cheese, eggs and cream should definitely be in the filling.

1. To make the pastry, sift the flour into a bowl and rub in the butter with your fingertips until the mixture resembles fine breadcrumbs. Stir in just enough water to bind to a soft dough.

2. Roll out the dough on a lightly floured work surface and use to line a 23-cm/9-inch flan tin. Press into the edges, trim the excess. Chill in the refrigerator for 15 minutes.

3. Preheat the oven to 200 °C/400 °F/Gas Mark 6. Prick the base with a fork, cover with a piece of greaseproof paper and fill with baking beans, then bake the base in the preheated oven for 10 minutes until lightly browned. Remove from the oven and take out the greaseproof paper and beans, then bake for a further 10 minutes.

4. Melt the butter in a frying pan, add the onion and fry for 2 minutes, then add the mushrooms and fry, stirring, for a further 3–5 minutes. Add the bacon, then spread the mixture evenly in the pastry case.

5. Put the eggs into a bowl with the cream and beat together, then season to taste with salt and pepper. Pour into the pastry case and sprinkle with the cheese. Bake for 20–25 minutes until golden brown and just set.

## INGREDIENTS

15 g/½ oz butter
1 small onion, finely chopped
115 g/4 oz closed-cup mushrooms, sliced
140 g/5 oz cooked bacon, diced, or lardons
2 eggs, beaten
200 ml/7 fl oz single cream
55 g/2 oz Gruyère cheese, grated
salt and pepper

### pastry

200 g/7 oz plain flour,
plus extra for dusting
100 g/3½ oz butter
2–3 tbsp cold water

# FOUGASSE
## OLIVE BREAD

MAKES 2 LOAVES

PREP TIME: 20–25 minutes,
plus rising

COOKING TIME: 25–30 minutes

### INGREDIENTS

*350 g/12 oz strong white flour,
plus extra for kneading*

*55 g/2 oz fine semolina flour,
plus extra for dusting*

*2¼ tsp easy-blend dried yeast*

*1½ tsp sugar*

*2 tsp salt*

*250 ml/9 fl oz lukewarm water*

*olive oil, for oiling and brushing*

*100 g/3½ oz black olives, stoned
and finely chopped*

*1½ tbsp herbes de Provence (optional)*

*tapenade or olive oil, to serve (optional)*

Fougasse is usually associated with Provence, but the bread also exists in different variations in other regions of the country. The classic version is shaped or slit like an ear of wheat and contains olives and herbs – typical ingredients from the French Mediterranean region.

1. Mix the strong white flour, semolina flour, yeast, sugar and salt together in a bowl and make a well in the centre. Gradually stir the water into the well, drawing in flour from the side until a soft, sticky dough forms. You might not need all the water, depending on the flour. Turn out the dough on to a lightly floured work surface and knead for 5–10 minutes or until it becomes smooth. Shape the dough into a ball, place it in an oiled bowl and roll it around so it is coated in oil. Cover the bowl with clingfilm and set aside in a warm place until the dough has doubled in volume.

2. Preheat the oven to 230 °C/450 °F/Gas Mark 8. Dust two baking trays with semolina flour and set aside. Turn out the dough on to a lightly floured work surface. Add the olives and herbs, if using, and quickly knead until they are evenly distributed. Divide the dough into two equal portions.

3. Using an oiled rolling pin, roll one piece of dough into an oval, 23–25 cm/ 9–10 inches long. Dust a sharp knife with semolina flour and make a long vertical slit in the centre of the dough, without cutting through the edges, then make three slits on each side in a herringbone pattern. Transfer the dough to a prepared baking tray. Shape the remaining dough and place on the other baking tray. Use oiled fingers to pull the slits apart, if necessary. Lightly brush the fougasses with oil, taking care to brush inside the slits. Place in the preheated oven, reduce the temperature to 200 °C/400 °F/Gas Mark 6 and bake for 25–30 minutes or until the loaves are golden brown and sound hollow when tapped on the base. Transfer to a wire rack to cool. Serve warm, with tapenade or olive oil.

# Garlic & Herb Bread Spirals

SERVES 6–8

PREP TIME: 30 minutes,
plus 2 hours to rise

COOKING TIME: 25 minutes

## INGREDIENTS

*500 g/1 lb 2 oz strong white flour,*
*plus extra for dusting*
*2¼ tsp easy-blend dried yeast*
*1½ tsp salt*
*350 ml/12 fl oz lukewarm water*
*2 tbsp oil, plus extra for greasing*
*85 g/3 oz butter, melted and cooled*
*3 garlic cloves, crushed*
*2 tbsp chopped fresh parsley*
*2 tbsp snipped fresh chives*
*beaten egg, for glazing*
*sea salt flakes, for sprinkling*

Garlic has been used since ancient times as a seasoning, but also as a remedy. Egyptian slaves used it as a tonic and to remove lice. The plant came from the Asian steppes across the Mediterranean Sea to Europe and since then it has been an important part of Southern French cuisine.

1. Brush a large baking tray with oil. Combine the flour, yeast and salt in a mixing bowl. Stir in the water and half the oil, mixing to a soft, sticky dough.

2. Turn out the dough on to a lightly floured work surface and knead until smooth and no longer sticky. Return to the bowl, cover and leave in a warm place for about 1 hour until doubled in size.

3. Meanwhile, preheat the oven to 240 °C/475 °F/Gas Mark 9. Mix together the butter, garlic, herbs and remaining oil. Roll out the dough to a 33 x 23-cm/ 13 x 9-inch rectangle and spread the herb mix evenly over the dough to within 1-cm/½-inch of the edge.

4. Roll up the dough from one long side and place on the prepared baking tray, join underneath. Cut into 12 thick slices and arrange, cut-side down, on the baking tray about 2 cm/¾ inch apart.

5. Cover and leave to rise in a warm place until doubled in size and springy to the touch. Brush with the beaten egg and sprinkle with sea salt flakes. Bake in the preheated oven for 20–25 minutes until golden brown and firm. Leave to cool on a wire rack.

# Baking *in* the Sun

From Portugal, Spain, Italy and Greece to Turkey – the countries of the Mediterranean have many things in common: lots of sun and sea and a food culture that helps itself to nature's rich treasures. For this reason, fresh fruit, nuts and olives find their way into the bakeries. Italy's baking culture, for example, can look back on a long tradition. More than 2,000 years ago, the focaccia we are familiar with today was already one of the favourite foods of the Etruscans living in central Italy. Even today, the Italian art of baking is a celebrated craft and is as creative as ever. Hardly anyone knows that the famous ciabatta was only invented around the end of the 20th century, by Arnaldo Cavallari. Ever since, there has been no stopping its triumphal march into the culinary world. Nowadays it is difficult to imagine an Italian meal without ciabatta. On the other hand, in contrast to the rather neutral-tasting bread common to the Mediterranean region, there is a variety of extremely sweet pastries and desserts. Tuscan Christmas cake, lemon polenta cake and succulent fig tartlets are just a few examples of the creations made possible in Mediterranean households by the fruits of nature.

Many different countries and many different cultures – the baking tradition varies a lot between Portugal and Turkey. However, all countries share a focus on fresh fruit and vegetables.

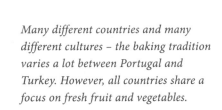

# Spanish

## CUSTARD FLAN

SERVES 8

PREP TIME: 40 minutes,
plus 40 minutes to chill

COOKING TIME: 1 hour

### INGREDIENTS

2 eggs

50 g/1¾ oz caster sugar

2 tsp vanilla extract
or 2 vanilla pods, scraped

2 tsp cornflour

200 ml/7 fl oz milk

200 ml/7 fl oz whipping cream

pinch of ground nutmeg

chopped blanched almonds and
fresh raspberries, to decorate

#### pastry

280 g/10 oz plain flour,
plus extra for dusting

2 tbsp caster sugar

125 g/4½ oz butter, diced,
plus extra for greasing

2–3 tbsp water

1 egg yolk

1 tbsp lemon juice

Different versions of pastry tarts with custard fillings have been known since the Middle Ages, especially in Western Europe. Spaniards love the combination of custard with fresh fruit – the flan in this recipe is enhanced for a special occasion with raspberries, cream and almonds.

1. To make the pastry, sift the flour into a large bowl. Stir in the sugar and rub in the butter until the mixture resembles fine breadcrumbs, then gradually add the water, egg yolk and lemon juice. Mix to a pliable dough.

2. Turn out the dough onto a lightly floured work surface and gently knead. Form into a ball, wrap in clingfilm and chill in the refrigerator for 30 minutes.

3. Preheat the oven to 190 °C/375 °F/Gas Mark 5. Lightly grease a 23-cm/ 9-inch round loose-based fluted tart tin. Take the dough from the refrigerator a few minutes before using, then roll out on a lightly floured work surface. Ease the pastry into the prepared tin and trim the edges. Transfer to the refrigerator to chill for 10 minutes. Place a piece of baking paper, large enough to cover the edges, onto the pastry, fill with baking beans and bake in the preheated oven for 10 minutes.

4. Remove the paper and baking beans and bake for a further 5 minutes. Remove from the oven and reduce the oven temperature to 150 °C/300 °F/ Gas Mark 2.

5. Meanwhile, put the eggs, sugar and vanilla extract into a large bowl and mix together. In a separate bowl, blend the cornflour with a little of the milk to form a smooth paste. Pour the remaining milk and half of the cream into a small saucepan. Add the cornflour mixture and stir until smooth and combined. Heat gently, stirring, until the milk is hot but not boiling. Gently whisk into the egg mixture until just combined.

6. Strain the mixture into the pastry case and sprinkle with nutmeg. Carefully transfer to the oven and bake for 35–40 minutes, or until just set. Remove from the oven and leave to cool completely. Whip the remaining cream until it holds soft peaks, then spread it over the cooled filling. Decorate with chopped almonds and fresh raspberries and serve immediately.

3.

3.

5.

6.

1.

2.

3.

4.

# Chocolate
## FILO PARCELS

Filo pastry is a popular staple in eastern Mediterranean kitchens. It is very similar to central European flaky pastry, but the leaves are thinner and more translucent. They are made singly and used singly by extremely skilled confectioners. Luckily, you can purchase them ready-made (either chilled or frozen).

1.  Preheat the oven to 190°C/375°F/Gas Mark 5. Grease a baking tray. Mix the nuts, mint and soured cream in a bowl. Add the apples, stir in the chocolate and mix well.

2.  Cut each pastry sheet into 4 squares. Brush 1 square with butter, then place a second square on top and brush with butter.

3.  Place 1 tablespoonful of the chocolate mixture in the centre, bring up the corners and twist together. Repeat until all of the pastry and filling have been used.

4.  Place the parcels on the prepared baking tray and bake in the preheated oven for about 10 minutes, until crisp and golden. Remove from the oven and leave to cool slightly.

5.  Dust with icing sugar and serve.

MAKES 18

PREP TIME: 15–20 minutes

COOKING TIME: 10 minutes

### INGREDIENTS

85 g/3 oz ground hazelnuts
1 tbsp finely chopped fresh mint
125 ml/4 fl oz soured cream
2 eating apples, peeled and grated
55 g/2 oz plain chocolate, melted
55–85 g/2–3 oz butter, melted, plus extra for greasing
9 sheets filo pastry, about 15 cm/6 inches square
icing sugar, sifted, for dusting

2.

2.

3.

# Lemon Polenta Cake

SERVES 8

PREP TIME: 20 minutes,
plus 20 minutes to cool

COOKING TIME: 30–35 minutes

In the 17th century, polenta, which is made from maize, was a 'poor people's food' that was found from Spain to as far as southern Russia. The solid porridge, made from coarsely ground grain, is a regional culinary tradition, especially in Italy, and creates desserts with a lovely coarse texture.

1. Preheat the oven to 180°C/350°F/Gas Mark 4. Grease a deep 20-cm/ 8-inch round cake tin and line with baking paper.

2. Beat together the butter and sugar until pale and fluffy. Beat in the lemon rind, lemon juice, eggs and ground almonds. Sift in the polenta and baking powder and stir until evenly mixed. Spoon the mixture into the prepared tin and smooth the surface. Bake in the preheated oven for 30–35 minutes, or until just firm to the touch and golden brown. Remove the cake from the oven and leave to cool in the tin for 20 minutes.

3. Meanwhile, to make the syrup, put the lemon juice, sugar and water into a small saucepan. Heat gently, stirring until the sugar has dissolved, then bring to the boil and simmer for 3–4 minutes, or until slightly reduced and syrupy. Turn out the cake on to a wire rack, then brush half of the syrup evenly over the surface. Leave to cool completely.

4. Cut the cake into slices, drizzle the extra syrup over the top and serve with crème fraîche.

## INGREDIENTS

*200 g/7 oz unsalted butter, plus extra for greasing*
*200 g/7 oz caster sugar*
*finely grated rind and juice of 1 large lemon*
*3 eggs, beaten*
*140 g/5 oz ground almonds*
*100 g/3½ oz quick-cook polenta*
*1 tsp baking powder*
*crème fraîche, to serve*

### syrup
*juice of 2 lemons*
*55 g/2 oz caster sugar*
*2 tbsp water*

# CRANBERRY & PINE NUT

# Biscotti

MAKES 18–20

PREP TIME: 15–20 minutes

COOKING TIME: 30–35 minutes

## INGREDIENTS

*butter or oil, for greasing*
*85 g/3 oz light muscovado sugar*
*1 large egg*
*140 g/5 oz plain flour, plus extra for dusting*
*½ tsp baking powder*
*1 tsp ground mixed spice*
*55 g/2 oz dried cranberries*
*55 g/2 oz pine nuts, toasted*

Biscotti are twice-baked biscuits of Italian origin, and this recipe is a classic version with cranberries and pine nuts. The name goes back to the medieval word *biscoctus*, meaning 'twice cooked'. The Roman scholar Pliny the Elder is said to have boasted they would be edible for centuries. Non-perishable food was especially useful on long journeys.

1. Preheat the oven to 180 °C/350 °F/Gas Mark 4. Grease a baking tray and line with baking paper.

2. Whisk together the sugar and egg in a large bowl until pale and thick enough to form a trail when the whisk is lifted.

3. Sift together the flour, baking powder and mixed spice into the bowl and fold into the mixture.

4. Stir in the cranberries and pine nuts and mix lightly to a smooth dough.

5. With lightly floured hands, shape the mixture into a long sausage, about 28 cm/11 inches long. Press to flatten slightly.

6. Lift the dough on to the baking tray and bake in the preheated oven for 20–25 minutes, until golden. (Do not switch off the oven after this first baking.)

7. Leave to cool for 3–4 minutes, then cut into 1.5-cm/⅝-inch-thick slices and arrange on the baking tray.

8. Bake in the oven for 10 minutes, or until golden. Remove from the oven, transfer to a wire rack and leave to cool completely.

2.

5.

6.

7.

1.

2.

3.

# Mascarpone *Cheesecake*

SERVES 10

PREP TIME: 45 minutes,
plus 3 hours to cool and chill

COOKING TIME:
1 hour–1 hour 10 minutes

## INGREDIENTS

**base**
*165 g/5¾ oz amaretti biscuits*
*90 g/3¼ oz sugar*
*40 g/1½ oz butter*
*40 g/1½ oz clear honey*

*300 g/10½ oz mascarpone cheese, at room temperature*
*600 g/1 lb 5 oz cream cheese, at room temperature*
*250 g/9 oz granulated sugar*
*5 eggs*
*1 egg yolk*
*100 ml/3½ fl oz whipping cream*
*1 tsp vanilla extract or 1 vanilla pod, scraped*
*finely grated zest of 1 orange*

People have been making cheesecakes with curd cheese or soured cream since the time of the ancient Romans. Many different versions have long been found across Europe. In this version, Italian biscuits and honey dominate and the filling contains a hefty portion of mascarpone. This mild, Italian soft cheese, made with cream, makes the cake creamier and gives a more intense flavour.

1.  Preheat the oven to 160 °C/325 °F/Gas Mark 3. To make the base, put the biscuits into a food processor with the sugar and pulse until reduced to fine crumbs. Add the butter and honey and process until incorporated. Press the mixture into the base of a 25-cm/10-inch springform cake tin.

2.  Put the mascarpone cheese, cream cheese and sugar into a large bowl and mix to combine. Add the eggs and egg yolk and beat until incorporated. Add the cream, vanilla extract and orange zest and stir until the mixture is well combined.

3.  Pour the mixture into the prepared tin and bake in the preheated oven for 1 hour–1 hour 10 minutes, until set but still soft in the middle. Turn off the oven but do not remove the cheesecake. After 1 hour, remove the cheesecake from the oven and transfer to a wire rack to cool completely. Unclip and remove the springform from the tin, leaving the cheesecake on the base of the tin, then transfer to the refrigerator to chill for at least 2 hours. Serve chilled.

# Torta Caprese

## CHOCOLATE CAKE

SERVES 12

PREP TIME: 20 minutes, plus 20 minutes to soak

COOKING TIME: 40 minutes

### INGREDIENTS

100 g/3½ oz raisins

finely grated rind and juice of 1 orange

175 g/6 oz butter, diced, plus extra for greasing

100 g/3½ oz plain chocolate, at least 70 per cent cocoa solids, broken into pieces

4 large eggs, beaten

100 g/3½ oz caster sugar

1 tsp vanilla extract

55 g/2 oz plain flour

55 g/2 oz ground almonds

½ tsp baking powder

pinch of salt

55 g/2 oz blanched almonds, lightly toasted and chopped

icing sugar, sifted, to decorate

For more than 3,000 years, the inhabitants of what is present-day Mexico have been making use of the cacao tree. In 1528, the Spanish conquistadors brought the fruit to Europe. But they did not like the taste of unsweetened chocolate. It only became popular in Europe after honey and cane sugar were added. Fine chocolate is the basis for this rich cake, which needs to be topped with only a little icing sugar.

1. Preheat the oven to 180°C/350°F/Gas Mark 4. Line a deep, loose-based, 25-cm/10-inch round cake tin with greaseproof paper. Grease the paper.

2. Put the raisins into a small bowl, add the orange juice and leave to soak for 20 minutes.

3. Melt the butter and chocolate together in a small saucepan over a medium heat, stirring. Remove from the heat and set aside to cool.

4. Put the eggs, sugar and vanilla extract into a large bowl and beat with an electric whisk until light and fluffy. Stir in the cooled chocolate mixture.

5. Drain the raisins if they have not absorbed all the orange juice. Sift together the flour, ground almonds, baking powder and salt into the egg and sugar mixture. Add the raisins, orange rind and blanched almonds and fold all the ingredients together.

6. Spoon into the prepared tin and smooth the surface. Bake in the preheated oven for 40 minutes, or until a cocktail stick inserted into the centre comes out clean and the cake starts to come away from the side of the tin. Leave to cool in the tin for 10 minutes, then remove from the tin, transfer to a wire rack and leave to cool completely. Dust the surface with icing sugar before serving.

2.

4.

5.

# LA COMIDA
# *de Picasso*

Lunchtime. But it's not just an ordinary lunch.
None other than Pablo Picasso is sitting in front
of an empty plate with a glass before him, staring
out at what appears to be nothing.

*Every moment of his life Pablo Picasso enjoyed being an artist – even at lunchtime. The bread loaves are a symbol of his extraordinary abilities.*

The mood in the photograph is curiously ordinary; it is only when we take a second glance at the picture, photographed by Robert Doisneau in 1952, that it reveals its true message: small loaves of bread caricature the genius painter's most important tools as a pair of oversized hands. Fingers as large as the paws of a monster taking a break. To boot, they allude to a French pun which – at least in the French language – puts the loaves and Picasso's hands on the same level. The loaves (pains) and the hands (mains) are a symbol for superhuman gifts or abilities. In fact, Picasso is obviously enjoying time out from his demanding work as an artist on the Côte d'Azur. What appears to be a humorous finger exercise for both artists, has in over 60 years become one of the best-selling photo motifs in the entire world. In France and Spain alone – Picasso's two principal places of residence – several million posters have been made from this photo. It may seem that artists chose to depict bread for purely aesthetic reasons, but this kind of bread played a crucial role in the Mediterranean region. The typical long bread, as seen in the photograph, has a long tradition probably going back to the 15th century. It was the custom in Spain, as well as in France, to roll the bread out into a long loaf on a work surface sprinkled with ground aniseed. These Mediterranean breads can be traced back to the Late Latin word focacia ('baked dough'), a derivation of the word focus ('hearth/stove', 'pan'). The Italian flat bread focaccia, the French fouace (or fouasse or fougasse) and the Spanish hogaza have the same etymological origin.

2.

3.

5

6.

6.

# Panforte

## CHRISTMAS CAKE

SERVES 14

PREP TIME: 30 minutes

COOKING TIME: 1½ hours

### INGREDIENTS

*115 g/4 oz hazelnuts*
*115 g/4 oz almonds*
*85 g/3 oz chopped mixed peel*
*55 g/2 oz ready-to-eat dried apricots, finely chopped*
*55 g/2 oz glacé pineapple, finely chopped*
*grated rind of 1 orange*
*55 g/2 oz plain flour*
*2 tbsp cocoa powder*
*1 tsp ground cinnamon*
*¼ tsp ground coriander*
*¼ tsp freshly grated nutmeg*
*¼ tsp ground cloves*
*115 g/4 oz caster sugar*
*175 g/6 oz clear honey*
*icing sugar, for dusting*

This popular spiced Christmas cake from the Tuscan city of Siena is called panforte and is similar to medieval recipes, such as gingerbread. It developed from a kind of a fruit cake that was a nutritious and non-perishable food in winter. The recipe was later refined using the spices that were traded in Siena and other places.

1. Preheat the oven to 180 °C/350 °F/Gas Mark 4. Line a 20-cm/8-inch round loose-based cake tin with baking paper.

2. Spread out the hazelnuts on a baking tray and toast in the preheated oven for 10 minutes until golden brown. Tip on to a tea towel and rub off the skins.

3. Meanwhile, spread out the almonds on a baking tray and toast in the oven for 10 minutes until golden. Watch carefully as they can burn easily.

4. Reduce the oven temperature to 150 °C/300 °F/Gas Mark 2. Chop all the nuts and place in a large bowl. Add the mixed peel, apricots, pineapple and orange rind to the nuts and mix well.

5. Sift together the flour, cocoa, cinnamon, coriander, nutmeg and cloves into the bowl and mix well.

6. Put the caster sugar and honey into a saucepan set over a low heat and cook, stirring constantly, until the sugar has dissolved. Bring to the boil and cook for a further 5 minutes until thickened and beginning to darken. Stir the nut mixture into the saucepan and remove from the heat.

7. Spoon the mixture into the prepared cake tin and smooth the surface. Bake in the oven for 1 hour, then remove from the oven and leave in the tin to cool completely. Carefully turn out of the tin and peel off the baking paper. Place on a cake plate, dust with icing sugar and cut into slices to serve.

# Cantucci

## BISCOTTI

MAKES 25–30

PREP TIME: 20 minutes

COOKING TIME: 20 minutes

### INGREDIENTS

*butter, for greasing*
*500 g/1 lb 2 oz plain flour,*
*plus extra for dusting*
*3 tsp baking powder*
*500 g/1 lb 2 oz caster sugar*
*pinch of salt*
*3 eggs*
*2 egg yolks*
*300 g/10½ oz roasted almonds*

Cantucci are almond biscuits from Tuscany that are twice baked. First they are baked in loaf shapes and then baked as cut slices. This makes them crumbly and they last a long time. The rather firm cantucci are enjoyed dunked in a coffee or a dessert wine.

1. Preheat the oven to 160 °C/325 °F/Gas Mark 3. Grease a baking tray and dust it with flour. Sift together the flour, baking powder, sugar and salt into a large bowl and make a well in the centre. Break 2 eggs into the well, add the egg yolks and gently fold into the flour mixture. Add the almonds and mix to combine.

2. Divide the dough into 2 or 3 pieces and shape each piece into a 5-cm/ 2-inch-high loaf shape. Place on the prepared baking tray. Beat the remaining egg and brush it over the tops of the loaves, then bake in the preheated oven for 15 minutes.

3. Remove the baked loaves from the oven (do not turn off the oven) and leave to stand until cool to the touch. Using a knife, cut each loaf into 2-cm/¾-inch slices. Place on the baking tray, cut-side down, and bake for 5 minutes, or until golden brown. Remove from the oven and leave to cool. Serve with coffee or dessert wine.

1.

2.

3.

2.

3.

3.

# Siphnopitta
## CHEESECAKE

Siphnopitta is the Greek version of cheesecake made with honey and slightly stronger tasting cheese. Traditionally, soft, unsalted sheep's or goat's cheese is used – but you can use Italian ricotta instead. The recipe is from the Cycladic island of Sifnos and is traditionally baked at Easter.

1.  Preheat the oven to 180 °C/350 °F/Gas Mark 4. Lightly grease a 30 x 20-cm/ 12 x 8-inch rectangular fluted tart tin. Sift together the flour and salt into a large bowl. Beat the butter into the flour mixture, then gradually add the water until the mixture comes together. Shape into a ball, wrap in clingfilm and chill in the refrigerator for about 30 minutes.

2.  Roll out the pastry on a lightly floured work surface, then ease it into the prepared tin, trimming the edges. Bake in the preheated oven for 10 minutes, then remove from the oven and leave to cool in the tin. Increase the oven temperature to 190 °C/375 °F/Gas Mark 5.

3.  Put the eggs, ricotta cheese, cinnamon and honey into a medium-sized bowl and mix to combine. Carefully pour the cheese mixture into the cooled pastry case and bake for about 30–35 minutes until firm and golden brown. Dust with cinnamon and leave to cool. Decorate with the orange slices, orange and lemon rind and mint sprigs and serve.

SERVES 6–8

PREP TIME: 25 minutes, plus 30 minutes to chill

COOKING TIME: 40–45 minutes

## INGREDIENTS

*290 g/10¼ oz plain flour, plus extra for dusting*

*½ tsp salt*

*250 g/9 oz butter, softened, plus extra for greasing*

*3–4 tbsp water*

*4 eggs*

*450 g/1 lb ricotta cheese*

*1 tsp ground cinnamon, plus extra for dusting*

*5 tbsp clear honey, or to taste*

### to decorate
*orange slices*
*chopped fresh orange and lemon rind*
*fresh mint sprigs*

# *Fig* TARTLETS

SERVES 4

PREP TIME: 10–15 minutes

COOKING TIME: 15–20 minutes

## INGREDIENTS

*250 g/9 oz ready-made
puff pastry
plain flour, for dusting
8 fresh ripe figs
1 tbsp caster sugar
½ tsp ground cinnamon
milk, for brushing
vanilla ice cream, to serve*

The fig, which has been cultivated throughout the Mediterranean since ancient times, is one of the oldest domesticated crops. Most figs are traditionally sold dried. Pastries with fresh figs, however, have a real taste of summer. When buying figs, check that they have the right consistency: ripe fruit is soft but not mushy.

1.  Preheat the oven to 190 °C/375 °F/Gas Mark 5. Line a baking tray with baking paper. Roll out the pastry on a lightly floured board to a thickness of 5 mm/¼ inch.

2.  Using a saucer as a guide, cut out four 15-cm/6-inch rounds and place on the prepared baking tray.

3.  Use a sharp knife to score a line around each round, about 1 cm/ ½ inch from the edge. Prick the centre of each round all over with a fork.

4.  Slice the figs into quarters and arrange 8 quarters over the centre of each pastry round.

5.  Mix together the sugar and cinnamon and sprinkle over the figs.

6.  Brush the edges of the pastry with milk and bake in the preheated oven for 15–20 minutes, until risen and golden brown. Serve the tartlets warm with ice cream.

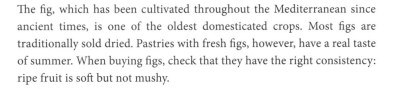

1.

2.

3.

4.

5.

# Honeyed

## BAKLAVA PASTRIES

MAKES 30

PREP TIME: 45 minutes

COOKING TIME: 45 minutes

### INGREDIENTS

*400 g/14 oz finely chopped mixed nuts, such as walnuts, almonds, pistachio nuts*

*450 g/1 lb ready-made filo pastry sheets*

*175 g/6 oz butter, melted, plus extra for greasing*

*2 tbsp caster sugar*

*1 tsp ground cinnamon*

### syrup

*325 g/11½ oz caster sugar*

*300 ml/10 fl oz water*

*1 tbsp lemon juice*

*3 tbsp clear honey*

*2 small cinnamon sticks*

Baklava is popular in Balkan and Middle Eastern cuisine: a rich, sweet pastry made from filo pastry and filled with nuts and sweetened with syrup or honey. This is the recipe for the Turkish version with honey and walnuts. It is popularly served on feast days.

1. Preheat the oven to 180 °C/350 °F/Gas Mark 4. Grease or line a baking tray with baking paper. Spread the nuts on the prepared tray and bake in the preheated oven for 5–10 minutes. Do not turn off the oven.

2. Meanwhile, place 1 layer of filo pastry in a 25 x 35-cm/10 x 14-inch baking tin. (Cover the unused sheets with a damp tea towel to prevent them drying out.) Brush the pastry with melted butter. Continue layering the pastry and brushing with butter until there are 5–7 layers of pastry in the tin.

3. Mix the nuts with the sugar and cinnamon. Sprinkle a third of the nut mixture over the pastry in the tin, then cover with 2–3 buttered layers of pastry. Sprinkle half of the remaining nut mixture over the pastry and cover with 2–3 layers of buttered pastry. Sprinkle the remaining nut mixture over the pastry, cover with 5–7 layers of buttered pastry and fold in all the overhanging edges. Using a sharp knife, cut the baklava into diamond shapes, cutting right through all the layers, then bake in the preheated oven for 25–30 minutes until golden brown.

4. Meanwhile, prepare the syrup. Put the sugar and water into a saucepan and heat over a low heat until the sugar has dissolved. Bring to the boil, then add the lemon juice, honey and cinnamon sticks. Reduce the heat and simmer for 10 minutes, then remove from the heat and leave to cool. Remove the baklava from the oven and immediately pour over the syrup. Leave to stand until the pastry has fully absorbed the syrup. The flavour of the baklava will mature after 1–2 days.

1.

3.

3.

3.

4.

4.

# DATE, PISTACHIO & HONEY SLICES

MAKES 12

PREP TIME: 30 minutes

COOKING TIME: 20–25 minutes

## INGREDIENTS

*250 g/9 oz dried dates, stoned and chopped*
*2 tbsp lemon juice*
*2 tbsp water*
*85 g/3 oz pistachio nuts, chopped*
*2 tbsp clear honey*
*milk, for glazing*

### pastry
*225 g/8 oz plain flour,
plus extra for dusting*
*25 g/1 oz golden caster sugar*
*150 g/5¼ oz butter*
*4–5 tbsp cold water*

Because of their high sugar content, long shelf life and the fact that they provide lots of energy for their size, the fleshy fruit of the date palm is still the ideal food for long journeys. In fact, in the Arab world the date has for centuries been packed as a provision for travelling through the desert. Together with the pithy pistachio and honey, they are also an extremely tasty, nutritious snack.

1. Put the dates, lemon juice and water into a saucepan and bring to the boil, stirring. Remove from the heat. Stir in the nuts and 1 tablespoon of the honey. Cover and leave to cool.

2. Preheat the oven to 200 °C/400 °F/Gas Mark 6. To make the pastry, put the flour, sugar and butter into a food processor and process to fine crumbs. Mix in just enough cold water to bind to a soft, not sticky, dough.

3. Divide the pastry into 2 pieces, then roll out each piece on a lightly floured work surface to a 30 x 20-cm/12 x 8-inch rectangle. Place 1 piece on a baking tray. Spread the date and nut mixture to within 1 cm/½ inch of the edge. Top with the other rectangle of pastry.

4. Firmly press the edges together to seal, then trim the excess and score the top of the pastry to mark out 12 slices. Glaze with the milk. Bake in the preheated oven for 20–25 minutes, or until golden. Brush with the remaining honey and turn out on to a wire rack to cool. Cut into 12 slices and serve.

# Ciabatta

## BREAD

MAKES 2 LOAVES

PREP TIME: 25 minutes,
plus 2 hours to rest and rise

COOKING TIME: 35 minutes

### INGREDIENTS

*butter, for greasing*
*175 ml/6 fl oz lukewarm water*
*1½ tsp easy-blend dried yeast*
*575 g/1 lb 4 oz plain flour*
*2½ tbsp olive oil*
*¾ tsp salt*

Crispy on the outside, delightfully airy inside and with a slight taste of olive oil: that's ciabatta. Letting the dough stand for a long time gives the bread its characteristic flavour and the gentle kneading gives the bread its large holes. The Italian bread is now a classic, but it's a recent classic. It was only made for the first time in 1982 by Arnaldo Cavallari in Rovigo in the Veneto region.

1.  Grease a baking tray. Pour the water into a large bowl, add the yeast and stir to dissolve. Add 115 g/4 oz of flour and mix thoroughly. Cover and leave to rest 30 minutes. Sift the remaining flour into a separate large bowl and make a well in the centre. Pour the yeast mixture into the flour, then add the oil.

2.  Mix together well, pulling in the flour from the side of the bowl to the centre, then knead for about 2 minutes until a spongy dough forms. Cover with a damp tea towel and leave to rise for about 1 hour, or until doubled in size.

3.  Add the salt and knead for 7–8 minutes until a smooth dough forms.

4.  Divide the dough into 2 pieces, shape each piece into a loaf and place on the prepared tray. Leave to rise for 30 minutes at room temperature.

5.  Meanwhile, preheat the oven to 230 °C/450 °F/Gas Mark 8. Bake the loaves in the preheated oven for 35 minutes until they are golden brown and sound hollow when tapped on the base. Transfer to a wire rack to cool.

1.

3.

4.

1.

2.

3.

# CHERRY TOMATO
# *Focaccia*
## *Bread*

Focaccia, baked with yeast dough, is a speciality of Liguria in northern Italy and its origins date back to the Etruscan era. It can be baked with a little olive oil, herbs and other ingredients. This flat bread is a forerunner of the pizza and is not eaten as a side dish but as a snack.

1. Mix together 2 tablespoons of the oil and all the garlic. Set aside. Mix together the flour, yeast, table salt and sugar in a large bowl. Add the remaining oil and the water. Mix to a dough. Turn out on to a lightly floured work surface and knead for 10 minutes until smooth and elastic, then knead in 1 tablespoon of the garlic-flavoured oil.

2. Oil a 17 x 25-cm/6½ x10-inch baking tin at least 4 cm/1½ inches deep. Press the dough into the base of the tin with your hands. Brush with the remaining garlic-flavoured oil, then scatter over the rosemary. Cover loosely with clingfilm and set aside in a warm place for about 1 hour until puffed up and doubled in size.

3. Preheat the oven to 230°C/450°F/Gas Mark 8. Scatter the tomatoes over the focaccia, squeezing in as many as you can, and press them into the dough. Sprinkle with the sea salt. Place in the preheated oven and immediately reduce the oven temperature to 200°C/400°F/Gas Mark 6. Bake for 25–30 minutes until golden brown and the bread sounds hollow when tapped on the base. Turn out on to a wire rack to cool. Serve warm or cold.

MAKES 1 LOAF

PREP TIME: 20 minutes, plus 1 hour to rise

COOKING TIME: 25–30 minutes

## INGREDIENTS

5 tbsp olive oil, plus extra for oiling
2 garlic cloves, crushed
350 g/12 oz strong white flour, plus extra for dusting
2¼ tsp easy-blend dried yeast
2 tsp table salt
1 tsp caster sugar
225 ml/8 fl oz lukewarm water
2 tsp finely chopped fresh rosemary
200–225 g/7–8 oz ripe red cherry tomatoes
¼ tsp sea salt flakes

# Feta & Olive Scones

MAKES 8

PREP TIME: 12–15 minutes

COOKING TIME: 12–15 minutes

## INGREDIENTS

*400 g/14 oz self-raising flour*
*¼ tsp salt*
*85 g/3 oz butter,*
*plus extra for greasing*
*40 g/1½ oz stoned black olives, chopped*
*40 g/1½ oz sun-dried tomatoes*
*in oil, drained and chopped*
*85 g/3 oz feta cheese*
*(drained weight), crumbled*
*200 ml/7 fl oz milk,*
*plus extra for glazing*
*pepper*

Olives have been eaten in Greece for thousands of years and the Greek sheep's cheese feta has been around since the days of the Byzantine empire. These scones just need a knob of butter and then this savoury treat is ready to enjoy.

1. Preheat the oven to 220 °C/425 °F/Gas Mark 7. Grease a baking tray.

2. Sift together the flour, salt and pepper to taste into a bowl and rub in the butter evenly with your fingers.

3. Stir in the olives, tomatoes and cheese, then stir in just enough milk to make a soft, smooth dough.

4. Roll out on a floured surface to a 3-cm/1¼-inch-thick rectangle. Cut into 6-cm/2½-inch squares. Place on the baking tray, brush with milk and bake in the preheated oven for 12–15 minutes until golden.

5. Serve the scones fresh and warm, with extra butter if needed.

2.

3.

4.

# Pitta Bread

SERVES 12

PREP TIME: 30 minutes,
plus 2 hours 10 minutes to rise

COOKING TIME: 10 minutes

### INGREDIENTS

1½ tsp easy-blend dried yeast

300 ml/10 fl oz lukewarm water

450 g/1 lb plain flour,
plus extra for dusting

1 tsp salt

1 tbsp vegetable oil,
plus extra for oiling

1½ tsp sugar

Soft pitta flat bread is widespread in the eastern Mediterranean and the Middle East. Freshly baked several times a day, it is served as an accompaniment to many meals. It is a simple, lightly salted dough with a little fat and is traditionally baked without a tray directly on the bottom of a stone oven.

1.  Put the yeast into a large bowl with the water and stir until dissolved. Add the remaining ingredients, mix to combine, then knead until a firm dough forms. Cover with a damp tea towel and leave to rise for at least 2 hours until doubled in size.

2.  Turn out the dough on to a lightly floured work surface, knock back, then use your hands to roll the dough into a 2-cm/¾-inch-thick roll. Cut the roll into 1-cm/½-inch slices. You should have 6–8 slices. Roll the slices into balls, cover with a damp tea towel and leave to rise for a further 10 minutes.

3.  Preheat the oven to 240°C/475°F/Gas Mark 9. Line a baking tray with baking paper, then oil the paper and dust it with flour. Roll out the balls on a lightly floured work surface into 15–20-cm/6–8-inch rounds.

4.  Place the rounds on the prepared baking tray and bake in the preheated oven for about 10 minutes until puffed. Remove from the oven and cover with a damp tea towel to keep the bread soft. The pittas can be stored in the refrigerator for a few days.

1.

2.

3.

# Feta & Spinach Parcels

In the Balkans, savoury pastry parcels are popular, especially stuffed with feta cheese and spinach. In Turkey they are called *borek*. It is everyday or festive food, depending on the filling. They taste particularly delicious fresh from the oven. But even when a day old, they are spicier and perfect for a party or a picnic.

1.  Preheat the oven to 200 °C/400 °F/Gas Mark 6. Oil a baking tray.

2.  Heat the oil in a wok or large frying pan, add the onions and fry, stirring, for 1–2 minutes. Add the spinach and stir until the leaves are wilted. Cook, stirring occasionally, for 2–3 minutes. Drain off any liquid and leave to cool slightly.

3.  Stir the egg, cheese and nutmeg into the spinach and season well with salt and pepper to taste.

4.  Brush 3 sheets of pastry with butter. Place another 3 sheets on top and brush with butter. Cut each sheet down the middle to make 6 long strips in total. Place a tablespoon of the spinach filling on the end of each strip.

5.  Lift one corner of pastry over the filling to the opposite side, then turn over the opposite way to enclose. Continue to fold over along the length of the strip to make a triangular parcel, finishing with the join underneath.

6.  Place the parcels on the prepared baking tray, brush with butter and sprinkle with the sesame seeds. Bake in the preheated oven for 12–15 minutes or until golden brown and crisp. Serve hot.

MAKES 6

PREP TIME: 25 minutes

COOKING TIME: 15–20 minutes

## INGREDIENTS

*2 tbsp olive oil,
plus extra for greasing*

*1 bunch spring onions, chopped*

*500 g/1 lb 2 oz spinach leaves,
roughly chopped*

*1 egg, beaten*

*125 g/4½ oz feta cheese (drained weight),
crumbled*

*½ tsp freshly grated nutmeg*

*6 sheets ready-made filo pastry*

*55 g/2 oz butter, melted*

*1 tbsp sesame seeds*

*salt and pepper*

# The Home of Traditional BAKING

When it comes to bread, the German-speaking countries are leaders of the pack. Nowhere else will you find so many types of bread. Last year, the German Bakers' Confederation recorded almost 3,000 bread specialities, including some with such whimsical names as 'Alpine Loaf', 'Cereal King' or 'Monk'. Bread and its quality are very important to the Germans. There are two daily meals in which bread plays an essential role. For breakfast, Germans usually have a very soft roll with jam, and in the evening the family gathers at the table and eats slices of bread topped with sausage or cheese, cucumber or tomato, according to each person's taste. For Germans, bread is the epitome of home, so it is not uncommon to find German emigrants yearning for typical German bread. However, that is not all: a cup of coffee in the afternoon with a delicious piece of cake is part of most German people's daily routine. Here too, they have a huge range to choose from, including fruit cakes, cream cakes and sponge cakes.

*Very different regions around Germany have developed completely different bread traditions. The further you travel to the south of Germany, the more you have big cakes and breads. There are also specialities like pretzels, a must in Munich's Oktoberfest.*

# Lebkuchen
## BISCUITS

MAKES 30

PREP TIME: 30 minutes

COOKING TIME: 15–20 minutes

### INGREDIENTS

*3 eggs*
*200 g/7 oz caster sugar*
*55 g/2 oz plain flour*
*2 tsp cocoa powder*
*1 tsp ground cinnamon*
*½ tsp ground cardamom*
*¼ tsp ground cloves*
*¼ tsp ground nutmeg*
*175 g/6 oz ground almonds*
*55 g/2 oz mixed peel,*
*finely chopped*

### to decorate

*115 g/4 oz plain chocolate,*
*broken into pieces*
*115 g/4 oz white chocolate,*
*broken into pieces*
*sugar crystals*

The German lebkuchen has evolved over a long period of time from honey cake and various spices. Since the 14th century, it has established itself as a traditional Christmas confectionery. It is baked without the use of yeast; the essential ingredients are various combinations of Asian spices. These had to be imported at a great expense and therefore it is mainly merchant towns that can claim a long tradition of lebkuchen baking.

1. Preheat the oven to 180 °C/350 °F/Gas Mark 4. Line several large baking trays with baking paper. Place the eggs and sugar in a heatproof bowl set over a saucepan of gently simmering water and whisk until thick and foamy. Remove the bowl from the pan and continue to whisk for 2 minutes.

2. Sift the flour, cocoa, cinnamon, cardamom, cloves and nutmeg into the bowl and stir in with the ground almonds and mixed peel. Drop heaped teaspoonfuls of the mixture on to the prepared baking trays, spreading them gently into smooth mounds.

3. Bake in the preheated oven for 15–20 minutes or until light brown and slightly soft to the touch. Leave to cool on the baking sheets for 10 minutes, then transfer the cookies to wire racks to cool completely.

4. Place the plain and white chocolate in two separate heatproof bowls, set the bowls over two pans of gently simmering water and heat until melted. Dip half the biscuits in the melted plain chocolate and half in the white chocolate. Sprinkle with sugar crystals and leave to set.

1.

5.

5.

# Plum Cake

SERVES 9

PREP TIME: 40 minutes,
plus 50 minutes to rise

COOKING TIME: 30 minutes

Baked with the use of yeast, the plum cake is a light and sweet treat that has an unmistakably fresh taste. It is a Central European confectionery, typical of the late-summer season, when blue-rock plums, a plum sub-species, are ripe and juicy. Some bakeries grace their plum cakes with a crumble topping, which is made out of puff pastry.

1.  Sift the flour into a bowl, then add the sugar. Make a well in the centre, add the egg and mix to combine, pulling in the flour mixture from the side of the bowl.

2.  Put the milk and butter into a small saucepan and heat over a low heat until the butter is melted. Remove from the heat and leave to cool to lukewarm. Crumble the yeast into the mixture, stir to dissolve and leave to stand for 5 minutes. Pour the yeast mixture into the flour mixture and knead well.

3.  Cover the bowl and leave to rise for at least 30 minutes until the dough has doubled in size.

4.  Preheat the oven to 180°C/350°F/Gas Mark 4 and grease a deep baking tin. Make 1–2 cuts in each plum half.

5.  Rub a little butter on your hands, then knock back the dough and press it into the prepared tin. Firmly press the plum halves, cut-side up, into the dough. Sprinkle over the cinnamon sugar and leave to stand for 15 minutes. Sprinkle the chopped hazelnuts over the plums, if using.

6.  Bake in the preheated oven for about 30 minutes, then remove from the oven and leave to cool slightly. Serve lukewarm with whipped cream or ice cream, if liked.

## INGREDIENTS

*200 g/7 oz plain flour*

*2 tablespoons granulated sugar*

*1 egg, beaten*

*100 ml/3½ fl oz milk*

*25 g/1 oz butter, plus extra for greasing*

*10 g/¼ oz fresh yeast (available in bakeries or online)*

*600 g/1 lb 5 oz plums, halved and stoned*

*50 g/1¾ oz cinnamon sugar (available online)*

*50 g/1¾ oz chopped hazelnuts (optional), for sprinkling*

*whipped cream or ice cream, to serve (optional)*

# STOLLEN

SERVES 8

PREP TIME: 1 hour, plus time to soak, rise and rest

COOKING TIME: 1 hour

## INGREDIENTS

*50 g/1¾ oz blanched almonds, roughly chopped*

*300 g/10½ oz raisins*

*100 g/3½ oz mixed peel*

*4 tbsp dark rum*

*400 g/14 oz strong white flour, plus extra for dusting*

*250 ml/9 fl oz lukewarm milk*

*40 g/1½ oz fresh yeast (available in bakeries or online), crumbled*

*3 tbsp clear honey*

*400 g/14 oz softened butter, diced, plus 100 g/3½ oz butter, melted*

*1 tsp salt*

*100 g/3½ oz marzipan, grated*

*2 tsp vanilla extract*

*grated zest of 1 lemon*

*150 g/5½ oz icing sugar, plus extra for dusting*

The shape of the stollen, which is made for Christmas, is a reminder of the Baby Jesus swaddling band. Known traditionally as Christmas bread, stollen was previously eaten for Lent and prepared with rapeseed oil. In 1430, the German nobility complained to the Pope about its unpleasant taste. However it was not until 1491 that His Excellency allowed for the use of butter in stollen. Later on, the court baker Heinrich Drasdo from Torgau further enhanced it with other richer ingredients and so the stollen, as we know it today, came into being.

1. Pour boiling water over the almonds and leave to soak for 10 minutes. Mix the raisins and mixed peel with the rum. Drain the almonds and mix with the rum and fruit mixture. Leave to soften overnight.

2. Mix together 200 g/7 oz of the flour with the milk, yeast and honey, knead to a dough, then dust with 1 tablespoon of the remaining flour. Leave to rise in a warm place for 30 minutes or until the surface of the dough splits.

3. Mix the remaining flour with the butter, salt, marzipan, vanilla extract, lemon zest and rum-soaked fruit and nuts, then add the dough and knead for 8 minutes. Cover the dough and leave to rise in a warm place for about 1 hour until doubled in size.

4. Meanwhile, preheat the oven to 200 °C/400 °F/Gas Mark 6. Dust a baking tray with flour. Turn out the dough on to a floured work surface, knead well and place on the prepared baking tray.

5. Bake in the middle of the preheated oven for about 1 hour, covering with baking paper or foil for the last 20 minutes of cooking if it is browning too quickly. Remove from the oven and brush with the melted butter. Dust with icing sugar, wrap in foil and leave to rest for about 2 weeks. Dredge with the icing sugar just before serving.

1.

3.

4.

2.

3.

6.

# Baumkuchen Small Cakes

The baumkuchen layer cake is a delicacy originating in Eastern Germany. It was originally baked in layers on a skewer over an open flame, with the skewer dipped up to 20 times in dough throughout the process. The finished cake resembles the annual rings of a tree, hence its name, which translates as 'tree cake'. This particular layer cake was created by chance in 1907, when an East Prussian confectioner accidentally dropped a few cake pieces into chocolate.

1. Preheat the grill to medium and grease a 25-cm/10-inch round spring-form cake tin.

2. Put the egg yolks, butter, icing sugar, vanilla sugar, flour and cornflour into a large bowl and mix to combine. Put the egg whites and salt into a separate bowl and whisk, gradually adding the caster sugar, until they hold soft peaks. Carefully fold into the mixture.

3. Spread a thin layer of the mixture on the base of the prepared tin and place under the preheated grill for 1 minute, or until golden brown. Remove from the grill, spread another thin layer of batter over the first layer and return to the grill. Repeat until all the mixture has been used up.

4. Turn out the cake on to a wire rack and leave to cool.

5. Meanwhile, to prepare the icing, put the chocolate into a bowl set over a saucepan of gently simmering water, add the vegetable fat and stir until melted.

6. Cut the cake into bite-sized triangles and use a fork to dip the wider ends in the chocolate mixture. Transfer to a wire rack and leave to cool.

MAKES 20

PREP TIME: 20 minutes

COOKING TIME: 20 minutes

## INGREDIENTS

6 egg yolks
200 g/7 oz softened butter, plus extra for greasing
100 g/3½ oz icing sugar
10 g/¼ oz vanilla sugar (available online)
100 g/3½ oz plain flour
50 g/1¾ oz cornflour
6 egg whites
pinch of salt
115 g/4 oz caster sugar

icing
200 g/7 oz plain chocolate, broken into pieces
1 tbsp vegetable fat

# HOME OF
# 3,000 *Breads*

The German and Austrian people are well known for being organised, reliable and economically successful but the culture is less well known for its diversity. However, in German and Austrian baking there are over 3,000 types of bread!

*Not only do thousands of bread recipes exist in Germany, but also lots of regional differences, which may vary from one village to another. Lots of bread recipes are still kept as family secrets, which often makes it very difficult to identify the origin.*

So, in terms of baking diversity, no other part of the world has a greater variety of bread. According to constantly growing statistics, in Germany alone there are around 3,000 different types of bread and more than 1,000 kinds of small bakes. As there have been no exact figures available, a 'bread-register' was established in Germany in 2011 in which experts collect and evaluate different recipes. Whether it's brown or white bread, this incredibly varied baking culture has a longstanding historical background. In the High Middle Ages, Germany and Austria were divided into hundreds of small duchies. These were all quite different from each other. This conglomerate of small states contrasted with countries like France and Britain, which were centrally governed. The fragmentation of Germany and its German neighbours meant that not only the bread, but also its forms varied considerably from one region to another. Sometimes, even neighbouring cities used completely different mixtures of ingredients and their individual compositions were well guarded in secret recipes. Bakers who did not maintain this confidentiality risked severe penalties. All the same, the strict medieval circumstances in Germany turned out to be a godsend for German baking culture. Today, interest in healthy bread with a unique flavour is stronger than ever. Consumption has also increased considerably in recent years. Statistics record an amount of around 70 kg/155 lb of bread consumed per capita each year. This is still a long way off from France which consumes more than 90 kg/ 200 lb per person, although the variety of bread there has increased only in recent years. However, it is a curious fact that of all bread types, brown bread and wholegrain bread are particularly popular. In the Middle Ages wealth determined which type of bread you could afford. Only the affluent sectors of the population could afford the expensive white varieties of finely ground wheat flour. This explains why the white wheat baguette, for example, was invented for the French nobility of the 17th century: the coarse wholemeal bread might hurt more 'sensitive palates'. In Germany too, people mostly ate brown bread made from coarsely ground wholegrain rye flour because it was much cheaper. Today it is exactly the opposite – the coarser and more natural the bread, the more likely it is to be regarded as a luxury product.

3.

3.

4.

# Little Black Forest Cakes

MAKES 10

PREP TIME: 40 minutes,
plus 1 hour to chill

COOKING TIME: 45 minutes

The Black Forest cherry cake, which enjoys a great popularity throughout Germany (presented here as a sliced version), is still a considerably young invention: this particular cream cake had its first mention in a cookery book in 1934. The recipe quickly captured the interest of the patisseries in Berlin and other major cities in Germany, Austria and Switzerland. Its origin, however, is unclear. The name is conceivably inspired by the typical Black Forest (Schwarzwald) female costume. The women of this region traditionally wore black dresses with white blouses and red hats.

1. Preheat the oven to 180°C/350°F/Gas Mark 4. Line a 20-cm/8-inch square baking tin with baking paper. Beat the eggs with the sugar until foaming. Mix together the flour, baking powder and cocoa powder, then sift into the egg mixture and mix to combine. Pour into the prepared baking tin and bake in the preheated oven for 30 minutes. Remove from the oven and leave to cool in the baking tin.

2. To make the filling, purée the cherries with the cherry juice. Add to a saucepan with the sugar, bring to the boil and cook for 5 minutes. Follow packet instructions for dissolving the gelatine leaves before adding to the cherry mixture.

3. Meanwhile, put the chocolate into a heatproof bowl set over a saucepan of gently simmering water and heat until melted. Spread evenly over the sponge. Leave to harden, then spread the cherry jelly evenly on top. Chill in the refrigerator for 1 hour.

4. To make the cream, put the kirsch into a saucepan with the icing sugar and heat over a medium heat. Dissolve the leaf gelatine as explained in Step 2 and add to the kirsch mixture. Whip the cream until it holds stiff peaks, then fold in the gelatine mixture. Spread the cream over the cherry jelly.

5. Cut the cake into 10 squares using a sharp knife. Place a cherry on each piece and sprinkle over some grated chocolate.

## INGREDIENTS

*3 eggs*
*100 g/3½ oz caster sugar*
*100 g/3½ oz plain flour*
*1 tsp baking powder*
*2 tsp cocoa powder*
*sour cherries or maraschino cherries and grated plain chocolate, to decorate*

### filling
*200 g/7 oz sour cherries or canned, stoned cherries*
*125 ml/4 fl oz cherry juice*
*50 g/1¾ oz jam sugar*
*2–3 gelatine leaves*
*70 g/2½ oz plain chocolate, finely chopped*

### cream
*2 tbsp kirsch*
*5 tbsp icing sugar*
*2 gelatine leaves*
*200 ml/7 fl oz whipping cream*

# Butter
## CAKE

MAKES 12

PREP TIME: 20 minutes

COOKING TIME: 30 minutes

### INGREDIENTS

*250 g/9 oz plain flour,*
*plus extra for sprinkling*

*250 g/9 oz caster sugar,*
*plus extra for sprinkling*

*70 g/2½ oz butter, plus extra for greasing*

*225 ml/8 fl oz single cream*

*1 tbsp baking powder*

*4 eggs*

### topping

*175 g/6 oz caster sugar, plus extra*
*for sprinkling*

*200 g/7 oz flaked almonds*

*25 g/1 oz chopped almonds*

*1 tbsp milk*

*175 g/6 oz butter, melted*

This cake is made of a sponge cake with a coating of butter and sugar, to which almonds are usually added. It is therefore referred to either as a butter cake or a sugar cake. This delicious treat can be easily produced in large quantities, which is why it is a very welcome and popular addition to all family parties in Germany.

1. Preheat the oven to 180 °C/350 °F/Gas Mark 4. Grease a deep 30 x 20-cm/ 12 x 8-inch rectangular baking tin and dust with flour, tipping out the excess. Put the flour, sugar, butter, cream, baking powder and eggs into a large bowl and beat with an electric whisk until combined. Spread evenly in the prepared tin and bake in the preheated oven for 15 minutes. Do not switch off the oven.

2. Meanwhile, make the topping. Put the sugar, flaked almonds, chopped almonds, milk and 100 g/3½ oz of the butter into a medium-sized bowl and mix to combine. Drizzle the remaining butter evenly over the cake.

3. Use a rubber palette knife to spread the topping evenly over the cake, then sprinkle with sugar. Return the cake to the oven and bake for a further 15 minutes. Remove from the oven and leave to cool in the tin, then cut into squares and serve.

1.

3.

3.

2.

3.

4.

# APPLE
# *Streusel Cake*

SERVES 8

PREP TIME: 15 minutes

COOKING TIME: 50 minutes

## INGREDIENTS

*400 g/14 oz eating apples, peeled, cored and diced*

*2 tbsp apple juice*

*140 g/5 oz light muscovado sugar*

*125 g/4½ oz unsalted butter, at room temperature, plus extra for greasing*

*2 large eggs, beaten*

*225 g/8 oz self-raising flour*

*1½ tsp mixed spice*

*40 g/1½ oz hazelnuts, peeled and finely chopped*

Apples are particularly widespread across Central Europe and have a long season, so apple cakes are always popular. These classic German treats can be made in umpteen variations with both freshly harvested and stored fruit. Firm and sour apple varieties are used most often, so as to give the already sweet cake a zesty and fresh aroma.

1. Preheat the oven to 190 °C/375 °F/Gas Mark 5. Grease a 20-cm/8-inch round springform cake tin and line with baking paper. Sprinkle the apples with the apple juice.

2. Reserve 1 tablespoon of the sugar, then put the remaining sugar and butter into a mixing bowl and beat until pale and fluffy. Gradually add the eggs, beating thoroughly after each addition. Sift together the flour and spice into the mixture and evenly fold in with a metal spoon.

3. Stir the apples and juice into the mixture, then spoon into the prepared tin and level the surface with a palette knife.

4. Mix the hazelnuts with the reserved sugar and sprinkle over the surface of the cake.

5. Bake in the preheated oven for 45–50 minutes until firm and golden brown. Leave to cool in the tin for 10 minutes, then turn out on to a wire rack to cool completely.

# Gugelhupf

## RING CAKE

SERVES 8

PREP TIME: 25 minutes

COOKING TIME: 1 hour

### INGREDIENTS

*4 eggs*
*150 g/5½ oz butter,*
*plus extra for greasing*
*150 g/5½ oz granulated sugar*
*2 tsp vanilla sugar (available online)*
*300 g/10½ oz plain flour,*
*plus extra for dusting*
*1 tbsp baking powder*
*3 tbsp rum*
*finely grated rind of 1 lemon*
*125 ml/4 fl oz milk*
*50 g/1¾ oz raisins*
*icing sugar, for dusting*

Essential to the Bundt Cake, or Gugelhupf, is the tall circular structure with a chimney-like opening in the middle – the bundt tin. This allows the dough to cook evenly. This particular cake style was already known in ancient Roman times. Gugelhupf marble cakes were a popular treat on the tables of the German and Austrian middle classes during the Biedermeier period, even though there was no single standardized recipe for them.

1.  Preheat the oven to 180 °C/350 °F/Gas Mark 4. Grease a bundt tin or ring tin and dust with flour, shaking off the excess.

2.  Separate the eggs. Put the butter, sugar, vanilla sugar and egg yolks into a bowl and beat until creamy. Sift together the flour and baking powder into a separate bowl. Put the egg whites into a clean, grease-free bowl and whisk until they hold stiff peaks.

3.  Stir the rum, lemon rind and flour mixture into the butter mixture. Add the milk and stir until bubbles form. Fold in the egg white and raisins.

4.  Put the mixture into the prepared tin and bake in the preheated oven for 50–60 minutes. Switch off the oven, open the oven door and leave the cake in the oven for 10 minutes. Turn out on to a wire rack and leave to cool completely. Sift the icing sugar over the cake, cut into slices and serve.

2.

3.

3.

3.

3.

5.

# Bee Sting *Cake*

SERVES 8

PREP TIME: 45 minutes,
plus time to rise and chill

COOKING TIME: 35 minutes

## INGREDIENTS

*40 g/1½ oz fresh yeast (available in bakeries
or online)*

*200 ml/7 fl oz lukewarm milk*

*500 g/1 lb 2 oz plain flour,
plus extra for sprinkling and dusting*

*50 g/1¾ oz caster sugar*

*2 eggs*

*50 g/1¾ oz butter*

*pinch of salt*

### almond topping

*70 g/2½ oz butter*

*2 tbsp double cream*

*50 g/1¾ oz caster sugar*

*100 g/3½ oz flaked almonds*

### filling

*500 ml/18 fl oz milk*

*1 vanilla pod*

*5 egg yolks*

*85 g/3 oz caster sugar*

*50 g/1¾ oz cornflour*

*250 g/9 oz softened butter*

According to a legend, a group of baker apprentices from Andernach on the Rhine used bee nests as weapons to defend their city in 1474, thus causing the attackers to flee. In order to commemorate this victory, they designed a special cake: the bee sting cake.

1. Crumble the yeast into the milk. Stir in 1 tablespoon of the flour and 1 tablespoon of the sugar. Sprinkle with a little flour and leave to rise in a warm place for 20–30 minutes. Sift the remaining flour into a large mixing bowl and stir in the eggs, the remaining sugar, the butter and salt. Add the yeast mixture to the flour mixture and knead to a smooth dough. Cover with clingfilm and leave to rise in a warm place until doubled in size.

2. Preheat the oven to 180 °C/350 °F/Gas Mark 4. Line a baking tray with baking paper. To make the almond topping, put the butter and cream into a saucepan over a low heat. Add the sugar and stir until dissolved, then stir in the almonds. Remove from the heat and leave to cool.

3. Turn out the dough on to a floured work surface and roll out to a rectangle the size of the baking tray. Place the dough on the prepared baking tray and spread with the almond topping. Leave to rest for 10 minutes, then bake in the middle of the preheated oven for 30–35 minutes.

4. Remove from the oven and leave to cool. Meanwhile, make the filling. Put the milk into a saucepan with the vanilla pod, bring to the boil and boil briefly. Remove from the heat, cover and leave to stand for about 20 minutes. Meanwhile, put the egg yolks and sugar into a bowl and beat until creamy, then stir in the cornflour. Strain the cooled vanilla milk into the egg mixture and beat until smooth. Return to the saucepan and heat over a low heat until thickened. Transfer to a bowl and stir until cool. Put the butter into a large bowl and beat with an electric whisk until fluffy, then slowly stir into the filling mixture.

5. Cut the cooled cake in half horizontally. Spread the filling on the bottom half and place the other half on top. Chill in the refrigerator for 1–2 hours. Trim the edges of the cake, then cut into slices and serve.

# Danube Wave Cake

SERVES 8–10

PREP TIME: 1 hour,
plus 4 hours to chill

COOKING TIME: 40 minutes

## INGREDIENTS

*325 g/11½ oz softened butter,
plus extra for greasing*
*325 g/11½ oz caster sugar*
*8 eggs*
*250 g/9 oz plain flour*
*250 g/9 oz cornflour*
*5 tsp baking powder*
*350 g/12 oz canned, drained cherries*
*3 tbsp cocoa powder*
*5 tbsp milk*

### crème pâtissière
*500 ml/18 fl oz milk*
*1tsp vanilla extract or 1 vanilla pod,
scraped*
*5 egg yolks*
*85 g/3 oz caster sugar*
*50 g/1¾ oz cornflour*

### icing
*200 g/7 oz plain chocolate*
*60 g/2¼ oz butter*
*125 ml/4 fl oz milk*

The Danube is one of the widest rivers in Germany. It became the inspiration for this cake, whose base consists of a light- and a dark-coloured batter. Cherries may also be placed firmly in the dark mixture in several places. When sliced, the cake reveals its wave-like structure. The icing is also often fashioned in such a way that it also resembles waves.

1. Put the butter and sugar into a large bowl and beat with an electric whisk until pale and fluffy. Add the eggs, one at a time, beating after each addition until combined. In a separate bowl, mix together the flour, cornflour and baking powder, then sift into the egg and butter mixture. Fold in carefully.

2. Preheat the oven to 200 °C/400 °F/Gas Mark 6. Grease a 35 x 20-cm/ 14 x 8-inch rectangular baking tin. Spread half the mixture in the prepared tin. Arrange the cherries evenly on top.

3. Mix the cocoa powder and milk into the remaining mixture and spread it over the cherries. Bake in the preheated oven for 20–25 minutes. Remove from the oven and leave to cool completely.

4. Meanwhile, to make the crème pâtissière, put the milk into a large saucepan and bring to the boil, then stir in the vanilla extract. Remove from the heat and leave to cool for 20 minutes. Put the egg yolks into a bowl with the sugar and beat with an electric whisk until thick and foaming. Add the cornflour and the cooled milk and mix to combine. Return to the pan and heat over a medium heat until thickened. Transfer to a bowl, then place the bowl in a larger bowl filled with ice cubes and chill for 2 hours.

5. Spread the crème pâtissière on the cooled cake. The cake and the crème should be the same temperature. Chill in the refrigerator for 2 hours.

6. For the icing, put the chocolate, butter and milk into a heatproof bowl set over a saucepan of barely simmering water and heat until the chocolate is melted. Pour over the cake and leave to cool until beginning to set. Use an icing comb or a fork to make a wavy pattern in the chocolate. Cut the cake into slices and serve chilled.

1.

5.

6.

2.

4.

5.

# Cinnamon Stars

Cinnamon stars are a Christmas speciality from Swabia (a region of Würt-temberg and Bavaria). The stars, sculpted out of dough and covered with icing, are baked at a low heat, so that the egg white icing just sets without changing colour and the dough remains relatively soft.

1. Whisk the egg whites in a clean, grease-free bowl until they hold stiff peaks. Stir in the sugar until thoroughly combined, then continue to whisk until thick and glossy.

2. Set aside 40 g/1½ oz of this mixture, then fold the hazelnuts and cinnamon into the remaining mixture to make a very stiff dough. Chill in the refrigerator for about 1 hour.

3. Preheat the oven to 140 °C/275 °F/Gas Mark 1. Line two baking trays with baking paper. Roll out the dough to a thickness of 1 cm/½ inch on a work surface heavily dusted with icing sugar.

4. Use a 5-cm/2-inch star-shaped cutter to cut the dough into shapes, frequently dusting the cutter with icing sugar to prevent sticking. Re-roll the trimmings as necessary until all the mixture has been used up.

5. Place the biscuits on the prepared baking trays, spaced well apart, and spread the top of each star with the reserved egg white mixture.

6. Bake in the preheated oven for 25 minutes or until the biscuits are still white and crisp on top but slightly soft and moist underneath. Turn off the oven and open the door to release the heat, but leave the biscuits in the oven for a further 10 minutes to dry out. Remove from the oven and transfer to wire racks to cool completely.

MAKES 20

PREP TIME: 25 minutes, plus 1 hour to chill

COOKING TIME: 25 minutes

## INGREDIENTS

2 egg whites
175 g/6 oz icing sugar, plus extra for dusting
250 g/9 oz ground roasted hazelnuts
1 tbsp ground cinnamon

# Redcurrant
## CAKE

SERVES 10–12

PREP TIME: 45 minutes,
plus 1 hour to chill

COOKING TIME: 30 minutes

### INGREDIENTS

1 kg/2 lb 4 oz redcurrants
55 g/2 oz granulated sugar
6 egg whites
175 g/6 oz caster sugar
175 g/6 oz ground hazelnuts

### pastry
350 g/12 oz plain flour,
plus extra for dusting
100 g/3½ oz icing sugar,
plus extra for dusting
pinch of salt
2 eggs
150 g/5½ oz butter,
plus extra for greasing
3 tbsp water

The redcurrant cake is a Central European classic of summertime baking. It is then that the beautiful red fruit of the redcurrant bush is fully ripe. Their slightly acidy flavour gives this cake an unmistakable 'kick', which, in this case, is enhanced with a hazelnut aroma.

1. To make the pastry, sift together the flour, icing sugar and salt into a large bowl. Add the eggs, butter and water, then mix together well. Turn out on to a lightly floured work surface and knead to a smooth dough. Wrap in clingfilm and chill in the refrigerator for 1 hour.

2. Preheat the oven to 180°C/350°F/Gas Mark 4. Grease a 28-cm/11-inch springform cake tin and dust with flour. Turn out the dough on to a lightly floured work surface and roll out to a thickness of 3 mm/⅛ inch. Ease into the prepared tin and prick several times with a fork.

3. Put the redcurrants into a large bowl, add the granulated sugar and carefully mix together. Put the egg whites into a clean, grease-free bowl and whisk until they hold stiff peaks, then add the caster sugar and gently fold in. Fold the egg white into the redcurrants, then fold in the hazelnuts.

4. Spoon the filling into the pastry case and bake in the preheated oven for 30 minutes. Remove from the oven and leave to cool. Carefully remove the cake from the tin, dust with icing sugar and serve.

2.

3.

4.

1.

3.

5.

# Berliner Doughnuts

MAKES 18–20

PREP TIME: 35 minutes,
plus 3–4 hours to stand and rise

COOKING TIME: 10–15 minutes

The success of the Berliner doughnuts – known in Bavaria and Austria as krapfen – dates back to the rise of Berlin as an industrial city and the capital of the German Empire, founded in 1871. This period saw the establishment of steam bakeries in many German towns, which quickly became widespread. Since these times, confectioners have created a great variety of the deep-fried sweet treats.

1. Put the yeast into a bowl with 100 ml/3½ fl oz of the milk and the salt, stir to dissolve and leave to stand for about 1 hour. Put the butter into a bowl with the caster sugar and vanilla sugar and beat with an electric whisk until pale and fluffy. Add the egg and the egg yolks, one at a time, beating after each addition until incorporated. Sift in the flour, then add the yeast mixture, vinegar and the remaining milk. Beat slowly until a soft dough forms.

2. Cover the dough with a damp tea towel and leave to rise in a warm place for about 2 hours until doubled in size.

3. Turn out the dough on to a lightly floured work surface, divide into 18–20 pieces and shape each piece into a ball. Leave to rise on the work surface, uncovered, for about 30 minutes until they develop a skin.

4. Meanwhile, heat enough oil for deep-frying in a large saucepan or deep-fryer to 180–190 °C/350–375 °F, or until a cube of bread browns in 30 seconds. Carefully slide the doughnuts into the oil and fry for 1½ minutes until golden brown. Turn them over and fry for a further 1½ minutes. Turn them over again and fry the top side for a further 30 seconds. To maintain the classic white line, do not move the doughnuts around during frying. Drain on kitchen paper and leave to cool.

5. Meanwhile, put some jam into a piping bag fitted with a plain nozzle and pipe into the centre of the doughnuts. Sprinkle with icing sugar and serve.

## INGREDIENTS

10 g/¼ oz fresh yeast (available in bakeries or online)
200 ml/7 fl oz cold milk
½ tsp salt
125 g/4½ oz butter
2½ tbsp caster sugar
1 tsp vanilla sugar (available online)
1 egg
2 egg yolks
500 g/1 lb 2 oz plain flour, plus extra for dusting
1 tbsp vinegar
sunflower oil, for deep-frying
raspberry or strawberry jam, for filling
icing sugar, for sprinkling

# Spiced Pear & Sultana Strudel

SERVES 6

PREP TIME: 35 minutes

COOKING TIME: 25 minutes

## INGREDIENTS

*85 g/3 oz unsalted butter,
melted, plus extra for greasing*

*3 firm ripe pears, peeled, cored and diced*

*finely grated rind and juice of ½ lemon*

*75 g/2¾ oz demerara sugar*

*1 tsp ground allspice*

*55 g/2 oz sultanas*

*55 g/2 oz ground almonds*

*6 sheets filo pastry (half a
250 g/9 oz pack)*

*icing sugar, sifted, for dusting*

The first written Strudel recipe dates back to 1698. A baker named Pueg from Vienna wrote down his 'secret', which has now been exposed in the National Library of Austria. The word itself explains the way of baking. 'Strudel' was the expression for cooking fruits and nuts inside a dough.

1. Preheat the oven to 200 °C/400 °F/Gas Mark 6 and grease a baking tray with butter.

2. Mix together the pears, lemon rind and juice, sugar, allspice, sultanas and half the almonds.

3. Place 2 sheets of filo pastry, slightly overlapping, on a clean tea towel.

4. Brush lightly with melted butter and sprinkle with a third of the almonds. Top with two more sheets, butter and almonds. Repeat once more.

5. Spread the pear mixture down one long side, to within 2.5 cm/1 inch of the edge.

6. Roll the pastry over to enclose the filling and roll up, using the tea towel to lift. Tuck the ends under.

7. Brush with a little melted butter and bake in the preheated oven for 20–25 minutes until golden and crisp.

8. Lightly dust the strudel with icing sugar. Serve the strudel warm or cold, cut into thick slices.

281

1.
2.
3.
4.
5.
6.
7.
8.

# Austrian Sacher Cake

SERVES 12

PREP TIME: 1½ hours

COOKING TIME: 1½ hours

### INGREDIENTS

*85 g/3 oz plain chocolate*

*2 tbsp water*

*6 eggs, separated*

*pinch of salt*

*100 g/3½ oz caster sugar*

*100 g/3½ oz butter,
plus extra for greasing*

*150 g/5½ oz plain flour, sifted,
plus extra for dusting*

*4 tsp vanilla extract*

*3 tbsp apricot jam*

### icing

*100 ml/3½ fl oz whipping cream*

*30 g/1 oz butter*

*150 g/5½ oz plain chocolate,
at least 70 per cent cocoa solids*

*70 g/2½ oz icing sugar*

*2 tbsp water*

In 1832, a 16-year-old Viennese chef's apprentice, Franz Sacher, invented the basic shape of the famed Sachertorte (Sacher cake). One day the head chef in charge of the kitchen of the emperor's Viennese residence was taken ill, and so Sacher had to step in and create a special dessert for the high-profile guests. But the cake remained unacknowledged until Sacher's son, Eduard, further developed and popularized it during his apprentice-ship at the Viennese confectioners Demel.

1. Preheat the oven to 180 °C/350 °F/Gas Mark 4. Grease a 23-cm/9-inch round springform cake tin and dust with flour. Put the chocolate and water into a heatproof bowl set over a saucepan of barely simmering water and heat until melted. Whisk the egg whites with the salt until they hold stiff peaks, then gradually add half the sugar, whisking after each addition until combined.

2. Put the butter and the remaining sugar into a separate large bowl and beat with an electric whisk until creamy, then add the egg yolks, one at a time, beating after each addition until combined. Add the flour, vanilla extract and melted chocolate. Carefully fold in the beaten egg whites.

3. Pour the mixture into the prepared tin and bake in the preheated oven for about 1½ hours, or until a skewer inserted into the centre comes out clean. Leave to cool in the tin, then turn out on to a wire rack to cool completely. Cut the cake in half horizontally.

4. Put the jam into a small saucepan and heat over a low heat until runny, then spread it evenly over the base layer of the cake. Place the second layer on top.

5. To make the icing, put the cream into a saucepan over a medium heat and bring to the boil. Remove from the heat and gradually add the butter and chocolate, stirring until melted. Put the sugar and the water into a sepa-rate saucepan over a medium heat and stir until dissolved. Add the sugar syrup to the chocolate mixture and stir to combine. Leave to cool slightly, then pour over the cake.

6. Use a palette knife to spread the icing evenly over the top and the sides of the cake. Leave to set firm and then decorate the surface, if desired. Chill in the refrigerator before serving.

2.

2.

4.

# FOR THE Love OF LIFE...

As with most traditional recipes in Europe, the origin of lebkuchen (German gingerbread) can be traced back many centuries. However, in people's minds, historical origins are usually less important than the memories that they associate with lebkuchen.

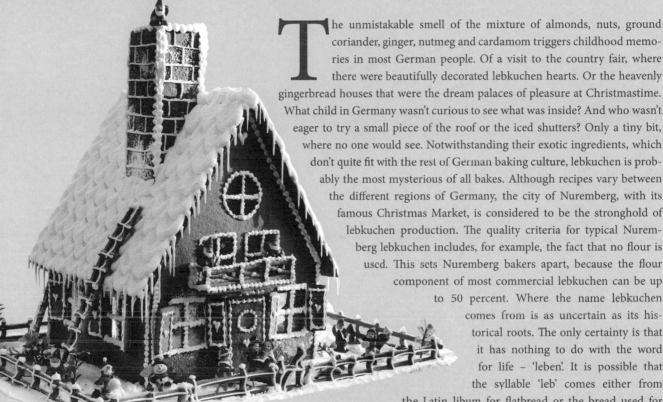

*Houses made from lebkuchen biscuits are real artworks and very often used as decorations in shop windows, especially in the south of Germany.*

The unmistakable smell of the mixture of almonds, nuts, ground coriander, ginger, nutmeg and cardamom triggers childhood memories in most German people. Of a visit to the country fair, where there were beautifully decorated lebkuchen hearts. Or the heavenly gingerbread houses that were the dream palaces of pleasure at Christmastime. What child in Germany wasn't curious to see what was inside? And who wasn't eager to try a small piece of the roof or the iced shutters? Only a tiny bit, where no one would see. Notwithstanding their exotic ingredients, which don't quite fit with the rest of German baking culture, lebkuchen is probably the most mysterious of all bakes. Although recipes vary between the different regions of Germany, the city of Nuremberg, with its famous Christmas Market, is considered to be the stronghold of lebkuchen production. The quality criteria for typical Nuremberg lebkuchen includes, for example, the fact that no flour is used. This sets Nuremberg bakers apart, because the flour component of most commercial lebkuchen can be up to 50 percent. Where the name lebkuchen comes from is as uncertain as its historical roots. The only certainty is that it has nothing to do with the word for life – 'leben'. It is possible that the syllable 'leb' comes either from the Latin libum for flatbread or the bread used for offerings, or from the old Germanic word for 'loaf', which is now a rarely used term that describes the 'body' of the bread. The ancient Egyptians already baked spiced honey cakes and placed the loaves in the graves of their dead to take along as provisions for their journey. However, we do not really know how the tradition of this sweet bread came to northern Europe, though there has been evidence of similar recipes in various monasteries in southern Germany. There, the so-called pfefferkuchen (pepper cake) was a dessert. As rare spices from distant lands were needed to make lebkuchen, it is probable that the monks brought these back from their travels. Later, the spices were ordered from merchants; for this reason, the lebkuchen tradition developed mainly along the major trade routes. In Germany, lebkuchen quickly became a coveted item, which is explained by its long shelf life. In southern Germany and Austria, bakers who specialized in making flat wafers were called zelter. The lebkuchen bakers were therefore called lebzelter. Incidentally, a lebzelter is mentioned in the tax records of the City of Munich in 1370.

1.

3.

4.

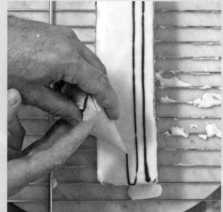

4.

# Esterházy SLICES

SERVES 12

PREP TIME: 50 minutes

COOKING TIME: 10 minutes

Esterházy slices are a variation of the Esterházy cake, which was created in the late 19th century by a Budapest confectioner for the Hungarian aristocratic Esterházy family who were renowned for their extravagant entertaining. The cake was named after Prince Paul III, Anton Esterházy, a diplomat and, in 1848, briefly Foreign Minister of the Austro-Hungarian Empire. The fame of the cake eventually reached Vienna where it soon became part of that city's legendary confectionery.

1. Preheat the oven to 200°C/400°F/Gas Mark 6. Grease a baking tray and dust it with flour. Whisk the egg whites in a clean, grease-free bowl until they hold soft peaks. Fold in the icing sugar, vanilla sugar and cinnamon and continue beating until the mixture holds stiff peaks. Stir in the ground hazelnuts. Spread the mixture evenly on the prepared baking tray, then bake in the preheated oven for 10 minutes. Remove from the oven, immediately cut the cake into four 7.5-cm/3-inch-wide slices and transfer to a wire rack to cool.

2. Meanwhile, to make the buttercream icing, put the butter into a large bowl and beat until creamy. Put the egg yolks, sugar and flour into a medium-sized saucepan and stir together until smooth. Pass through a sieve to remove any lumps, if necessary. Stir in the milk and the rum, place over a medium heat and bring to the boil, stirring constantly. Remove from the heat, cover and leave to cool, then stir into the butter.

3. Spread a slice of the cake with the buttercream and top with another slice of cake. Repeat until all the slices are used, ending with a slice of cake.

4. To make the icing, put the egg white, icing sugar and lemon juice into a bowl and stir to combine. Spread over the top layer of cake. Mix the cocoa powder with the water until smooth. Put into a piping bag and pipe in long lines on top of the icing. Draw a skewer through the icing to create a feathered pattern. Cut into slices and serve.

## INGREDIENTS

butter, for greasing
plain flour, for dusting
6 egg whites
125 g/4½ oz icing sugar
60 g/2¼ oz vanilla sugar (available online)
pinch of ground cinnamon
150 g/5½ oz ground hazelnuts

buttercream icing
200 g/7 oz butter
3 egg yolks
1½ tbsp granulated sugar
40 g/1½ oz plain flour
250 ml/9 fl oz milk
splash of rum or kirsch

icing
½ egg white
200 g/7 oz icing sugar
juice of ½ lemon
2 tbsp cocoa powder
1 tsp water

# Linzer Torte

SERVES 10–12

PREP TIME: 45 minutes, plus time to rest and mature

COOKING TIME: 30–40 minutes

### INGREDIENTS

*150 g/5½ oz butter, plus extra for greasing*

*2 eggs*

*1 tbsp kirsch or cherry brandy*

*150 g/5½ oz plain flour, plus extra for dusting*

*150 g/5½ oz caster sugar*

*pinch of salt*

*pinch of ground cinnamon*

*¼ tsp ground cloves*

*150 g/5½ oz coarsely ground almonds*

*2 tsp cocoa powder*

*250 g/9 oz cherry jam*

The recipe for Linzer torte (a cake named after the city of Linz in Upper Austria) is the oldest cake recipe in the world. It was first published in 1653 in a cookery book of Countess Anna Margarita Sagramosa from Verona. It was popularized by Johann Konrad Vogel, a baker from Franconia in Germany, who emigrated to Linz in 1822. He manufactured this delicacy in large quantities, also shipping his products to other locations.

1.  Melt the butter in a small saucepan. Put the eggs into a small bowl with the kirsch and beat together.

2.  Mix together the flour, sugar, salt, cinnamon and cloves in a separate bowl, then add the butter and mix to combine. Add the almonds and the cocoa powder. Slowly add the egg mixture, mixing until a smooth dough forms. Cover the bowl and transfer to the refrigerator to rest for at least 48 hours.

3.  Preheat the oven to 160 °C/325 °F/Gas Mark 3 and grease a 25-cm/10-inch fluted flan tin. Turn out the dough on to a lightly floured work surface. Roll out three quarters of the dough into a round that has a thickness of 1 cm/½ inch. Place in the prepared tin, working it about 2.5 cm/1 inch up the sides of the tin. Spread a 5-mm/¼-inch layer of jam on the dough.

4.  Roll out the remaining dough and use a pastry wheel to cut it into 1-cm/ ½-inch-wide strips. Lay the strips on top of the jam in a lattice pattern. Bake in the middle of the preheated oven for 30–40 minutes.

5.  Remove from the oven and leave to cool completely, then wrap in foil and leave to rest for at least 1 week. Linzer torte is never served fresh out of the oven and improves with time.

3.

3.

4.

# Spiced Fruit Loaf

MAKES 1 LOAF

PREP TIME: 20 minutes,
plus rising

COOKING TIME: 1 hour 10 minutes

### INGREDIENTS

*450 g/1 lb strong white flour,
plus extra for dusting*

*pinch of salt*

*2 tsp mixed spice*

*115 g/4 oz unsalted butter, diced*

*2¼ tsp easy-blend dried yeast*

*100 g/3½ oz golden caster sugar*

*115 g/4 oz dried currants*

*115 g/4 oz raisins*

*50 g/1¾ oz chopped mixed peel*

*finely grated rind of 1 orange*

*1 egg, beaten*

*150 ml/5 fl oz milk, warmed*

*vegetable oil, for oiling*

Fruit breads are very common in the south of Germany during the weeks of Advent. In some regions in Germany and Austria it is served to all family members on Christmas Eve after coming back from church. Dried pears and butter are served with the bread.

1.  Sift the flour, salt and mixed spice into a bowl and rub in the butter until the mixture resembles breadcrumbs. Stir in the yeast, sugar, dried fruit, mixed peel and orange rind, then add the egg and warm milk and bring together to form a soft dough.

2.  Knead the dough briefly on a lightly floured surface. Dust a clean bowl with flour and add the dough. Cover the bowl and leave to rise in a warm place for 2 hours.

3.  Preheat the oven to 180 °C/350 °F/Gas Mark 4 and oil a 900-g/2-lb loaf tin. Knead the dough again briefly, then place it in the prepared tin, cover and leave to rise for 20 minutes. Bake in the preheated oven for 1 hour 10 minutes – the loaf should be golden and well risen. Leave to cool in the tin before slicing and serving.

1.

2.

3.

1.

2.

4.

# Onion Tart

This savoury onion tart is typically served in Germany as a snack to go with young wine, also known in German as Federweisser. Vineyard workers and participants of wine festivals especially enjoy eating it warm.

1. To make the pastry, put 100 g/3½ oz of the flour into a bowl and make a well in the centre. Pour the milk into the well and crumble in the yeast. Add the sugar, stir to combine, then cover and leave to rise for 15 minutes.

2. Add the remaining flour and the butter to the yeast mixture and knead until a smooth dough forms. Cover with a damp tea towel and leave to rise for 1 hour until doubled in size. Turn out on to a lightly floured work surface and roll out into a round.

3. Preheat the oven to 160 °C/325 °F/Gas Mark 3. Grease a 28-cm/11-inch fluted flan tin. Ease the pastry into the prepared tin.

4. Halve the onions and slice them into thin strips. Melt the butter in a frying pan, add the pancetta and sauté for 1–2 minutes, then add the onions and season to taste with salt and pepper. Sauté for a further 5–6 minutes until the onions are translucent, then remove from the heat and leave to cool. Spread the mixture in the pastry case.

5. Beat the eggs with the cream, season with salt and pepper and pour over the onion and pancetta mixture in the pastry case. Bake in the preheated oven for 50 minutes until golden brown. If the surface is browning too quickly, cover with foil. Serve hot or cold.

SERVES 10–12

PREP TIME: 35 minutes, plus 1¼ hours to rise

COOKING TIME: 50 minutes

## INGREDIENTS

*4 mild onions*
*1 tbsp butter*
*70 g/2½ oz smoked pancetta*
*3 eggs*
*350 ml/12 fl oz double cream*
*salt and pepper*

### pastry
*350 g/12 oz plain flour,*
*plus extra for dusting*
*125 ml/4 fl oz lukewarm milk*
*20 g/¾ oz fresh yeast (available in bakeries or online)*
*1 tsp sugar*
*25 g/1 oz butter, melted,*
*plus extra for greasing*

1.

2.

4.

# Spring Onion & Cheese
# TART

SERVES 8

PREP TIME: 35 minutes,
plus 1 hour to rest

COOKING TIME: 50 minutes

The spring onion is harvested in the early spring, almost too early in fact, at a time when the bulb is only beginning to grow. With its crisp, fresh taste, it serves to refine a number of dishes such as this hearty tart. When contrasted with that of a fully grown common onion, the flavour of a spring onion is very mild and their stems are characterized by a slight leek flavour.

1. To make the pastry, mix together the flour, salt and butter in a bowl. Add the water, a little at a time, mixing after each addition until a stiff dough forms. Wrap in clingfilm and leave to rest for 1 hour.

2. Preheat the oven to 180 °C/350 °F/Gas Mark 4. Oil a 25-cm/10-inch rectangular fluted flan tin. Put the oil into a frying pan over a medium heat, add the spring onions and fry for about 5 minutes until translucent. Remove from the heat and leave to cool.

3. Beat the eggs in a large bowl, then add the cheese and ham and mix to combine. Add the cream and spring onions and mix together well. Stir in the nutmeg, then season to taste with salt and pepper.

4. Ease the pastry into the prepared tin and prick the base all over with a fork. Pour the filling into the pastry case and bake in the bottom of the preheated oven for 45 minutes until the surface of the tart is golden brown and a skewer inserted into the centre comes out clean. Serve the tart hot or cold.

## INGREDIENTS

*1 tbsp oil, plus extra for oiling*
*3–4 spring onions, finely chopped*
*3 eggs*
*150 g/5½ oz Emmenthal cheese, grated*
*150 g/5½ oz cooked ham, diced*
*200 ml/7 fl oz double cream*
*pinch of nutmeg*
*salt and pepper*

## pastry
*200 g/7 oz plain flour*
*pinch of salt*
*125 g/4½ oz butter, at room temperature*
*124 ml/4 fl oz water*

# Baking *in the* SCANDINAVIAN STYLE

Cake, bread and biscuits are an essential part of everyday life in Scandinavia. Undoubtedly, the climate conditions in northern Europe mean that hearty and filling foods are important in the typical Scandinavian diet. A light snack between meals not only helps to boost energy levels but can also lift the spirits, especially during a dark winter. Crispbreads spread with lots of butter and cakes with the obligatory blueberry topping are a favourite throughout Scandinavia, particularly during the 'white nights' around the summer solstice when the night sky never becomes truly dark. It was once believed that the morning dew at this time of the year had healing powers. The dew would be collected in bottles and used for bread baking, because the bread would rise even higher and taste even better.

*The typical Scandinavian way of living is beautiful, but sometimes with very rough weather conditions – which is perhaps one reason why many families are enthusiastic about high quality home baking. A good cake is always an opportunity to assemble friends and family around a table.*

# Princess Cake

SERVES 12

PREP TIME: 30 minutes,
plus time to chill

COOKING TIME: 40 minutes

## INGREDIENTS

*butter, for greasing*
*breadcrumbs, for coating*
*4 eggs*
*225 g/8 oz granulated sugar*
*60 g/2¼ oz plain flour*
*80 g/2¾ oz potato flour*
*1 tsp baking powder*
*icing sugar, for dusting*

### filling

*250 ml/9 fl oz double cream*
*4 egg yolks*
*3 tbsp potato flour or 2 tbsp cornflour*
*2 tbsp granulated sugar*
*2 tsp vanilla extract*
*475 ml/16 fl oz whipping cream, whipped*

### topping

*300 g/10½ oz marzipan*
*green food colouring*
*yellow food colouring*
*pink marzipan rose and*
*green marzipan leaves, to decorate*

This cake was first made by Jenny Åkerström. She was the housekeeping teacher of Princess Margaretha, Princess Martha and Princess Astrid of Sweden, and she published a cookery book in their honour in 1929. But the recipe for the princess cake was only published in the 1948 edition of the book, under the name of green cake. It remains unclear why the marzipan is coloured green, but the cake certainly looks striking.

1. Preheat the oven to 190 °C/375 °F/Gas Mark 5. Grease a 23-cm/9-inch round cake tin, then coat the base and side with breadcrumbs. Put the eggs and granulated sugar into a mixing bowl and beat with an electric whisk until light and fluffy.

2. Sift together the plain flour, potato flour and baking powder and carefully fold into the egg mixture until thoroughly combined. Pour the mixture into the prepared tin and bake in the bottom of the preheated oven for 40 minutes or until golden and a skewer inserted into the centre comes out clean. Transfer to a wire rack to cool.

3. To make the filling, put the double cream, egg yolks, potato flour and sugar into a small saucepan and whisk together. Cook over a low heat, stirring constantly, until thick. Remove from the heat and stir in the vanilla extract.

4. To make the topping, knead the marzipan until soft, then gradually add the green and yellow food colourings until it is light green in colour. Use your hands to flatten the marzipan into a round, then place between two sheets of baking paper or on a work surface dusted with icing sugar and roll it out into a 2-mm/⅛-inch thick round with a diameter of 30 cm/ 12 inches.

5. Slice the cooled cake into 3 layers horizontally, cutting the top layer a little thinner than the others. Assemble the cake by spreading half the filling on the bottom layer. Add the second layer of cake and spread with the remaining filling. Top with the whipped cream, then add the final layer of cake, gently forming it into a dome shape. Take care that not too much cream is hanging over the sides.

6. Lay the marzipan round on top of the cake, shaping it around the sides until the whole cake is covered. Trim any excess marzipan from the base of the cake with a very sharp knife. Dust the top with icing sugar and decorate with the marzipan rose and leaves. Chill until ready to serve.

2.

3.

4.

4.

1.

2.

4.

# Semla Buns

MAKES 14–16

PREP TIME: 35 minutes,
plus 1 hour 10 minutes to rise

COOKING TIME: 10 minutes

Semla buns are sweet rolls filled with a marzipan mixture and topped with whipped cream. In Scandinavia, it is a traditional pastry on Shrove Tuesday, the day before Lent begins. The Semlor were therefore called 'Fat Tuesday' and were originally served in dishes with hot milk. Some cafés still serve them this way.

1.  Gently heat the milk with the cardamom in a saucepan, then remove from the heat, crumble in the yeast and stir to dissolve. Break the egg into a bowl and gradually beat in the butter. Add the sugar and salt. Sift the flour into a large bowl and add the egg and butter mixture. Add the yeast mixture and knead until a smooth, elastic dough forms. Cover with a damp tea towel and leave to rise for about 1 hour until doubled in size.

2.  Preheat the oven to 200 °C/400 °F/Gas Mark 6. Dust a baking tray with flour. Divide the dough into 14–16 pieces, roll each piece into a ball and place on the prepared baking sheet. Dust with flour, then cover and leave to rise for a further 10 minutes.

3.  Whisk the egg yolk with a little milk and brush over the surface of the buns. Bake in the middle of the preheated oven for 6–7 minutes. Remove from the oven and leave to cool.

4.  Cut off the top of the buns horizontally and set aside. Use your fingers to hollow out the buns, reserving the crumbs. To make the filling, mix the reserved crumbs with the marzipan paste and milk until a soft paste forms. Spoon the paste into the buns, pipe over the whipped cream and place a reserved top on each bun. Dust with icing sugar and serve.

## INGREDIENTS

300 ml/10 fl oz milk,
plus extra for brushing

1 tbsp ground cardamom

50 g/1¾ oz fresh yeast (available in bakeries or online)

1 egg

150 g/5½ oz softened butter

140 g/5 oz caster sugar

½ tsp salt

600 g/1 lb 5 oz plain flour,
plus extra for dusting

1 egg yolk

icing sugar, for dusting

### filling

400 g/14 oz marzipan paste
(available online)

dash of milk

400 ml/14 fl oz whipping cream, whipped

# Appelkaka
## Cake

SERVES 12

PREP TIME: 20 minutes

COOKING TIME: 50 minutes

### INGREDIENTS

*3 tbsp biscotti crumbs, for coating*

*225 g/8 oz softened butter,
plus extra for greasing*

*275 g/9¾ oz caster sugar*

*4 eggs*

*175 g/6 oz plain flour*

*1 tsp baking powder*

*4–6 apples, cut into wedges*

*2 tsp ground cinnamon mixed
with 1 tbsp granulated sugar*

*140 g/5 oz almonds, chopped*

When, after a long summer, it starts to get cool again and the apples are ripe, this juicy Swedish apple cake is simply a must. Fresh apples, cinnamon and almonds lend it a unique flavour, often crowned with whipped cream or vanilla sauce.

1. Preheat the oven to 180 °C/350 °F/Gas Mark 4. Grease a 25-cm/10-inch round springform cake tin and generously coat with biscotti crumbs. Put the butter and sugar into a bowl and beat until smooth and creamy. Add the eggs, one at a time, beating after each addition until combined. Sift together the flour and baking powder into the mixture and stir in.

2. Spread the mixture in the prepared tin. Toss the apple wedges with the cinnamon and sugar mixture and arrange on the cake mixture.

3. Sprinkle with the almonds and bake in the preheated oven for 50 minutes or until a skewer inserted in the centre comes out clean. Remove from the oven, cut into pieces and serve warm or cold.

# ALMOND STICKS

Almond sticks are a fun and crunchy delight, especially for children: even a small bite is enough to enjoy the sweet, nutty flavour. It takes a bit more of an effort to make than normal snacks, but they're worth it.

1. Preheat the oven to 180 °C/350 °F/Gas Mark 4. Line a large baking tray with baking paper. Put the butter and sugar into a bowl and whisk until pale and fluffy. Add 2 eggs and the almond extract and stir until combined. Sift together the flour and the salt into a separate bowl, add to the butter and sugar mixture and knead until a smooth dough forms.

2. Turn out the dough on to a lightly floured work surface and roll out to a thickness of 2 cm/¾ inch. Using a sharp knife, cut out 25–30 strips, each measuring 2 x 5 cm/1 x 2 inches.

3. Beat the remaining eggs in a shallow bowl. Put the almonds into a separate bowl. Dip the dough strips into the beaten eggs, then into the chopped almonds. Generously sprinkle with sugar and place on the prepared baking tray.

4. Bake in the preheated oven for 8–10 minutes, then remove from the oven and transfer to a wire rack to cool. The almond sticks can be stored in an airtight container for up to 1 week.

MAKES 25–30

PREP TIME: 20–25 minutes

COOKING TIME: 8–10 minutes

## INGREDIENTS

225 g/8 oz softened butter

100 g/3½ oz caster sugar, plus extra for sprinkling

4 eggs

1 tsp almond extract

375 g/13 oz plain flour, plus extra for dusting

¼ tsp salt

200 g/7 oz almonds, chopped

2.

# TIME *for* SEMLOR

*Stockholm wouldn't be known as the capital of Scandinavian baking without the semla bun. It has become a tradition to take a break, drink a cup of coffee and eat a semla bun. In Sweden this sort of break is called 'fika'.*

The people of Stockholm have the greatest respect for the legendary 'bun man'. Nobody knows his name, what he looks like or when he will show up in the streets. But one thing is certain: the 'bun man' targets a bakery every day, buys a legendary Swedish semla bun, eats it and then rates it comprehensively in the newspapers or on his blog on the Internet. A bakery with a good review won't be complaining about a lack of business in the days and weeks that follow. The semla bun, with its cream and marzipan filling, was traditionally only served between Shrove Tuesday and Easter. But the semla bun is so popular that immediately after Christmas all the shop windows are so full of them that you'd think there weren't any other specialities in Sweden. Therefore, it was inevitable that someone like the 'bun man' should come along and start reviewing this particular treat. This is how the critic describes what makes a particularly good semla bun: 'The ingredients must be perfect, the marzipan flavourful but not intrusive and the cream should look freshly whipped. Everything should be well presented and the proportions must be just right.' If these conditions are met, there's nothing to prevent a perfect 'fika'. You do not know what 'fika' is? Fika can be had or held in the late morning and also in the early or late afternoon. In any case, there should always be time for fika, even if the term doesn't actually exist in Scandinavian languages. There is no official translation for 'fika', but there is a very precise definition for it – as a very famous Swedish furniture store once put it in its baking book entitled Fika: 'It is a break with coffee and pastries, a cornerstone of Swedish food culture. A moment of relaxation among friends, family or colleagues. 'Fika' is for any time, any place, anywhere. In Sweden any time is fika time.'

Fika is not necessarily a national custom in all Scandinavian countries. However taking time out for a cup of coffee is a much-loved habit everywhere, be it Denmark, Sweden or Norway. Taking a short break clearly increases productivity at work – whether it's in the factory, at the office or at school. And – of course – also at home!

3.

4.

5.

# Tosca CAKE

SERVES 8

PREP TIME: 20 minutes

COOKING TIME: 35–40 minutes

## INGREDIENTS

150 g/5½ oz plain flour,
plus extra for dusting

1 tsp baking powder

½ tsp salt

125 g/4½ oz butter, melted,
plus extra for greasing

1 tsp vanilla extract or 1 vanilla pod,
scraped

5 tbsp milk

3 eggs

150 g/5½ oz caster sugar

### topping

60 g/2¼ oz butter

125 g/4½ oz caster sugar

5 tbsp whipping cream

2 tbsp plain flour

pinch of salt

85 g/3 oz flaked almonds

¼ tsp almond extract

1 tsp vanilla extract or 1 pod, scraped

Scandinavia's popular Tosca cake is thought to be named after Giacomo Puccini's opera about the love and suffering of ordinary people, first performed in 1900. The cake is very easy to make and so is good to bake for guests. Just pop it in the oven as your guests are arriving and let them enjoy the smell of the light cake with its caramelized almond topping as it bakes.

1. Preheat the oven to 180 °C/350 °F/Gas Mark 4. Grease a 23-cm/9-inch springform cake tin and dust with flour. Line the base with baking paper, then grease the paper.

2. Sift together the flour, baking powder and salt into a bowl and set aside. Mix together the butter, vanilla extract and milk in a separate bowl and set aside in a warm place so that the butter remains liquid.

3. Put the eggs and sugar into a large bowl and beat with an electric whisk until pale and thick. Add the flour mixture and the milk mixture alternately, mixing after each addition. Do not over-mix. Transfer to the prepared tin and bake in the preheated oven for 20–25 minutes, until the top is just set.

4. Meanwhile, prepare the topping. Combine the butter, sugar, cream, flour and salt in a saucepan and heat over a medium–high heat, stirring, until the butter is melted. Add the almonds, bring to a simmer and cook for about 1 minute, then remove from the heat. Stir in the almond extract and vanilla extract and set aside.

5. Remove the cake from the oven. Increase the oven temperature to 200 °C/400 °F/Gas Mark 6. Gently spread the topping on the cake. Return to the oven and bake for a further 15 minutes, until the topping is golden brown. Leave to cool, then slice and serve.

# Kladdkaka

## CHOCOLATE CAKES

MAKES 9

PREP TIME: 15 minutes

COOKING TIME: 15–20 minutes

### INGREDIENTS

*2 eggs*
*275 g/9¾ oz caster sugar*
*50 g/1¾ oz plain flour*
*pinch of salt*
*4 tbsp cocoa powder*
*125 g/4½ oz butter, melted, plus extra for greasing*
*icing sugar, for dusting*
*cranberries, to decorate*
*whipped cream, to serve (optional)*

This sticky and sweet chocolate cake is very popular in Sweden. It is made with plenty of sugar and just a little flour. It's a bit like a brownie, but softer and denser, especially in the middle. Serve with whipped cream or vanilla ice cream.

1.  Preheat the oven to 180 °C/350 °F/Gas Mark 4. Lightly grease 9 holes of a fluted muffin tin. Beat the eggs and sugar in a large bowl, then gradually beat in the flour and salt.

2.  Stir the cocoa powder into the butter and carefully mix into the mixture.

3.  Pour the mixture into the prepared holes of the tin and bake in the pre-heated oven for 15–20 minutes until slightly crispy on the outside and a skewer inserted into the centre comes out sticky. Remove from the oven and leave to cool.

4.  Dust with icing sugar, decorate with cranberries and serve with whipped cream, if using.

1.

2.

3.

1.

2.

4.

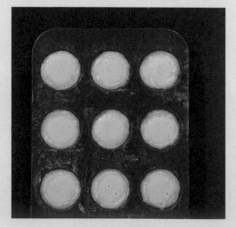

# Mazarin

## TARTLETS

MAKES 12

PREP TIME: 30 minutes,
plus time to chill

COOKING TIME: 10–15 minutes

### INGREDIENTS

*100 g/3½ oz butter*
*2 eggs*
*100 g/3½ oz caster sugar*
*150 g/5½ oz flaked almonds,*
*plus extra to decorate*
*1 tsp bitter almond oil*
*or almond extract*
*rose petals, to decorate*

### pastry

*150 g/5½ oz plain flour,*
*plus extra for dusting*
*½ tsp baking powder*
*85 g/3 oz caster sugar*
*115 g/4 oz butter, plus extra for greasing*
*1 egg*
*1 tsp vodka*

### icing

*150 g/5½ oz icing sugar*
*2 tbsp milk or water*

These tartlets, named after the Italian/French cardinal and politician Jules Mazarin (1602–1661), are also simply called mazarins. The cardinal was a gourmet and encouraged an exchange of recipes in Europe. The Swedish mazarins probably evolved from other European almond tartlets several decades before. They are considered to be a particular favourite with baking connoisseurs.

1.  To make the pastry, put the flour, baking powder, sugar, butter, egg and vodka into a large bowl and mix together until a soft dough forms. Add a little water if needed to achieve the correct consistency. Cover with clingfilm and chill in the refrigerator for several hours.

2.  Preheat the oven to 180 °C/350 °F/Gas Mark 4. Grease a 12-hole muffin tin. Turn out the dough on to a lightly floured work surface and roll out to a thickness of 5 mm/¼ inch. Use a round cutter to cut out 12 rounds large enough to line the holes, then gently ease into the prepared tin.

3.  Melt the butter in a small saucepan. Put the eggs and sugar into a bowl and beat together, then add the almonds and the almond oil and beat until combined. Stir in the melted butter.

4.  Pour the filling into the pastry cases and bake in the preheated oven for 10–15 minutes until golden brown. Remove from the oven and leave to cool.

5.  Meanwhile, to make the icing, put the icing sugar and milk into a bowl and mix well. Generously coat the cooled tartlets with the icing and leave to set. Decorate with flaked almonds and rose petals.

# ICED CARROT

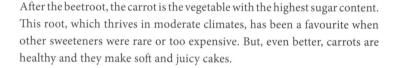
*Cake*

SERVES 16

PREP TIME: 20–25 minutes

COOKING TIME: 40–45 minutes

## INGREDIENTS

*175 ml/6 fl oz sunflower oil,
plus extra for greasing*
*175 g/6 oz light muscovado sugar*
*3 eggs, beaten*
*175 g/6 oz grated carrots*
*85 g/3 oz sultanas*
*55 g/2 oz walnut pieces*
*grated rind of 1 orange*
*175 g/6 oz self-raising flour*
*1 tsp bicarbonate of soda*
*1 tsp ground cinnamon*
*½ tsp grated nutmeg*
*strips of orange zest,
to decorate*

### icing
*200 g/7 oz cream cheese*
*100 g/3½ oz icing sugar*
*2 tsp orange juice*

After the beetroot, the carrot is the vegetable with the highest sugar content. This root, which thrives in moderate climates, has been a favourite when other sweeteners were rare or too expensive. But, even better, carrots are healthy and they make soft and juicy cakes.

1.  Preheat the oven to 180 °C/350 °F/Gas Mark 4. Grease a 23-cm/9-inch square cake tin and line with baking paper.

2.  Beat together the oil, sugar and eggs in a large bowl. Stir in the grated carrots, sultanas, walnut pieces and orange rind.

3.  Sift together the flour, bicarbonate of soda, cinnamon and nutmeg into the bowl, then mix evenly into the carrot mixture.

4.  Spoon the mixture into the prepared tin and bake in the preheated oven for 40–45 minutes until well risen and firm to the touch.

5.  Leave to cool in the tin for 5 minutes, then turn out onto a wire rack to cool completely.

6.  To make the icing, combine the cheese, sugar and orange juice in a bowl and beat until smooth. Spread over the top of the cake and swirl with a palette knife.

7.  Decorate with strips of orange zest and serve cut into squares.

2.

3.

5.

6.

2.

4.

5.

# Troika *Cake*

SERVES 8

PREP TIME: 35 minutes

COOKING TIME: 35–40 minutes

This is a Norwegian recipe for rich, dense chocolate cake with raspberry jam, whipped cream and marzipan. The name *troika* means 'set of three' in Russia, which reflects the three distinct layers of the cake.

1. Preheat the oven to 180 °C/350 °F/Gas Mark 4. Line a 30-cm/12-inch square baking tin with baking paper, then grease the paper.

2. Mix together the flour, cocoa powder, sugar, baking powder, bicarbonate of soda and salt in a large bowl.

3. Add the eggs, vanilla extract, buttermilk and butter and beat until smooth. Transfer the mixture to the prepared tin and bake in the preheated oven for 35–40 minutes until a skewer inserted into the centre comes out clean. Transfer to a wire rack and leave to cool completely.

4. Using a large knife, carefully cut the cake in half horizontally. Place 1 piece on a work surface and spread with the jam. Whip the cream with the sugar and vanilla extract until it holds stiff peaks. Reserve a quarter of the cream, then spread the remainder evenly over the jam. Cover with the second piece of cake and transfer to the refrigerator.

5. Gradually work a few drops of food colouring into the marzipan until it is pale pink in colour. Thinly roll it out on a work surface dusted with icing sugar to a 30-cm/12-inch square. Take the cake out of the refrigerator and spread the remaining cream over the top. Place the marzipan layer on top and press gently. Use a sharp knife to trim any excess. Serve chilled.

## INGREDIENTS

280 g/10 oz plain flour
140 g/5 oz cocoa powder
250 g/9 oz caster sugar
1½ tsp baking powder
2½ tsp bicarbonate of soda
½ tsp salt
4 eggs
1 tsp vanilla extract
5 tbsp buttermilk
125 g/4½ oz butter, melted, plus extra for greasing

### filling and topping
200 g/7 oz raspberry jam
200 ml/7 fl oz whipping cream
2 tbsp caster sugar
1 tsp vanilla extract
red food colouring
250 g/9 oz marzipan
icing sugar, for dusting

# Skoleboller Buns

MAKES 12

PREP TIME: 45 minutes, plus 1 hour 20 minutes to rise

COOKING TIME: 15–20 minutes

## INGREDIENTS

*70 g/2½ oz butter, melted, plus extra for greasing*
*300 ml/10 fl oz lukewarm milk*
*2 tsp easy-blend dried yeast*
*50 g/1¾ oz caster sugar*
*½ tsp salt*
*1 tsp ground cardamom*
*500 g/1 lb 2 oz plain flour*
*35 g/1¼ oz desiccated coconut, for sprinkling*

### vanilla filling

*250 ml/9 fl oz milk*
*2 tbsp plain flour*
*2 tbsp vanilla sugar or 1 tsp vanilla extract*
*2 egg yolks, beaten*

### icing

*100 g/3½ oz icing sugar*
*2 tbsp lemon juice*

The recipe for the Norwegian skoleboller is from the 1950s. At the time people were looking for a simple pastry that schoolchildren could eat in their hands. The flat yeast dough bun gets its special taste from the spice cardamom. It is then filled with vanilla cream and topped with a sugar glaze after baking.

1.  Mix together the butter, milk and yeast in a large bowl. Add the sugar, salt, cardamom and flour, kneading until a smooth dough forms. Cover with a damp tea towel and leave to rise for at least 1 hour until doubled in size.

2.  Shape the dough into small balls and use your thumb to make a hollow in the centre of each.

3.  To make the vanilla filling, put the milk, flour, vanilla sugar and egg yolks into a saucepan over a medium heat, mix to combine, then bring to the boil and cook, stirring constantly, until thickened. Transfer to a bowl and leave to cool.

4.  Meanwhile, preheat the oven to 220 °C/425 °F/Gas Mark 7. Grease a large baking tray. Spoon the filling into the hollows in the dough balls. Place the balls on the prepared tray and bake in the preheated oven for 10–15 minutes until golden brown. Remove from the oven and transfer to a wire rack to cool.

5.  Meanwhile, to make the icing, mix together the icing sugar and lemon juice in a small bowl. Coat the buns with the icing, sprinkle with the coconut and serve.

1.

3.

3.

3.

4.

5.

# Sarah Bernhardt Biscuits

MAKES 30–35

PREP TIME: 1 hour,
plus 8 hours to cool

COOKING TIME: 15 minutes

These extravagant biscuits are named after Sarah Bernhardt (1844–1923), an eccentric French actress absolutely adored by her audiences. One of the first international stars, she performed in Denmark on one of her tours, and the Danes thanked her with this recipe.

1. To make the ganache, put the cream, honey, salt and vanilla extract into a saucepan. Bring to the boil, then remove from the heat. Add the chocolate and stir with a wooden spoon until melted. Cover with clingfilm and leave to cool overnight.

2. Preheat the oven to 160 °C/325 °F/Gas Mark 3. Line two baking trays with baking paper. Line a tray with greaseproof paper.

3. To make the macaroons, put the marzipan paste, sugar, almond extract and salt into a bowl and mix until well combined. Add the egg whites, one at a time, mixing well after each addition until combined.

4. Put the macaroon mixture into a piping bag fitted with a plain 1-cm/¼-inch nozzle and pipe 2-cm/¾-inch rounds on the baking paper-lined baking trays. Bake in the preheated oven for 12 minutes.

5. Transfer the macaroons to the prepared tray. Fill a piping bag with the ganache and pipe a little mound on each macaroon. Sandwich pairs of macaroons together and chill in the refrigerator for about 30 minutes.

6. To make the icing, put the plain chocolate into a heatproof bowl set over a saucepan of barely simmering water and heat until melted. Remove from the heat, stir in the oil and leave to cool slightly.

7. Remove the macaroons from the refrigerator and dip into the chocolate icing. Leave to cool and set. Finally drizzle melted white chocolate over the plain chocolate icing.

8. Keep the biscuits in the refrigerator and bring to room temperature before serving.

## INGREDIENTS

### ganache
475 ml/16 fl oz double cream
3 tbsp clear honey
pinch of salt
1 tsp vanilla extract
450 g/1 lb plain chocolate

### almond macaroons
250 g/9 oz marzipan paste
(available online)
90 g/3¼ oz caster sugar
1 tsp almond extract
½ tsp salt
2 egg whites

### icing
175 g/6 oz plain chocolate,
at least 70 per cent cocoa solids
2 tbsp vegetable oil
55 g/2 oz white chocolate, melted

# Cinnamon *Swirls*

MAKES 12

PREP TIME: 20 minutes,
plus 1 hour 10 minutes to rise

COOKING TIME: 20–30 minutes

## INGREDIENTS

*25 g/1 oz butter, cut into small pieces,
plus extra for greasing*
*225 g/8 oz strong white flour*
*½ tsp salt*
*2¼ tsp easy-blend dried yeast*
*1 egg, lightly beaten*
*125 ml/4 fl oz lukewarm milk*
*2 tbsp maple syrup, for glazing*

### filling
*55 g/2 oz butter, softened*
*2 tsp ground cinnamon*
*50 g/1¾ oz soft light brown sugar*
*50 g/1¾ oz currants*

These Swedish cinnamon swirls are sold throughout Scandinavia and across the globe. They probably originated between the two World Wars, as more baking ingredients became available. They are favourites at afternoon coffee parties in Sweden. According to tradition, guests must first eat a filling cinnamon swirl before helping themselves to cakes.

1.  Grease a baking tray and a bowl. Sift the flour and salt into a separate mixing bowl and stir in the yeast. Rub in the chopped butter with your fingertips until the mixture resembles breadcrumbs. Add the egg and milk and mix to a dough.

2.  Form the dough into a ball, place in the greased bowl, cover and leave to stand in a warm place for about 40 minutes, or until doubled in volume. Knock back the dough for 1 minute, then roll out to a 30 x 23-cm/12 x 9-inch rectangle.

3.  To make the filling, cream together the butter, cinnamon and sugar until light and fluffy. Spread the filling over the dough, leaving a 2.5-cm/1-inch border. Sprinkle the currants evenly over the top. Roll up the dough from one of the long edges and press down to seal.

4.  Preheat the oven to 190 °C/375 °F/Gas Mark 5. Cut the roll into 12 slices and place, cut-side down, on the prepared baking sheet. Cover and leave to stand for 30 minutes.

5.  Bake in the preheated oven for 20–30 minutes or until the swirls are well risen. Brush with maple syrup and leave to cool slightly before serving.

1.

3.

4.

1.

2.

2.

# Seeded Rye
# BREAD

MAKES 1 LOAF

PREP TIME: 25 minutes
plus 1–1½ hours to rise

COOKING TIME: 30–35 minutes

Rye is the classic grain used for making bread in northern Europe, where it has been a staple food for centuries and is eaten for most of the meals of the day. Compared with wheat bread, rye bread is darker, has a stronger taste, keeps better and is much healthier. The rye and wheat bread mixture is seasoned with caraway, also typical of this dark bread.

1. Lightly oil a baking tray. Mix the rye flour, white flour, salt, caraway seeds and yeast in a large bowl and make a well in the centre. Mix together the butter, honey and water and pour into the well. Mix with a knife to a soft, sticky dough.

2. Turn out the dough onto a floured work surface and knead for 10 minutes, or until smooth and elastic. Shape into an oval and place on the prepared baking tray. Slash the top in a diamond pattern, lightly dust with flour and leave in a warm place for 1–1½ hours or until doubled in size.

3. Meanwhile, preheat the oven to 190 °C/375 °F/Gas Mark 5. Bake the loaf in the preheated oven for 30–35 minutes or until the crust is a rich brown colour and the base sounds hollow when tapped with your knuckles. Transfer to a wire rack to cool.

## INGREDIENTS

250 g/9 oz rye flour,
plus extra for dusting

250 g/9 oz strong white flour

1½ tsp salt

1 tbsp caraway seeds

2¼ tsp easy-blend dried yeast

25 g/1 oz butter, melted

2 tbsp honey, warmed

300 ml/10 fl oz lukewarm water

sunflower oil, for oiling

# Sweet Treats
## *from* EASTERN EUROPE
## & RUSSIA

Eastern European and Russian baking is mainly known for its savoury bread and meat pies, but this region also has a flair for delicious, sweet treats, such as the chocolate babka loaf and the vodka coffee cake. Another popular speciality is pierogi, which is a ravioli-like dumpling that is hugely popular in Poland and Russia. These come with different fillings, both sweet as well as savoury, and are served either as a main dish or a dessert. A big part of the Eastern European baking tradition dates back to pre-Christian times, when flatbreads and also pancakes were the symbol of the sun, a bountiful harvest and a happy family.

*Bread and salt is a welcome greeting
ceremony in many central and eastern
European cultures. It is customary to give
newcomers bread and salt to wish prosper-
ity and fertility in a settled home. In the
19th century a lot of immigrants brought
this tradition to other continents.*

# Chocolate Babka Loaf

SERVES 8

PREP TIME: 30 minutes, plus 1½ hours to chill and 1 hour to rise

COOKING TIME: 50 minutes

## INGREDIENTS

*6 egg yolks*

*175 g/6 oz butter, melted, plus extra for greasing*

*1 tsp vanilla extract*

*100 g/3½ oz caster sugar*

*½ tsp salt*

*275 ml/9 fl oz milk*

*5 tsp easy-blend dried yeast*

*475 g/1 lb 1 oz plain flour, plus extra for dusting*

*icing sugar, for dusting*

### chocolate filling

*225 g/8 oz plain chocolate, at least 70 per cent cocoa solids, roughly chopped*

*1 tbsp cocoa powder*

*½ tsp ground cinnamon*

*100 g/3½ oz caster sugar*

*100 g/3½ oz walnuts, roughly chopped*

This sweet loaf is traditionally baked for Easter in the Christian regions of Eastern Europe. Many Jews living there took the recipe with them when they emigrated to North America and other countries. The Polish and Belarussian word *babka* means 'grandmother', and it is said that the wavy pattern of the dough is reminiscent of her wrinkles.

1. Whisk the egg yolks in a bowl, then gradually add the butter and vanilla extract. Add the sugar and salt and stir to combine. Heat the milk in a small saucepan until lukewarm. Add the yeast and stir to dissolve.

2. Sift the flour into a large bowl, then pour in the egg mixture and milk, stirring constantly. Mix until a smooth, elastic dough forms. Transfer to a bowl, cover with clingfilm and chill in the refrigerator for 1½ hours.

3. Meanwhile, make the chocolate filling. Put the chocolate, cocoa powder and cinnamon into a food processor and process until fine crumbs form. Combine the chocolate mixture with the sugar.

4. Grease a 25-cm/10-inch loaf tin and line a baking tray with baking paper. Turn out the dough on to a lightly floured work surface, then roll out to a 25-cm/10-inch square and place on the prepared tray. Spread the chocolate mixture evenly on the dough and top with the walnuts, then fold the dough over slightly at two opposite sides of the square and press down. Place in the prepared tin, with the joins at the base of the tin, cover with a damp tea towel and leave to rise for 1 hour.

5. Meanwhile, preheat the oven to 180 °C/350 °F/Gas Mark 4. Bake the loaf in the middle of the preheated oven for 40–45 minutes until golden brown. Remove from the oven, leave to cool for 10 minutes, then turn out of the tin on to a wire rack and leave to cool completely. Dust with icing sugar and serve.

1.

5.

6.

# Sweet Pierogi

MAKES 25–30

PREP TIME: 35 minutes,
plus 5 minutes to stand

COOKING TIME: 45–50 minutes

Pierogi are a national dish in Poland. Originally a peasant food, they were later taken up by other parts of society. The dumplings, made from unleavened dumpling dough, are first cooked with the filling and then baked or fried. Either savoury or sweet, they can be made in a variety of shapes and flavours and are also found in neighbouring countries.

1. Grind the linseeds in a mortar with a pestle, then add to a small bowl with the water. Whisk to combine, then leave to stand until thick. Sift together the flour and salt into a large bowl. Make a well in the flour and add the oil and the linseed mixture. Mix until well combined, then turn out on to a floured work surface and knead until a dough forms.

2. Put the dough into a bowl, cover with a tea towel and leave to stand for about 5 minutes.

3. Meanwhile, to make the filling, chop the dried prunes into small pieces. Put them into a saucepan with the water, sugar and lemon juice and stir until well combined. Add the cinnamon stick and cook over a medium heat, stirring frequently, for about 20 minutes until the water is almost completely absorbed. Remove the cinnamon stick, transfer the mixture to a small bowl and leave to cool.

4. To make the caramel sauce, mix together the sugar, cream, milk, butter and salt in a saucepan over a medium–low heat. Cook, whisking gently, for 5–7 minutes until thickened. Add the vanilla extract and cook for a further 1 minute. Remove from the heat and leave to cool.

5. Roll out the dough on a lightly floured work surface to a thickness of 3 mm/⅛ inch, then use a 8-cm/3-inch round cookie cutter to cut into 25–30 rounds, re-rolling the trimmings as needed. Put 1–2 tablespoons of filling on to each round. Fold over the dough and pinch to seal. Meanwhile, bring a large saucepan of water to the boil. Submerge batches of the sealed pierogi in the boiling water for 2–3 minutes until they float. Remove and dry on kitchen paper.

6. Heat enough oil for deep-frying in a large saucepan to 180–190°C/ 350–375°F, or until a cube of bread browns in 30 seconds. Add batches of the pierogis and deep-fry for 2–3 minutes until golden brown. Serve hot with the caramel sauce.

## INGREDIENTS

*1 tbsp linseeds*
*2 tbsp water*
*275 g/9¾ oz plain flour, plus extra for dusting*
*½ tsp salt*
*2 tbsp oil*

### filling
*325 g/11½ oz dried prunes*
*250 ml/9 fl oz water*
*50 g/1¾ oz caster sugar*
*1 tbsp lemon juice*
*1 cinnamon stick*
*vegetable oil, for deep-frying*

### caramel sauce
*200 g/7 oz brown sugar*
*4 tbsp whipping cream*
*4 tbsp milk*
*55 g/2 oz butter*
*pinch of salt*
*1 tbsp vanilla extract*

# Vodka Coffee
## CAKE

SERVES 8

PREP TIME: 15 minutes

COOKING TIME: 1 hour

### INGREDIENTS

*275 g/9¾ oz plain flour,
plus extra for dusting*

*2 tsp baking powder*

*½ tsp salt*

*50 g/1¾ oz cornflour*

*25 g/1 oz cocoa powder*

*60 g/2¼ oz butter,
plus extra for greasing*

*200 g/7 oz caster sugar*

*4 eggs*

*1 tsp vanilla extract*

*175 ml/6 fl oz milk*

*125 ml/4 fl oz vegetable oil*

*3 tbsp vodka*

*3 tbsp coffee liqueur*

*icing sugar and fresh raspberries,
to decorate*

### icing

*2 tbsp coffee liqueur*

*25 g/1 oz icing sugar*

In this cake, as in the drink Russian Coffee, the aromatic coffee has a strong flavour that is beautifully balanced by the sweet and mild vodka. In Poland and Russia, vodka has been traditionally distilled from rye since the 14th century and is very popular throughout Eastern Europe.

1. Preheat the oven to 180°C/350°F/Gas Mark 4. Grease a bundt tin and dust with flour, shaking out any excess.

2. Mix together the flour, baking powder, salt, cornflour and cocoa powder in a large bowl. Put the butter and sugar into a separate bowl and beat together, then add the eggs, one at a time, beating after each addition until incorporated. Add the vanilla extract, milk, oil, vodka and liqueur and mix to combine. Fold in the flour mixture.

3. Pour the mixture into the prepared tin and bake in the preheated oven for 1 hour. Leave to cool in the tin for 5 minutes, then turn out on to a wire rack and leave to cool completely.

4. To make the icing, mix the liqueur with the sugar and brush on to the top and sides of the cake. Dust with icing sugar, and serve decorated with the raspberries.

2.

3.

4.

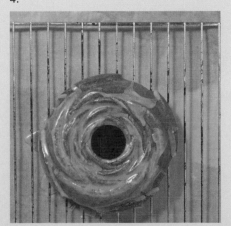

# Where Tradition Meets VARIETY

Israel's multicultural society is reflected in its baking culture, which has German, French, Arabic and Eastern influences, the blend of which accounts for the large variety of flavours. When seeing a rugelach pastry for the first time, who would not think of the French croissant? Jerusalem, especially, is considered an important stronghold of the art of baking. Since many immigrants to Israel were no longer able to cook and bake with the foods and fruit typical of their homelands, they were forced to adapt many traditional recipes to suit the local produce.

With so many different people in one country, over the last 50 years Israel's baking culture has evolved a lot in terms of taste and ingredients. The result is a very Mediterranean way of baking, but also with influences from all over the world.

# JEWISH HONEY
# CAKE

**SERVES 8–10**

**PREP TIME:** 25 minutes

**COOKING TIME:** 45–55 minutes

## INGREDIENTS

*275 g/9¾ oz plain flour*

*2 tsp ground cinnamon*

*½ tsp ground ginger*

*½ tsp ground mixed spice*

*1 tsp baking powder*

*½ tsp bicarbonate of soda*

*2 eggs*

*150 g/5½ oz soft light brown sugar*

*250 g/9 oz clear honey*

*125 ml/4 fl oz vegetable oil,
plus extra for greasing*

*125 ml/4 fl oz dark rum*

*100 g/3½ oz walnut pieces*

This honey cake is the traditional cake for the Jewish New Year, marking a sweet start to the New Year. This cake is also popular throughout the Middle East in a variety of different forms. Honey, as we know it, has existed since Roman times, when it was considered a valuable medicine and was reserved for holidays and special occasions.

1.  Preheat the oven to 180 °C/350 °F/Gas Mark 4. Lightly grease a bundt tin. Set aside 1 tablespoon of the flour, then sift together the remaining flour, the cinnamon, ginger, mixed spice, baking powder and bicarbonate of soda into a bowl.

2.  Put the eggs and the sugar into a separate bowl and stir to combine. Whisk in the honey, oil and rum. Carefully whisk in the flour mixture and mix until the dough is thick and smooth.

3.  Toss the walnuts in the reserved flour and stir into the mixture. Pour the mixture into the prepared tin and bake in the preheated oven for about 45–55 minutes until a skewer inserted into the centre of the cake comes out clean. Leave to cool in the tin for about 10 minutes, then remove from the tin and transfer to a wire rack to cool for a further 30 minutes. Cut into slices and serve.

2.

# Hamantaschen

This pastry is an integral part of Jewish culture. It is traditionally eaten for the Feast of Purim and evokes the deliverance of the Jewish people. Haman, the highest Persian official at the time, wanted to kill all the Jews in the country. But he didn't succeed and was instead executed. The pastry, also called 'Haman's Ears', alludes to the fact that he lost his ears before the execution.

1. Line two large baking trays with non-stick baking paper. Put the butter and sugar into a bowl and beat with an electric whisk until light and fluffy. Add the orange zest, orange juice and vanilla extract, then add 2 of the eggs, one at a time, beating after each addition until incorporated.

2. Sift together the flour, baking powder and salt into a separate bowl. Gradually add the flour mixture to the butter mixture, mixing on low speed until just combined. Wrap the dough in clingfilm and chill in the refrigerator for at least 1 hour.

3. Roll out the dough on a floured work surface to a thickness of 3 mm/ ⅛ inch. Using a round 7-cm/3-inch fluted cutter, cut out 40 rounds, re-rolling the trimmings as necessary, and place on the prepared baking trays. Chill in the refrigerator for about 30 minutes until firm. Preheat the oven to 180 °C/350 °F/Gas Mark 4.

4. Meanwhile, grind the poppy seeds in a mortar with a pestle and put them into a medium-sized saucepan. Add the milk and honey and cook over a medium–low heat for about 20 minutes, stirring occasionally, until thickened. Remove from the heat and leave to cool completely.

5. Remove the chilled rounds and the apricot jam from the refrigerator. Pipe either 2 teaspoons of poppy-seed filling or jam into the centre of each round. Beat the remaining egg with 1 teaspoon of water. Brush the edges of the rounds with the egg wash, then fold in the sides to form a triangle. Pinch the dough to enclose the filling.

6. Place the pastries on the prepared trays and bake in the middle of the preheated oven for 12–15 minutes until golden. Leave to cool on the trays for 5 minutes, then transfer to wire racks to cool completely. The pastries can be stored in an airtight container for up to 1 week.

MAKES 40

PREP TIME: 40 minutes, plus 1½ hours to chill

COOKING TIME: 35–40 minutes

## INGREDIENTS

*140 g/5 oz poppy seeds*
*125 ml/4 fl oz milk*
*85 g/3 oz honey*
*150 g/5½ oz apricot jam, chilled*

### pastry

*250 g/9 oz butter, softened*
*325 g/11½ oz caster sugar*
*2 tsp orange zest*
*2 tbsp freshly squeezed orange juice*
*1 tsp vanilla extract or 1 vanilla pod, scraped*
*3 eggs*
*550 g/1 lb 4 oz plain flour, plus extra for dusting*
*4 tsp baking powder*
*½ tsp salt*

# Rugelach

The crescent-shaped rugelach is of Ashkenazic origin: its Yiddish name and a similar Polish pastry suggest it has Eastern European origins. Although it is a year-round treat in Jewish cuisine, it is most popular in November/December for the Hanukkah festival. It is fun and easy to make and there are many possible variations for the filling.

1.  To make the pastry, put the butter and cream cheese into a bowl and beat with an electric whisk. Mix together the flour and salt and slowly add to the mixture until a smooth dough forms. It will be quite sticky. Wrap in clingfilm and chill in the refrigerator overnight.

2.  Preheat the oven to 180°C/350°F/Gas Mark 4 and lightly grease two or three baking trays. Divide the dough into 3 pieces, and return 2 pieces to the refrigerator.

3.  Using a floured rolling pin, roll out the dough on a lightly floured work surface to a 3-mm/⅛-inch-thick round with a diameter of about 28 cm/11 inches.

4.  Mix three quarters of the sugar with the cinnamon in a small bowl. Using a palette knife, spread a third of the jam on the dough round, then sprinkle over a third of the chopped nuts and the cinnamon sugar. Cut the round into 16 wedges.

5.  Starting at the wide end, roll each wedge around the filling, then bend into a crescent shape. Place the crescents on one of the prepared baking trays, spaced about 2.5 cm/1 inch apart, with the ends tucked underneath.

6.  Repeat with the remaining 2 pieces of dough.

7.  Brush the crescents with milk and sprinkle with the remaining sugar. Bake in the preheated oven for 20–25 minutes until golden. Remove from the oven and transfer to a wire rack to cool. The rugelach can be stored in an airtight container for up to 3 days.

MAKES 48

PREP TIME: 45 minutes, plus 8 hours to chill

COOKING TIME: 20–25 minutes

## INGREDIENTS

100 g/3½ oz sugar
1 tsp cinnamon
250 g/9 oz raspberry jam
150 g/5½ oz walnuts, finely chopped

### pastry

250 g/9 oz softened butter, plus extra for greasing
250 g/9 oz cream cheese
250 g/9 oz plain flour, plus extra for dusting
½ tsp salt
milk, for brushing

3.

3.

4.

# A Taste OF Asia

Asia is not the first region that springs to mind when you think about baking, but this vast area does have a wide and varied baking history. The Chinese are fond of cakes made of rice, such as the nian gao cake, which is eaten during the Chinese New Year and is similar to the Japanese mochi cake. It is served as a sweet or savoury cake and is sometimes flavoured with cream and cinnamon. So those who think Asian baking is not very diverse are very much mistaken, as there is now a growing tradition of varied, interesting baking and in many parts of Asia, European-style traditional baking with flour is becoming more common.

*Wheat flour is used in many Asian cuisines, producing a successful combination of Western-inspired Asian bakes.*

# Mango & Rice
## TART

SERVES 6

PREP TIME: 1 hour,
plus 4 hours to chill and rest

COOKING TIME: 30 minutes

### INGREDIENTS

*200 g/7 oz jasmine rice*
*140 g/5 oz sugar*
*350 ml/12 fl oz water*
*100 ml/3½ fl oz coconut milk*
*1 tsp salt*
*2–3 ripe mangos, peeled
and thinly sliced*

### pastry

*200 g/7 oz plain flour, plus extra
for dusting*
*75 g/2¾ oz caster sugar*
*1 tsp vanilla extract*
*2 egg yolks*
*100 g/3½ oz butter, diced, plus
extra for greasing*
*2 tbsp water*

At home in the tropical rainforests, the mango tree can grow to be over 40 metres/130 feet high and its fruits can weigh up to 2 kilograms/4½ pounds. The fruit has a unique and sweet aromatic fragrance, which is why the Hindus have been offering it to the gods for thousands of years. In Thailand, mango with sweet rice and coconut is a popular dessert. Here, we offer it as a tart inspired by the tropics.

1. To make the pastry, sift together the flour and sugar into a large bowl and add the vanilla extract and the egg yolks. Add the butter and water and knead until a dough forms. Turn out the dough onto a lightly floured work surface and knead until smooth. Wrap in clingfilm and chill in the refrigerator for 1 hour.

2. Preheat the oven to 180°C/350°F/Gas Mark 4. Grease a 26-cm/10½-inch round, fluted tart tin. Roll out the dough on a lightly floured work surface and ease it into the tart tin. Line with baking paper, fill with baking beans and bake in the preheated oven for 12 minutes. Take out of the oven, remove the paper and weights and return to the oven for a further 10 minutes. Remove from the oven and leave to cool.

3. Meanwhile, place the rice in a saucepan of boiling water and cook for 10–12 minutes or according to packet instructions, until soft. Drain the rice thoroughly and set aside, cover and keep warm. Put the sugar and water into a saucepan and heat until a syrup forms. Pour the syrup into a baking tray and stir in the coconut milk and salt. Add the hot rice to the coconut mixture – this will cause the mixture to become quite liquid. Leave the rice mixture in the tray for about 3 hours to absorb the coconut milk.

4. Pour the rice mixture into the pastry case and spread evenly. Arrange the sliced mangos decoratively on top of the tart and chill in the refrigerator until ready to serve.

2.

3.

4.

2.

2.

3.

# Fortune

## COOKIES

Traditionally, these crunchy, sweet fortune cookies contain a slip of paper with an inspirational phrase or prophecy inside. Their origins lie in Japan, where a similar pastry was mentioned in records there from the 19th century. Before the First World War, Japanese caterers on the American West Coast gave them away to their guests, however they became more popular in Chinese-American restaurants.

1.  Write down fortunes or sayings on small strips of paper. Preheat the oven to 180°C/350°F/Gas Mark 4 and line a large baking tray with baking paper.

2.  Mix together all the ingredients in a large bowl. Using a wooden spoon, drop 20 mounds of batter onto the prepared baking tray, spaced well apart to allow room for spreading. Bake in the preheated oven for 10–15 minutes.

3.  As soon as you remove the cookies from the oven, place a paper strip in the centre of each one, then fold the cookie over the handle of a wooden spoon. Place each folded cookie on the rim of a bowl and press the edges together on either side of the bowl to make the traditional fold. Transfer to a wire rack and leave to cool.

MAKES 20

PREP TIME: 10 minutes

COOKING TIME: 10–15 minutes

### INGREDIENTS

*2 egg whites*
*½ tsp vanilla extract or 1 vanilla pod, scraped*
*½ tsp almond extract*
*3 tbsp vegetable oil*
*125 g/4½ oz plain flour*
*1½ tsp cornflour*
*pinch of salt*
*125 g/4½ oz caster sugar*
*3 tsp water*

# ANOTHER WORLD

## *of* Baking

When people think of classic baking, delicacies from countries such as France or Italy spring to mind, with Asian baking being less well known. This makes the variety of Asian recipes more surprising, though many of them have been developed in only the last 100 years.

*Naan bread has a plain taste that makes it a great accompaniment to spicy food, yogurt and tasty dips. It is a surprising fact that this variety of bread was developed in Turkey where it is consumed in the same way.*

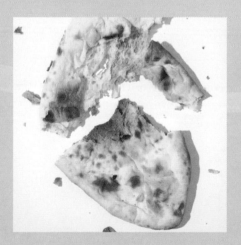

Although moon cakes and fortune cookies appear in Chinese records dating back to the 13th and 14th centuries, in a food culture dominated by rice dishes, cakes and bread made from grain play a more subordinate role. For this reason, a ceremonial meal without rice cakes in all their various shapes and sizes and in all possible combinations, such as with fruit, cannot be imagined. Their colour and exact composition are attuned to the Yin and Yang in order to achieve balance. The composition also depends on the region and the festival. The idea of desserts and cakes in the Western sense evolved much later. Instead, soup was often served as the final course in many south-east Asian countries – the idea being to fill the last remaining space in the stomach. Although bread made with flour does exist from northern China to Beijing, it is also a more expensive food. In Thailand, Laos and Vietnam, wheat breads are baked in steam ovens. The flatbreads are ready in 20 minutes and are spread with minced meat and baked vegetables. The most popular bakes in China and in Japan are a Western import: French croissants are the epitome of a luxury food.

In other parts of Asia this is quite different: In South Asia (India, Pakistan, Bangladesh) and Central Asia (Afghanistan, Uzbekistan, Tajikistan), as well as in the Near East (Iran, Kurdistan), the baking culture is mainly determined by a naan type of bread. This is usually eaten as an accompaniment to hot food. Naan has a flat, pitta-like shape and is elongated prior to baking. The inner part is flat while the outer edge is a little thicker. It resembles a pizza base. Unlike other Indian breads, naan bread is made from leavened dough, either by adding yogurt or yeast, and also baking powder. The basic ingredients were originally millet and yeast, but nowadays naan bread is often made with wheat flour. Traditionally, naan bread is baked over an open fire. This natural baking method, which calls for a great deal of care, is what gives it its characteristic flavour. The word 'naan' has both Persian and Afghan roots. In both languages, it simply means 'bread'.

# Ginger Tartlets

MAKES 8

PREP TIME: 25 minutes

COOKING TIME: 15 minutes

## INGREDIENTS

*200 g/7 oz ginger biscuits*
*50 g/1¾ oz blanched almonds*
*100 g/3½ oz butter, melted*
*300 ml/10 fl oz double cream*
*100 g/3½ oz cream cheese*
*4 tbsp freshly squeezed orange juice*
*2 tbsp icing sugar*
*1 tsp finely grated orange zest*
*fresh raspberries, to decorate*

Ginger is originally from the Asian tropics and is used both as a spice and a medicine. It has a pleasing, aromatic smell and a spicy, pungent flavour. Ginger was often used to replace pepper, which was scarce in the Middle Ages, but it also lends a special fragrance to sweet treats. Tartlets spiced with ginger are widespread in the English-speaking world.

1. Preheat the oven to 160°C/325°F/Gas Mark 3. Put the ginger biscuits and almonds into a food processor and process until they resemble coarse crumbs.

2. Transfer to a bowl, add the butter and stir until well combined. Divide the mixture among eight individual 7.5-cm/3-inch fluted moulds, pressing the mixture against the base and sides. Place the moulds on a baking tray and bake in the preheated oven for 15 minutes. Leave to cool slightly, then carefully remove the tartlet cases from the moulds and leave to cool completely.

3. Put the cream, cream cheese, orange juice, icing sugar and orange zest into a large bowl and mix to combine. Gently beat until smooth. Spoon the mixture into the tartlet cases, decorate with fresh raspberries and serve.

1.

2.

1.

3.

4.

# Chocolate
# Samosas

MAKES 16

PREP TIME: 1 hour,
plus 1 hour to chill

COOKING TIME: 10–15 minutes

For centuries, samosas have been a popular filled pastry in South Asia, Arabia and East Africa. The folded triangles can be filled with a variety of ingredients, typically cooked leftovers, and then deep fried. Here, they've been turned into a delightful dessert.

1. To make the filling, put the cream into a small saucepan and bring to the boil over a medium heat. Put the chocolate chips into a bowl, pour over the boiling cream and stir until melted. Chill in the refrigerator for 1 hour.

2. Sift the flour into a mixing bowl, add the ghee and rub in. If the dough is too stiff, gradually add a little cold water. Keep covered with a damp cloth.

3. Divide the dough into 16 equal-sized pieces and roll out each piece into a long rectangle. Put 1 teaspoon of the filling onto one end of the rectangle and fold over the dough repeatedly to make a triangle shape.

4. Heat enough oil for deep-frying in a large saucepan to 180–190 °C/ 350–375 °F, or until a cube of bread browns in 30 seconds. Add the samosas, in batches if necessary, and cook over a medium heat until crisp and golden. Do not overcrowd the pan, and take care that the oil is brought back to the correct temperature in between each batch. Drain on kitchen paper and leave to cool for 5 minutes. Serve warm.

## INGREDIENTS

filling
*250 ml/9 fl oz whipping cream*
*250 g/9 oz plain chocolate chips*

*250 g/9 oz plain flour*
*100 ml/3½ fl oz ghee or vegetable oil*
*oil, for deep-frying*

# Gulab Jamun

## SYRUP DUMPLINGS

Gulab Jamun is a classic Indian dessert served at large celebrations. Little balls of milk dough are deep fried and then soaked in flavoured syrup. The name goes back to the Persian word *gulab* for 'rose', and it probably refers to the shape of the Jambul berries.

MAKES 12–14

PREP TIME: 25 minutes, plus 2 hours to soak

COOKING TIME: 5 minutes

### INGREDIENTS

1.5 litres/2¾ pints water
450 g/1 lb caster sugar
1 tbsp ground cardamom
2 tbsp rosewater
275 g/9¾ oz powdered milk
185 g/6½ oz plain flour
1½ tsp baking powder
250 ml/9 fl oz whipping cream
oil, for oiling and deep-frying

1.  Put the water and sugar into a saucepan, bring to the boil and boil until the sugar is dissolved. Remove from the heat and add the cardamon and rosewater. Mix well and set aside.

2.  Put the powdered milk, flour and baking powder into a bowl and mix together well. Gradually add the cream, a little at a time, kneading the mixture until you have a medium–soft dough that is not sticky. Do not add all the cream unless it is needed to achieve the correct consistency.

3.  Divide the dough into walnut-sized balls and roll between lightly oiled hands until smooth. Meanwhile, heat enough oil for deep-frying in a large saucepan to 180–190 °C/350–375 °F, or until a cube of bread browns in 30 seconds. Add the dumplings in batches and fry, stirring frequently to brown all over.

4.  Remove the cooked dumplings from the oil using a slotted spoon and place in the sugar syrup. Leave the dumplings to soak in the syrup for at least 2 hours before serving.

1.

2.

3.

1.

2.

3.

# Hokkaido Milk Loaf

SERVES 6–8

PREP TIME: 25 minutes,
plus about 2 hours to rise

COOKING TIME: 45 minutes

Milk and milk powder from the Japanese island of Hokkaido were originally used for this bread, giving it its name. In Japan, Korea and other East Asian countries it is a staple food. But it is more than just a simple soft and sweet white bread – its special texture and fluffiness are legendary.

## INGREDIENTS

*oil, for oiling*
*300 g/10½ oz strong bread flour*
*30 g/1 oz plain flour*
*1¼ tsp easy-blend dried yeast*
*3 tbsp powdered milk*
*50 g/1¾ oz caster sugar*
*1 tsp salt*
*½ egg, beaten*
*175 ml/6 fl oz milk*
*5 tbsp whipping cream*

1. Lightly oil a large bowl. Put all the ingredients into a separate large bowl and mix using the dough hook of an electric beater until a walnut-sized piece of dough can be rolled out thinly enough for light to pass through it.

2. Place the dough in the prepared bowl, cover with oiled clingfilm and leave to stand for about 1 hour until doubled in size. Knock back the dough, then divide it into 3 equal-sized pieces, shape each piece into a round and leave to rise for a further 20 minutes. Preheat the oven 180 °C/350 °F/Gas Mark 4.

3. Flatten the dough and roll up each portion like a Swiss roll. Place the rolls side by side in a 450 g/1 lb loaf tin and leave to rise until the dough fills the tin four fifths full. Bake in the preheated oven for 45 minutes. Remove from the oven and leave to cool on a wire rack. Cut into slices and serve.

# Moon Cakes

In ancient times Chinese emperors used to make offerings to the moon in autumn. This tradition evolved into the Mid-Autumn Festival, which is still celebrated in China today, and the moon cakes as a delicacy definitely form part of it. Formerly the pastries were also used to pass on secret information. Like a puzzle, the filling of the cakes would reveal a message when correctly put together.

1. Mix together the flour, powdered milk, baking powder and salt in a bowl. Put 3 of the eggs, the sugar, vanilla extract and the melted butter into a separate bowl and beat with an electric whisk for about 5 minutes until creamy. Stir in the dry ingredients and knead until a smooth dough forms. Wrap in clingfilm and chill in the refrigerator overnight.

2. To make the filling, mix together the jam, dates, coconut and raisins.

3. Preheat the oven to 190 °C/375 °F/Gas Mark 5. Line two baking trays with baking paper.

4. Remove the dough from the refrigerator and divide into 15–20 pieces. Shape each piece into a round and place 1 tablespoon of the filling in the centre of each round. Fold the edges over the filling and press together.

5. Dust a 5-cm/2-inch moon cake press or round cutter with flour. Take the filled balls of dough and, one at a time, press them in the moon cake press, then remove. Alternatively, use the cutter to cut out rounds.

6. Lightly whisk the remaining egg with the water and brush over the moon cakes, then place them on the prepared baking trays. Bake in the preheated oven for 30 minutes or until the cakes are golden brown.

MAKES 15–20

PREP TIME: 20–30 minutes, plus overnight chilling

COOKING TIME: 30 minutes

## INGREDIENTS

650 g/1 lb 7 oz plain flour
60 g/2¼ oz powdered milk
1 tbsp baking powder
1 tsp salt
4 eggs
250 g/9 oz caster sugar
1 tsp vanilla extract or 1 vanilla pod, scraped
125 g/4/½ oz butter, melted
2 tbsp water, for glazing

### filling
200 g/7 oz apricot jam
100 g/3½ oz dried dates, chopped
55 g/2 oz desiccated coconut
70 g/2½ oz raisins

4.

5.

MOONLIGHT

# Romance

It's not exactly simple, but in China August used to be regarded as the second month of autumn, and every year the Moon Festival falls on the 15th day of the eighth month of the lunar calendar.

*The production of moon cakes varies much from region to region. However, they are always nicely decorated and sold in beautiful cake boxes that are even more important than the cake itself.*

Are you still not sure when it takes place? It doesn't matter! The main thing to note is that in mid to late September, the Moon Festival turns daily life in China upside down. Whoever can't calculate the date just has to wait until the cities are decorated with countless colourful paper lanterns in every conceivable shape and size. They are everywhere – in front of every house, in every street, in every shop. Small gifts are bought, especially the 10-cm/4-inch moon cakes that have all kinds of different decoration and and come in various sorts of packaging. A Moon Festival definitely wouldn't be the same without moon cakes.

There are different theories as to how the custom originated. One of them suggests that moon cakes were originally used to convey secret messages from house to house by hiding little notes in the filling. Or the fillings were like a puzzle that, when put together, revealed a secret message. They were, so to speak, a forerunner of today's fortune cookies. Another theory claims that the people wanted to express their respect for Chang'e, the mystery woman on the moon, by giving away exquisitely prepared desserts. In any case, the Moon Festival can be compared with harvest festivals and is celebrated with sumptuous foods. The status of the cake can be compared with goose or turkey for Christmas or maybe chocolate for Valentine's Day. Its decisive, leading role makes it simply indispensable during the festival. The sheer multitude of flavours and exquisite packaging of the moon cake definitely make it a cultural highlight. Usually they are filled with lotus paste and curdled egg yolks, but there are also many sweet versions based on all kinds of recipes. The surfaces of the cakes are decorated with motifs symbolizing heaven. The moon cake must be round because this signifies the reunion of lovers for the Chinese. The moon brings people closer together emotionally, because – no matter where they are in the world – they all look up at its silvery light in the same sky.

1.

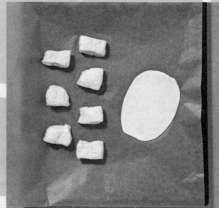

2.

3.

# Naan Bread

Naan comes from a Persian word meaning (flat) 'bread'. For at least two centuries, it has been the typical bread in the western and southern parts of Asia. It is traditionally baked in a stone oven. It is round, soft and puffs up making light bubbles in the dough. It is always served hot and can be spread with butter or dipped in a sauce.

1. Sift together the flour and salt into a mixing bowl. Gradually add the yogurt and mix with your hands. Gradually add enough water to make a soft, slightly sticky dough. Cover the bowl and leave to stand at room temperature for 1 hour.

2. Divide the dough into 8 equal pieces, shape each piece into a ball, then flatten the balls into 20-cm/8-inch ovals.

3. Preheat the grill to high. Put the butter and garlic into a small saucepan and heat over a low heat. Stir in the coriander and keep warm.

4. Place the bread under the preheated grill and cook for 8–10 minutes, turning halfway through, or until puffed up and there are little brown spots on the surface. Remove from the heat, brush with the butter mixture and serve immediately.

MAKES 8

PREP TIME: 25 minutes, plus 1 hour to stand

COOKING TIME: 8–10 minutes

## INGREDIENTS

*250 g/9 oz plain flour*
*2½ tsp salt*
*3 tbsp natural yogurt*
*100 ml/3½ fl oz lukewarm water*
*40 g/1½ oz butter*
*1 garlic clove, peeled and crushed*
*2 tbsp chopped fresh coriander*

# Baking IN THE Antipodes

The history of the British colonization of Australia began with the founding of New South Wales in 1788. Sheep farming was essentially the main source of nourishment for the settlers, who would often eat lamb for each meal every day of the week. The staple diet of the farm workers consisted of mutton, tea and damper, a kind of bread made of flour, salt and water, which was baked directly in the embers of an open fire. The Honourable Robert Dundas Murray made the following remark in his work *A Summer at Port Philip* (published in 1843): 'You're eating mutton and damper today – tomorrow they'll be serving mutton and damper as well, and for the rest of the year your meal will consist of good old mutton – be it boiled, grilled or stewed.' The 'ritual' of afternoon tea was adopted from England, whereby tea would be served alongside the classic scones. In Australia, scones and tea would typically also include pumpkin purée instead of, or as well as, jam.

*In a country once governed by Great Britain, it's no wonder that scones, biscuits, cakes and bread feature highly in Australia's baking repertoire.*

# Hokey Pokey

## BISCUITS

MAKES 15–20

PREP TIME: 25 minutes,
plus time to cool

COOKING TIME: 20–25 minutes

The biscuit dough is incredibly quick and easy to make and it smells delicious as it bakes in the oven. The name 'hokey pokey' comes from a vanilla and caramel-flavoured ice cream with the same name. It was also used in the 19th century by Italian street vendors selling ice cream on the streets of the UK and the United States.

1. Preheat the oven to 180°C/350°F/Gas Mark 4. Line a large baking tray with baking paper. Put the butter, sugar, golden syrup and milk into a saucepan and heat, stirring constantly, until the butter is melted and the mixture is just below boiling point. Remove from the heat and leave to cool to lukewarm.

2. Sift together the flour and bicarbonate of soda into a bowl, add to the cooled mixture and stir well.

3. Roll heaped tablespoons of the mixture into balls. Place the balls on the prepared tray, then flatten them with a floured fork to make 7.5-cm/ 3-inch rounds.

4. Bake in the preheated oven for 15–20 minutes, or until golden brown. Leave to cool on the tray for 1–2 minutes, then carefully transfer to a wire rack to cool completely.

5. Dip the biscuits halfway vertically into the melted chocolate and sprinkle the chocolate with the chopped nuts. Transfer to greaseproof paper to set.

## INGREDIENTS

*125 g/4⅓ oz butter*
*100 g/3½ oz granulated sugar*
*1 tbsp golden syrup*
*1 tbsp milk*
*175 g/6 oz plain flour,*
*plus extra for flouring*
*1 tsp bicarbonate of soda*
*200 g/7 oz white chocolate, melted*
*55 g/2 oz walnuts, very finely chopped*

1.

2.

3.

# Anzac
## BISCUITS

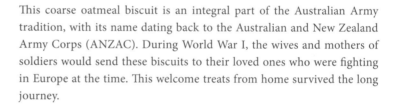

MAKES 18–20

PREP TIME: 20 minutes

COOKING TIME: 20–25 minutes

### INGREDIENTS

*90 g/3¼ oz porridge oats*
*150 g/5½ oz plain flour*
*175 g/6 oz soft light brown sugar*
*90 g/3¼ oz desiccated coconut*
*125 g/4½ oz butter*
*2 tbsp golden syrup*
*¾ tsp bicarbonate of soda*
*3 tbsp water*
*halved, melted caramels and chocolate buttons, to decorate*

This coarse oatmeal biscuit is an integral part of the Australian Army tradition, with its name dating back to the Australian and New Zealand Army Corps (ANZAC). During World War I, the wives and mothers of soldiers would send these biscuits to their loved ones who were fighting in Europe at the time. This welcome treats from home survived the long journey.

1. Preheat the oven to 150 °C/300 °F/Gas Mark 2. Line a baking tray with baking paper. Mix together the porridge oats, flour, sugar and coconut in a large bowl.

2. Melt the butter and golden syrup in a saucepan over a low heat. Mix the bicarbonate of soda with the water and stir into the butter mixture. Remove the pan from the heat, add the contents to the oat mixture and mix until a moist, firm batter forms.

3. Place tablespoons of the mixture on to the prepared tray, lightly pressing each mound with the back of the spoon until the biscuits are about 5 cm/ 2 inches in diameter.

4. Bake in the preheated oven for approximately 12–15 minutes until golden brown. Leave to cool on the tray for 1–2 minutes, then carefully transfer to a wire rack to cool completely.

5. To decorate, place half a melted caramel on each biscuit and top with a chocolate button. The biscuits can be stored in an airtight container for up to 1 week.

2.

2.

# Lamingtons

MAKES 8–10

PREP TIME: 40 minutes,
plus at least 8 hours to chill

COOKING TIME: 35–45 minutes

### INGREDIENTS

*280 g/10 oz plain flour,*
*plus extra for dusting*

*3 tsp baking powder*

*¼ tsp salt*

*140 g/5 oz butter,*
*plus extra for greasing*

*150 g/5½ oz granulated sugar*

*1 tsp vanilla extract*
*or 1 vanilla pod, scraped*

*2 eggs*

*125 ml/4 fl oz milk*

#### icing

*200 g/7 oz icing sugar*

*30 g/1 oz cocoa powder*

*125 ml/4 fl oz milk*

*25 g/1 oz butter*

*280 g/10 oz desiccated coconut*

If you haven't eaten Lamingtons during your childhood, you didn't grow up in Australia. They were first served by the Scottish nobleman Lord Lamington, Governor of Queensland from 1896 to 1901.

1. Preheat the oven to 180 °C/350 °F/Gas Mark 4. Lightly grease a 20 x 30-cm/ 8 x 12-inch rectangular cake tin and dust it with flour. Mix together the flour, baking powder and salt in a large bowl.

2. Put the butter, sugar and vanilla extract into a separate bowl and whisk until pale and fluffy. Gradually add the eggs, flour mixture and milk, making alternate additions and stirring carefully to combine.

3. Spread the mixture evenly in the prepared tin and bake in the preheated oven for 30–40 minutes, until a cocktail stick inserted into the centre of the cake comes out clean.

4. Remove from the oven, transfer to a wire rack and leave to cool for 5 minutes. Cut the cake into 8–10 rectangles and chill in the refrigerator overnight.

5. To make the icing, mix together the icing sugar and cocoa powder in a bowl. Heat the milk in a saucepan, then add the butter and stir until melted. Pour the warm liquid into the sugar mixture, stirring well until thickened but still runny.

6. Using a fork, dip the cake rectangles in the icing to cover them completely, then place them on a wire rack set over a piece of baking paper. Put the coconut into a shallow bowl, then add the cakes, one at a time, and turn in the coconut until completely covered. The cakes can be kept in an airtight container for up to 1 week.

2.

2.

6.

# Boston BUN

Traditionally, this recipe makes use of leftover, very lightly seasoned mashed potatoes. Raisins and a thick layer of icing and desiccated coconut are added to this modern version of the cake, which is made in both Australia and New Zealand.

1. Preheat the oven to 180°C/350°F/Gas Mark 4. Lightly grease a 20-cm/ 8-inch round cake tin. Ensure the potatoes are cold and smooth – push them through a sieve if necessary. Put the potatoes and sugar into a large bowl and whisk together. Add the raisins and whisk the mixture until smooth.

2. Sift together the flour, baking powder and cinnamon into a separate bowl, then add to the potato mixture alternately with the milk.

3. Transfer the mixture to the prepared tin, using a palette knife to spread it evenly, and bake in the preheated oven for 40–50 minutes. Remove from the oven and transfer to a wire rack to cool in the tin.

4. To make the icing, mix together the sugar, lemon juice, butter and coconut. Use a spoon to press the mixture through a sieve, then spread it over the top of the cake in a thick layer. Carefully remove the cake from the tin, cut into slices and serve.

SERVES 8

PREP TIME: 20 minutes

COOKING TIME: 40–50 minutes

## INGREDIENTS

*115 g/4 oz mashed potatoes*
*225 g/8 oz granulated sugar*
*150 g/5½ oz raisins*
*250 g/9 oz plain flour*
*3 tsp baking powder*
*1 tsp ground cinnamon*
*250 ml/9 fl oz milk*

### icing
*185 g/6½ oz icing sugar*
*2 tsp lemon juice*
*30 g/1 oz butter, melted, plus extra for greasing*
*3 tsp desiccated coconut*

1.

3.

# Coffee
## SCROLLS

MAKES 12–15

PREP TIME: 40 minutes,
plus 1 hour to rise

COOKING TIME: 25 minutes

### INGREDIENTS

*425 ml/15 fl oz milk, plus
extra for brushing*
*125 ml/4 fl oz vegetable oil*
*100 g/3½ oz granulated sugar*
*2¼ tsp easy-blend dried yeast*
*450 g/1 lb plain flour,
plus extra for dusting*
*1 tsp baking powder*
*1 tsp bicarbonate of soda*
*½ tsp salt*
*90 g/3¼ oz butter*
*100 g/3½ oz soft light brown sugar*
*70 g/2½ oz sultanas*
*ground cinnamon, for sprinkling*

### icing

*100 g/3½ oz icing sugar, sifted*
*1 tsp vanilla extract
or 1 vanilla pod, scraped*
*2–3 tbsp milk, plus extra if needed*
*2–3 tsp espresso coffee*
*pinch of salt*

These cinnamon rolls are similar to the English Chelsea Bun, but with the addition of a coffee-flavoured icing, which prevents them tasting too sweet. They are a popular breakfast food in Australia – especially for late weekend breakfasts when enjoyed with a cup of strong coffee.

1. Put the milk and oil into a large saucepan with the granulated sugar and heat over a medium heat until hot but not boiling. Remove from the heat and leave to cool until lukewarm. Add the yeast and stir to dissolve. Add the flour and mix well. Cover with clingfilm and leave to rise for 1 hour at room temperature.

2. Preheat the oven to 180 °C/350 °F/Gas Mark 4 and line a baking tray with some baking paper. Add the baking powder, bicarbonate of soda and salt to the flour mixture and mix to combine.

3. Turn out the dough on to a work surface dusted with flour and roll out to a 70 x 30-cm/28 x 12-inch rectangle. Spread the butter, brown sugar, sultanas and cinnamon evenly over the dough. Roll up widthways and brush the ends with a little milk to seal them.

4. Using a sharp knife, cut the roll into 2-cm/¾-inch-thick slices and place on the baking tray, leaving enough space between the slices to allow for spreading. Bake in the middle of the preheated oven for about 20 minutes.

5. Meanwhile, prepare the icing. Mix together all the ingredients in a bowl. The glaze should remain fluid. If it's too thick, add a little milk. Spread the warm rolls with the icing and serve immediately.

1.

3.

4.

# Peach Melba
# *Meringue*

Auguste Escoffier, the chef at London's Savoy Hotel, created a new dessert to celebrate the 1892 première of *Lohengrin* at Covent Garden. The combination of a peach and two scoops of vanilla ice cream drizzled with raspberry sauce was intended to represent the pose held by the swan at the end of the first act. The Australian opera singer Nellie Melba loved this dessert and it was soon referred to as Peach Melba. Here it is used as a filling for a meringue roll.

1.  Preheat the oven to 150 °C/300 °F/Gas Mark 2. Brush a 35 x 25-cm/14 x 10-inch Swiss roll tin with oil and line with greaseproof paper.

2.  To make the raspberry coulis, process the raspberries and icing sugar to a purée. Press through a sieve into a bowl and reserve.

3.  To make the meringue, sift the cornflour into a bowl and stir in the sugar. In a separate, grease-free bowl, whisk the egg whites until they hold stiff peaks, then whisk in the vinegar. Gradually whisk in the cornflour and sugar mixture until stiff and glossy.

4.  Spread the mixture evenly in the prepared tin, leaving a 1-cm/½-inch border. Bake in the centre of the preheated oven for 20 minutes, then reduce the heat to 110 °C/225 °F/Gas Mark ¼ and cook for a further 25–30 minutes, or until puffed up. Remove from the oven. Leave to cool for 15 minutes. Turn out on to a sheet of baking paper and carefully remove the greaseproof paper from the meringue.

5.  To make the filling, place the peaches in a bowl with the raspberries. Add 2 tablespoons of the coulis and mix. In a separate bowl, whisk together the crème fraîche and cream until thick. Spread over the meringue. Scatter the fruit over the cream, leaving a 3-cm/1¼-inch border at one short edge. Using the baking paper, lift and roll the meringue, starting at the short edge without the border and finishing with the join underneath. Transfer to a plate and serve with the coulis.

SERVES 8

PREP TIME: 25 minutes, plus 15 minutes to cool

COOKING TIME: 50 minutes

## INGREDIENTS

*sunflower oil, for brushing*

**raspberry coulis**
*350 g/12 oz fresh raspberries*
*115 g/4 oz icing sugar*

**meringue**
*2 tsp cornflour*
*300 g/10½ oz caster sugar*
*5 large egg whites*
*1 tsp cider vinegar*

**filling**
*3 peaches, peeled, stoned and chopped*
*250 g/9 oz fresh raspberries*
*200 ml/7 fl oz crème fraîche*
*150 ml/5 fl oz double cream*

1.

2.

3.

# Damper Bread

The damper is a classic bread made by Australian cattlemen, who would bake a few, long-lasting ingredients in the glow of the campfire when they were in the outback alone for weeks on end. As the temperature of the coals tended to vary, the men would knock on the thick bread to check when it was ready. If the bread made a hollow sound, it was good to go. Different flavours can be created by adding Parmesan cheese, olives or dried fruit.

1.  Preheat the oven to 200°C/400°F/Gas Mark 6. Line a baking tray with non-stick baking paper. Sift together the flour and salt into a large bowl. Use your fingertips to rub the butter into the flour until the mixture resembles fine breadcrumbs.

2.  Turn out on to a floured work surface. Add the water, cutting in with a knife until the mixture comes together. Knead gently until smooth.

3.  Shape into an 18-cm/7-inch round and place on the prepared tray. Use a sharp knife that has been dipped in flour to mark 8 wedges on top. Sprinkle over the poppy seeds and bake in the preheated oven for 30 minutes, or until the damper is cooked through and sounds hollow when tapped on the base. Transfer to a wire rack for 5 minutes to cool. Serve warm or at room temperature.

SERVES 8

PREP TIME: 20 minutes

COOKING TIME: 30 minutes

## INGREDIENTS

450 g/1 lb plain flour,
plus extra for dusting

pinch of salt

85 g/3 oz butter

175 ml/6 fl oz water,
plus extra if needed

200 g/7 oz poppy seeds

# Louise *Cake*

SERVES 6–8

PREP TIME: 30 minutes

COOKING TIME: 25–30 minutes

## INGREDIENTS

140 g/5 oz butter, at room
temperature, plus extra for greasing

175 g/6 oz caster sugar

3 egg yolks, at room temperature

2 tsp vanilla extract or 2 vanilla pods,
scraped

250 g/9 oz plain flour

2 tsp baking powder

225 g/8 oz raspberry jam

### coconut meringue topping

3 egg whites

pinch of salt

60 g/2¼ oz caster sugar

85 g/3 oz desiccated coconut

1 tsp vanilla extract

The Louise Cake has been a popular dessert in New Zealand for a long time. A thin layer of sponge cake is topped with raspberry jam and coconut meringue and then baked. The charming trio goes perfectly with a cup of tea.

1.  Preheat the oven to 180 °C/350 °F/Gas Mark 4. Lightly grease a 20-cm/8-inch round springform cake tin. Put the butter and sugar into a large bowl and whisk until fluffy. Add the egg yolks and whisk until incorporated. Add the vanilla extract, then fold in the flour and baking powder. The batter should be quite crumbly in texture.

2.  Spread the batter evenly in the prepared tin and bake in the preheated oven for 10–15 minutes until golden.

3.  Remove from the oven and use a palette knife to spread the jam over the entire surface of the cake.

4.  Meanwhile, to make the topping, put the egg whites into a bowl with the salt and whisk until they hold soft peaks. Using a wooden spoon, carefully fold in the sugar and coconut. Add the vanilla extract and lightly stir to incorporate. Use a palette knife to spread the meringue over the jam.

5.  Bake in the oven for a further 10–15 minutes until the meringue is light golden brown. Make sure that the meringue doesn't burn. Remove the cake from the oven and leave to cool in the tin for 10 minutes.

6.  Unclip and remove the springform, leaving the cake on the base of the tin, then transfer to a wire rack to cool completely. Transfer the cake to a plate, cut into slices and serve.

2.

3.

4.

# INDEX

Africa 108–9
  African Ginger Biscuits 110
afternoon tea 116, 125
Alfajores Caramel Biscuits 100
almonds
  almond macaroons 319
  Almond Sticks 303
  Appelkaka Cake 302
  Apricot & Almond Tarte 189
  Bee Sting Cake 271
  Butter Cake 264
  Cantucci Biscotti 230
  Lebkuchen Biscuits 252
  Lemon Polenta Cake 219
  Linzer Torte 288
  Mazarin Tartlets 311
  Stollen 256
  Torta Caprese Chocolate
    Cake 224
  Tosca Cake 307
  Vanilla Macaroons 175
Amaranth Alegrias Biscuits 98
Anzac Biscuits 364
apples
  Appelkaka Cake 302
  Apple Pie 22
  Apple Streusel Cake 267
  Chocolate Filo Parcels 217
  Dorset Apple Cake 118
  Tarte Tatin 176
Apricot & Almond Tarte 189
Arepas Flatbreads 105
Asia 338–9, 344–5
Australia 360–1
Austria 260, 261
  Austrian Sacher Cake 282

bacon
  Quiche Lorraine 209
bagels 11, 62–3
  Bagels 69
baguettes 170, 204–5
  Baguettes 206
baking 11, 13
bicarbonate of soda 13
Banana Bread 38
Baumkuchen Small Cakes 259
Bedouin 108
Bee Sting Cake 271
Berliner Doughnuts 279
Berry Muffins 46

Bible 13
biscuits
  African Ginger Biscuits 110
  Alfajores Caramel Biscuits 100
  Almond Sticks 303
  Amaranth Alegrias Biscuits 98
  Anzac Biscuits 364
  Black & White Biscuits 48
  Cantucci Biscotti 230
  Chocolate Shortbread 146
  Cinnamon Stars 275
  Cranberry & Pine Nut Biscotti 220
  Garibaldi Biscuits 94
  Gingernuts 140
  Hokey Pokey Biscuits 363
  Lebkuchen Biscuits 252
  Mexican Wedding Biscuits 80
  Polvorones Biscuits 99
  Sarah Bernhardt Biscuits 319
  Snickerdoodles 32
Black & White Biscuits 48
Black Bottom Pecan Pie 17
blackberries
  Berry Muffins 46
Blondies, Fudge 27
blueberries
  Berry Muffins 46
  Blueberry & Cranberry Squares 26
  Summer Fruit Tartlets 201
Boston Bun 369
Boston Cream Pie 45
Brandy Snaps 134
bread 11, 13, 227, 250, 261, 345
  Arepas Flatbreads 105
  Bagels 69
  Baguettes 206
  Banana Bread 38
  Brioche 190
  Cherry Tomato Focaccia Bread 243
  Chocolate Babka Loaf 326
  Ciabatta Bread 240
  Courgette Bread 70
  Crumpets 157
  Crusty White Loaf 158
  Damper Bread 375
  English Muffins 161
  Garlic & Herb Bread Spirals 211
  Hokkaido Milk Loaf 353
  Irish Soda Bread 167
  Mixed Seed Bread 164
  Moroccan Country Bread 114

  Naan Bread 359
  Olive Fougasse Bread 210
  Pan de Muerto Sweet Bread 91
  Pitta Bread 246
  Plum Cake 255
  Seeded Rye Bread 323
  Sourdough Bread 64
  Spiced Fruit Loaf 290
  Stollen 256
  Stromboli with Salami,
    Roasted Peppers & Cheese 67
Brigadeiros Chocolate Sweets 92
Brioche 190
Brownies, Chocolate & Cherry 56
Bulgaria 11
buns
  Chelsea Buns 145
  Cinnamon Swirls 320
  Coffee Scrolls 370
  Hot Cross Buns 133
  Sally Lunn Bun 122
  Semla Buns 301
  Skoleboller Buns 316
butter
  Butter Cake 264
  buttercream filling 203
  buttercream icing 287
  Canadian Butter Tarts 58
buttermilk
  Chocolate Chip Muffins 52
  Irish Tea Cake 168
  Red Velvet Cake 36

cakes 250, 345
  Appelkaka Cake 302
  Apple Streusel Cake 267
  Austrian Sacher Cake 282
  Baumkuchen Small Cakes 259
  Bee Sting Cake 271
  Boston Bun 369
  Boston Cream Pie 45
  Butter Cake 264
  Cherry Cake 150
  Danube Wave Cake 272
  Devil's Food Cake 30
  Dorset Apple Cake 118
  Esterházy Slices 287
  Fruit Cake 149
  Gugelhupf Ring Cake 268
  Iced Madeira Cake 137
  Jewish Honey Cake 334

Kladdkaka Chocolate Cakes 308
Lamingtons 366
Linzer Torte 288
Little Black Forest Cakes 263
Louise Cake 376
Mantecada 97
Maple & Pecan Bundt Cake 55
Oaxacan Coconut & Caramel
    Cake 79
Panforte Christmas Cake 229
Plum Cake 255
Princess Cake 298
Red Velvet Cake 36
Redcurrant Cake 276
Torta de Hojas Layer Cake 81
Tosca Cake 307
Tres Leches Cream Cake 76
Troika Cake 315
Victoria Sponge Cake 128
Vodka Coffee Cake 330
Canada 14
    Canadian Butter Tarts 58
Cantucci Biscotti 230
caramel
    Alfajores Caramel Biscuits 100
    caramel sauce 329
    Oaxacan Coconut & Caramel
        Cake 79
    Sweet Caramel Pasteles 82
carrots
    Iced Carrot Cake 312
cheese
    Feta & Olive Scones 244
    Feta & Spinach Parcels 249
    Quiche Lorraine 209
    Spring Onion & Cheese Tart 295
    Spring Onion & Parmesan
        Cornbread 73
    Stromboli with Salami, Roasted
        Peppers & Cheese 67
cheesecake
    Mascarpone Cheesecake 223
    New York Cheesecake 18
    Siphnopitta Cheesecake 233
    Strawberry & Cream
        Cheesecake 121
Chelsea Buns 145
cherries
    Cherry Bakewell Tartlets 132
    Cherry Cake 150
    Chocolate & Cherry Brownies 56

Chocolate Petits Fours 197
Danube Wave Cake 272
Little Black Forest Cakes 263
Mini Cherry Pies 61
Cherry Tomato Focaccia Bread 243
Chilean Pineapple Cake 88
China 11, 356-7
chocolate
    Austrian Sacher Cake 282
    Baumkuchen Small Cakes 259
    Black & White Biscuits 48
    Boston Cream Pie 45
    Brigadeiros Chocolate Sweets 92
    Chocolate & Cherry Brownies 56
    Chocolate Babka Loaf 326
    Chocolate Chip Cookies 24
    Chocolate Chip Muffins 52
    Chocolate Cupcakes 21
    Chocolate Filo Parcels 217
    Chocolate Petits Fours 197
    Chocolate Samosas 349
    Chocolate Shortbread 146
    Danube Wave Cake 272
    Devil's Food Cake 30
    Hokey Pokey Biscuits 363
    Kladdkaka Chocolate Cakes 308
    Lebkuchen Biscuits 252
    Little Black Forest Cakes 263
    Millionaire's Shortbread 141
    Mississippi Mud Pie 51
    Mousse au Chocolate Tartlets 193
    Peanut Butter S'Mores 42
    Sarah Bernhardt Biscuits 319
    Torta Caprese Chocolate Cake 224
    Troika Cake 315
    White Chocolate & Rose Cupcakes 131
Ciabatta Bread 240
cinnamon
    cinnamon & maple filling 33
    Cinnamon Spiced Orange Beignets 188
    Cinnamon Stars 275
    Cinnamon Swirls 320
    Doughnuts with Cinnamon Sugar 25
    Snickerdoodles 32
Classic Vanilla Cupcakes 43
coconut
    Anzac Biscuits 364
    Boston Bun 369
    Coconut Kisses 101
    Lamingtons 366
    Louise Cake 376

Oaxacan Coconut & Caramel Cake 79
coffee
    Coffee Scrolls 370
    Vodka Coffee Cake 330
condensed milk
    Brigadeiros Chocolate Sweets 92
    Key Lime Pie 35
    Millionaire's Shortbread 141
    Torta de Hojas Layer Cake 81
    Tres Leches Cream Cake 76
cookies
    Chocolate Chip Cookies 24
    Fortune Cookies 343
cornmeal
    Spring Onion & Parmesan
        Cornbread 73
Courgette Bread 70
cranberries
    Blueberry & Cranberry Squares 26
    Cranberry & Pine Nut Biscotti 220
    Kladdkaka Chocolate Cakes 308
cream
    Black & White Biscuits 48
    Boston Cream Pie 45
    Brandy Snaps 134
    Chilean Pineapple Cake 88
    Chocolate Cupcakes 21
    Chocolate Samosas 349
    Crème Brûlée Tartlets 182
    eggnog whipped cream 28
    Ginger Tartlets 346
    Gulab Jamun Syrup Dumplings 350
    Little Black Forest Cakes 263
    Mississippi Mud Pie 51
    Mousse au Chocolate Tartlets 193
    New York Cheesecake 18
    Onion Tart 293
    Peach Melba Meringue 373
    Princess Cake 298
    Quiche Lorraine 209
    Raspberry Charlotte 194
    Sarah Bernhardt Biscuits 319
    Semla Buns 301
    Spanish Custard Flan 214
    Spicy Jalapeño Cornbread 106
    Strawberry & Cream Cheesecake 121
    Tres Leches Cream Cake 76
    Troika Cake 315
cream cheese
    Iced Carrot Cake 312
    Irish Tea Cake 168

Pumpkin Whoopie Pies 33
Red Velvet Cake 36
Rugelach 336
Strawberry & Cream Cheesecake 121
Summer Fruit Tartlets 201
Crème Brûlée Tartlets 182
crème fraîche
(see soured cream)
crème pâtissière 178, 272
Croissants 172
Crumpets 157
Crusty White Loaf 158
cupcakes 41
Chocolate Cupcakes 21
Classic Vanilla Cupcakes 43
White Chocolate & Rose Cupcakes 131

Damper Bread 375
Danube Wave Cake 272
dates
Date & Walnut Loaf 154
Date, Pistachio & Honey Slices 239
Moon Cakes 354
Day of the Dead 87
Devil's Food Cake 30
Dorset Apple Cake 118
doughnuts
Berliner Doughnuts 279
Doughnuts with Cinnamon Sugar 25
Mexican Sopapillas 84
dried fruit
Fruit Cake 149
Panforte Christmas Cake 229
Spiced Fruit Loaf 290
dumplings
Gulab Jamun Syrup Dumplings 350
Sweet Pierogi 329

Eastern Europe 324–5
Éclairs, Strawberry 181
eggs
Baumkuchen Small Cakes 259
Egypt 11, 108, 153
English Muffins 161
Esterházy Slices 287
evaporated milk
Pumpkin Pie 28
Tres Leches Cream Cake 76

Feta & Olive Scones 244
Feta & Spinach Parcels 249

Fig Tartlets 234
Finland 11
Fortune Cookies 343
Fougasse 210
Fraisier 203
France 170–1, 204–5
Fruit Cake 149
Fudge Blondies 27

Garibaldi Biscuits 94
Garlic & Herb Bread Spirals 211
Germany 11, 250–1, 260, 261, 284–5
ginger
African Ginger Biscuits 110
Ginger Tartlets 346
Gingernuts 140
golden syrup
Anzac Biscuits 364
Black Bottom Pecan Pie 17
Brandy Snaps 134
Canadian Butter Tarts 58
Hokey Pokey Biscuits 363
Greece 11, 13
Guava Bars 83
Gugelhupf Ring Cake 268
Gulab Jamun Syrup Dumplings 350

Hamantaschen 335
hazelnuts
Apple Streusel Cake 267
Chocolate Filo Parcels 217
Cinnamon Stars 275
Esterházy Slices 287
Redcurrant Cake 276
herbs
Garlic & Herb Bread Spiral 211
Hokey Pokey Biscuits 363
Hokkaido Milk Loaf 353
honey
Date, Pistachio & Honey Slices 239
Hamantaschen 335
Honeyed Baklava Pastries 236
Jewish Honey Cake 334
Hot Cross Buns 133

Iced Carrot Cake 312
Iced Madeira Cake 137
India 11
Ireland 166
Irish Soda Bread 167
Irish Tea Cake 168

Israel 332–3

jam
Austrian Sacher Cake 282
Berliner Doughnuts 279
Hamantaschen 335
Linzer Torte 288
Louise Cake 376
Moon Cakes 354
Rugelach 336
Troika Cake 315
Jewish Honey Cake 334

Key Lime Pie 35
Kladdkaka Chocolate Cakes 308

Lamingtons 366
Latin America 74–5
lebkuchen 284–5
Lebkuchen Biscuits 252
Lemon & Poppy Seed Madeleines 198
Lemon Meringue Pie 127
Lemon Polenta Cake 219
Lemon Tarte 187
Liebig, Justus 13
limes
Key Lime Pie 35
Linzer Torte 288
Little Black Forest Cakes 263
Louise Cake 376

macadamia nuts
Fudge Blondies 27
macaroons 184–5
almond macaroons 319
Coconut Kisses 101
Vanilla Macaroons 175
Madeira Cake, Iced 137
Mango Rice Tart 340
Mantecada 97
maple syrup
cinnamon & maple filling 33
Maple & Pecan Bundt Cake 55
marzipan
Fraisier 203
Princess Cake 298
Semla Buns 301
Troika Cake 315
mascarpone
Blueberry & Cranberry Squares 26
Mascarpone Cheesecake 223

Strawberry & Cream Cheesecake 121
Strawberry Éclairs 181
Strawberry Shortcake 138
Mazarin Tartlets 311
Mediterranean 212–13
meringue
    Lemon Meringue Pie 127
    Louise Cake 376
    Peach Melba Meringue 373
Mexico 87
    Mexican Corncake 103
    Mexican Sopapillas 84
    Mexican Wedding Biscuits 80
milk
    Bee Sting Cake 271
    crème pâtissière 178, 272
    Hokkaido Milk Loaf 353
    South African Milk Tarts 113
    Tres Leches Cream Cake 76
Millionaire's Shortbread 141
Mini Cherry Pies 61
Mississippi Mud Pie 51
Mixed Seed Bread 164
Moon Cakes 354
Moon Festival 356–7
Moroccan Country Bread 114
Mousse au Chocolate Tartlets 193
muffins
    Berry Muffins 46
    Chocolate Chip Muffins 52
    English Muffins 161
    Raspberry Crumble Muffins 139
mushrooms
    Quiche Lorraine 209

Naan Bread 359
New York Cheesecake 18
nuts
    Honeyed Baklava Pastries 236
    Panforte Christmas Cake 229

oats
    Anzac Biscuits 364
    Guava Bars 83
Oaxacan Coconut & Caramel Cake 79
olives
    Feta & Olive Scones 244
    Olive Fougasse Bread 210
onions
    Onion Tart 293
    Spicy Jalapeño Cornbread 106

Spring Onion & Cheese Tart 295
Spring Onion & Parmesan
    Cornbread 73
oranges
    Cinnamon Spiced Orange
        Beignets 188
    Ginger Tartlets 346
ovens 11, 108

Pan de Muerto Sweet Bread 91
Panforte Christmas Cake 229
pastries 170
    Chocolate Filo Parcels 217
    Chocolate Samosas 349
    Cinnamon Spiced Orange Beignets 188
    Croissants 172
    Date, Pistachio & Honey Slices 239
    Feta & Spinach Parcels 249
    Hamantaschen 335
    Honeyed Baklava Pastries 236
    Moon Cakes 354
    Rugelach 336
    Sausage Rolls 163
    Strawberry Éclairs 181
    Sweet Caramel Pasteles 82
    Tarte Tatin 176
    Vanilla Millefeuille 178
Peach Melba Meringue 373
Peanut Butter S'Mores 42
peanuts
    Amaranth Alegrias Biscuits 98
pears
    Spiced Pear & Sultana Strudel 280
pecan nuts
    Black Bottom Pecan Pie 17
    Maple & Pecan Bundt Cake 55
    Mexican Wedding Biscuits 80
    Snickerdoodles 32
peppers
    Spicy Jalapeño Cornbread 106
    Stromboli with Salami, Roasted
        Peppers & Cheese 67
Picasso, Pablo 226–7
Pierogi, Sweet 329
pies 152–3
    Apple Pie 22
    Black Bottom Pecan Pie 17
    Key Lime Pie 35
    Lemon Meringue Pie 127
    Mini Cherry Pies 61
    Mississippi Mud Pie 51

Pumpkin Pie 28
pine nuts
    Cranberry & Pine Nut Biscotti 220
pineapple
    Chilean Pineapple Cake 88
pistachio nuts
    Date, Pistachio & Honey Slices 239
Pitta Bread 246
Plum Cake 255
polenta
    Arepas Flatbreads 105
    Lemon Polenta Cake 219
    Mantecada 97
    Mexican Corncake 103
    Spicy Jalapeño Cornbread 106
    Spring Onion & Parmesan
        Cornbread 73
Polvorones Biscuits 99
potatoes
    Boston Bun 369
Princess Cake 298
prunes
    Sweet Pierogi 329
Pumpkin Pie 28
Pumpkin Whoopie Pies 33

Quiche Lorraine 209

raisins
    Boston Bun 369
    Gugelhupf Ring Cake 268
    Stollen 256
raspberries
    Berry Muffins 46
    Ginger Tartlets 346
    Peach Melba Meringue 373
    Raspberry Charlotte 194
    Raspberry Crumble Muffins 139
    Summer Fruit Tartlets 201
Red Velvet Cake 36
redcurrants
    Berry Muffins 46
    Redcurrant Cake 276
rice
    Mango Rice Tart 340
ricotta
    Siphnopitta Cheesecake 233
Rome 11, 13, 108
rosewater
    White Chocolate & Rose Cupcakes 131
Rugelach 336

# INDEX

Russia 324–5
Rye Bread, Seeded 323

salami
   Stromboli with Salami, Roasted
      Peppers & Cheese 67
Sally Lunn Bun 122
Sarah Bernhardt Biscuits 319
Sausage Rolls 163
Scandinavia 296–7, 305
Scones 142
   Feta & Olive Scones 244
seeds
   Damper Bread 375
   Lemon & Poppy Seed Madeleines 198
   Mixed Seed Bread 164
   Seeded Rye Bread 323
semla buns 305
   Semla Buns 301
shortbread
   Chocolate Shortbread 146
   Millionaire's Shortbread 141
   Strawberry Shortcake 138
Siphnopitta Cheesecake 233
Skoleboller Buns 316
Snickerdoodles 32
Sourdough Bread 64
soured cream
   Devil's Food Cake 30
   Maple & Pecan Bundt Cake 55
South African Milk Tarts 113
Spanish Custard Flan 214
Spiced Fruit Loaf 290
Spiced Pear & Sultana Strudel 280
Spicy Jalapeño Cornbread 106
spinach
   Feta & Spinach Parcels 249
Spring Onion & Cheese Tart 295
Spring Onion & Parmesan Cornbread 73
Stollen 256
strawberries
   Fraisier 203
   Strawberry & Cream Cheesecake 121
   Strawberry Éclairs 181
   Strawberry Shortcake 138
   Summer Fruit Tartlets 201
Stromboli with Salami, Roasted
      Peppers & Cheese 67
Strudel, Spiced Pear & Sultana 280
sugar
   Doughnuts with Cinnamon Sugar 25

sultanas
   Canadian Butter Tarts 58
   Chelsea Buns 145
   Coffee Scrolls 370
   Hot Cross Buns 133
   Iced Carrot Cake 312
   Irish Tea Cake 168
   Spiced Pear & Sultana Strudel 280
Summer Fruit Tartlets 201
Sweet Caramel Pasteles 82
Sweet Pierogi 329
sweetcorn
   Mexican Corncake 103

Tarte Tatin 176
tarts
   Apricot & Almond Tarte 189
   Canadian Butter Tarts 58
   Cherry Bakewell Tartlets 132
   Crème Brûlée Tartlets 182
   Fig Tartlets 234
   Ginger Tartlets 346
   Lemon Tarte 187
   Mango Rice Tart 340
   Mazarin Tartlets 311
   Mousse au Chocolate Tartlets 193
   Onion Tart 293
   South African Milk Tarts 113
   Spanish Custard Flan 214
   Spring Onion & Cheese Tart 295
   Summer Fruit Tartlets 201
   Tarte Tatin 176
tomatoes
   Cherry Tomato Focaccia Bread 243
Torta Caprese Chocolate Cake 224
Torta de Hojas Layer Cake 81
Tosca Cake 307
Tres Leches Cream Cake 76
Troika Cake 315

United Kingdom 116
United States of America 14

vanilla
   Classic Vanilla Cupcakes 43
   Skoleboller Buns 316
   Tres Leches Cream Cake 76
   Vanilla Macaroons 175
   Vanilla Millefeuille 178
Victoria Sponge Cake 128
Vikings 11

Vodka Coffee Cake 330

walnuts
   Chocolate Babka Loaf 326
   Courgette Bread 70
   Date & Walnut Loaf 154
   Hokey Pokey Biscuits 363
   Iced Carrot Cake 312
   Jewish Honey Cake 334
   Rugelach 336
   Torta de Hojas Layer Cake 81
White Chocolate & Rose Cupcakes 131
Whoopie Pies, Pumpkin 33

yeast 13
yogurt
   Naan Bread 359
   Raspberry Crumble Muffins 139

In this beautifully illustrated book, American pastry chef Edward Gee explains the techniques that produce perfect results every time, whether baking small or family cakes, breads, biscuits, brownies, macaroons or buns. Since Edward was a small boy of eight, he has loved baking for his family and he has gone on to develop a passion for creating sweet treats for all occasions. Many years later - as an Executive Pastry Chef in big American luxury hotels like the Buena Vista Palace, The Swan and Dolphin Hotel or the Waldorf Astoria - he has now realized his dream to write down his favourite recipes for others to bake and enjoy too. With a baking teacher's precision and a cook's passion, Edward Gee brings the baking world to you. 'With easy step-by-step instructions, I can ensure you're always on the right track'.

BAKE is the result of an international collaboration between the renowned worldwide publisher Parragon and 99pages, an innovative publishing house based in Europe. Both partners have created a beautiful design with stunning photography, featuring 180 famous baking recipes from all over the world, including the USA, Europe, Latin America, Asia, Australasia and Africa. All of the recipes provide a background into international baking traditions, while also giving practical advice to develop the reader's baking skills. And the cakes, biscuits, breads, and buns in this book have two things in common - they look beautiful and taste fantastic.

Books produced by 99pages regularly cause a sensation at international cookbook competitions and are enthusiastically received by critics. Edouard Cointreau, President of the Gourmand World Cookbook Awards, says '99pages are one of the greatest surprises on the international cookbook market.'

# 99PAGES

# PICTURE ACKNOWLEDGEMENTS

The publisher would like to thank the following for permission to reproduce copyright material on the following pages: page 10: Woman grinding corn to make unleavened bread © Richard Hook/Getty Images; page 10: Barley / corn, on white background, cut out © 2010 Creative Crop (Digital Vision)/Getty Images; page 11: Detail of a Harvest Scene. From the tomb of Sennedjem. Mural painting, 19th Dynasty. Necropolis of Deir el-Medina on the West Bank at Luxor, Egypt © Leemage (Universal Images Group)/Getty Images; page 11: Woman with a shovel, 1497 © SSPL/Getty Images; page 13: German chemist Justus Liebig, created Baron von Liebig, (1803 - 1873). Original Artwork: Engraving by J B Hunt after a painting by Trantschold. © Hulton Archive/Getty Images; page 13: Advertisement for Royal Baking Powder by the Royal Baking Powder Company in New York, New York, 1888. © Jay Paull (Archive Photos)/Getty Images; page 14: Political map © Sylvain Sonnet (Photographer's Choice RF)/Getty Images; page 15: American Flag © Jose Luis Pelaez (The Image Bank)/Getty Images; page 15: USA, California, Route 66, Barstow, Route 66 Motel; © Alan Copson (AWL Images)/Getty Images; page 15: Autumn High Resolution Isolated Dry Maple Leaf © Miroslav Boskov (E+)/Getty Images; page 15: The Chrysler Building New York City © 2009 Matthew Mawson (Flickr Select)/Getty Images; page 40: Pink cup cake with cherry on the top on white background, cut out © Creative Crop (Digital Vision)/Getty Images; page 41: Large and small red white and blue cupcakes arranged as an American Flag ©Thatcher Keats (Photonica)/Getty Images; page 41: Hands icing cupcake on table © Line Klein(Cultura)/Getty Images; page 62: Bagel pieces © C Squared Studios (Photodisc)/Getty Images; page 63: Baker taking bagels out of oven in kitchen of bakery, portrait © Mitch Tobias (The Image Bank)/Getty Images; page 63: Neon sign advertising seafood specialties and bagels at delicatessen. © Dennis K. Johnson (Lonely Planet Images)/Getty Images; page 74: Political map © Sylvain Sonnet (Photographer's Choice RF)/Getty Images; page 75: Smashed donkey pinata on floor with candy © Jeffrey Coolidge (Stone)/Getty Images; page 75: Chichen Itza in Mexico. © Xavier Arnau (Vetta)/Getty Images; page 75: Girl wearing a sombrero in Puerto Penasco Mexico during spring. © 2011 Bill Dwyer (Flickr Select)/Getty Images; page 86: Day of the Dead statuettes © Inti St Clair (Blend Images)/Getty Images; page 87: Mexican crafts with skeletons in old town, Albuquerque, New Mexico, USA © Danita Delimont (Gallo Images)/Getty Images; page 87: Mexico, young woman wearing Day of the Dead skull mask © Livia Corona (Stone+)/Getty Images; page 108: Political map © Sylvain Sonnet (Photographer's Choice RF)/Getty Images; page 109: South African giraffes (Giraffa camelopardalis giraffa) running © Art Wolfe (Lifesize)/Getty Images; page 109: Happy maasai with small son outside the village. © Britta Kasholm-Tengve (the Agency Collection)/Getty Images; page 109: Sunrise in savannah, Massai Mara National Park. © 2011 Luis Sánchez Martín (Ismart Photography)/(Flickr)/Getty Images; page 116: Political map © Sylvain Sonnet (Photographer's Choice RF)/Getty Images; page 152: Presentation and tasting of a giant pie, in Denby dale, England. Frontpage of French newspaper Le Petit Journal Illustre, 1928. Private Collection. © Leemage (Universal Images Group)/Getty Images; page 153: Woman holding pie with oven mittens © Angela Wyant (Stone+)/Getty Images; page 166: Political map © Sylvain Sonnet (Photographer's Choice RF)/Getty Images; page 166: Sheep grazing on rural hillside © Henglein and Steets (Cultura)/Getty Images; page 170: Political map © Sylvain Sonnet (Photographer's Choice RF)/Getty Images; page 184: Macaroons © 2012 Neil Langan UK (Photolibrary)/Getty Images; page 185: Colorful French Macarons © Dan Moore (E+)/Getty Images; page 185: France, market, macaroons © Jacques LOIC (Photononstop)/Getty Images; page 212: Political map © Sylvain Sonnet (Photographer's Choice RF)/ Getty Images; page 213: Black bull billboard © Shanna Baker (Photographer's Choice RF)/Getty Images; page 213: The view along the Lycian coast trail from Kayakoy to Oludeniz, Turkey © Ron Watts (First Light)/Getty Images; page 213: Didyma, an ancient Ionian sanctuary, in modern Didim, Turkey, containing the Temple of Apollo, the Didymaion. © Chris Cheadle (All Canada Photos)/Getty Images; page 226: Pablo Picasso At Lunch, Vallauris, 1952. © Robert DOISNEAU(2011Gamma-Rapho)/(Masters)/Getty Images; page 227: Salted pretzel stick © Foodcollection/Getty Images; page 250: Political map © Sylvain Sonnet (Photographer's Choice RF)/Getty Images; page 251: Alp digl Plaz, ascent to Alp Flix, Kanton of Grisons, Switzerland © Iris Kuerschner (LOOK)/Getty Images; page 251: Girl with map at Brandenburger Tor © Chris Tobin (Digital Vision)/Getty Images; page 251: German man in lederhosen drinking beer, Hofbrauhaus, Munich, Bavaria, Germany © Laurie Noble (The Image Bank)/Getty Images; page 260: Man breaking bread © Andrew Carmichael (Stone)/Getty Images; page 261: Man kneading bread dough © Howard George (Arthur Woodcroft)/(The Image Bank)/ Getty Images; page 261: Bread and pastries in shop window. © Richard I'Anson (Lonely Planet Images)/Getty Images; page 284: Leb-kuchenherz, heart-shaped cookies made from Lebkuchen, sold during Oktoberfest. © Dan Herrick (Lonely Planet Images)/Getty Images; page 284: Gingerbread house on white background, close-up © Dag Sundberg (Photographer's Choice)/Getty Images; page 296: Political map © Sylvain Sonnet (Photographer's Choice RF)/Getty Images; page 297: Fishermans Cabin (Rorbuer), Nusfjord, Lofoten Islands, Norway © Banana Pancake (Photolibrary)/Getty Images; page 297: A basket of blueberries, Sweden. © Huerta, Anna/Getty Images; page 297: A moose laying down Sweden. © Plattform/Getty Images; page 304: Storkyrkan (Cathedral) and Stortorget (Parliament). Stockholm. Sweden © Nils-Johan Norenlind (age fotostock)/Getty Images; page 305: Celebration of Fat/ Shrove Tuesday with semlor. © 2010 Karin Andersson (Flickr Open)/Getty Images; page 305: Cup of cappuccino with spoon and sugar packet © Inti St. Clair (Inti St.Clair, Inc.)/(Photodisc)/Getty Images; page 324: Political map © Sylvain Sonnet (Photographer's Choice RF)/Getty Images; page 325: Loaf of homemade sourdough bread, small bowl of salt and knife. © 2012 Sarka Babicka (Flickr)/ Getty Images; page 325: Wooden nesting dolls © Alan Kearney (Brand X Pictures)/Getty Images; page 325: Saint Basil's Cathedral and The Kremlin in Moscow © Dmitry Mordvintsev (E+)/Getty Images; page 332: Political map © Sylvain Sonnet (Photographer's Choice RF)/Getty Images; page 333: Israel, Judean Mountains, Old Jerusalem, Dome of the Rock © Bertrand Gardel (hemis.fr)/Getty Images; page 333: Jerusalem road sign © Joel Carillet (E+)/Getty Images; page 333: People prays and walk in front of the western wall, wailing wall or kotel. © 2011 Beatriz Pitarch (Flickr)/Getty Images; page 338: Political map © Sylvain Sonnet (Photographer's Choice RF)/Getty Images; page 339: Taj Mahal facade © David Henderson (OJO Images)/Getty Images; page 339: Shanghai Citys-cape During the Daytime © 2009 Andrew Rowat (Stone)/Getty Images; page 339: Pagoda and Dragon Snow Mountain © Adam Crowleyd (Digital Vision)/Getty Images; page 344: Naan Bread © Ferran Traite Soler (E+)/Getty Images; page 345: Men making bread at bakery. © Dennis Walton (Lonely Planet Images)/Getty Images; page 345: naan and ginger mango chutney. © Jessica Boone (Photodisc)/Getty Images; page 356: Homemade Mooncake for Chinese mid-autumn festival. ©MelindaChan (Flickr)/Getty Images; page 357: mooncake handmade ©Vietnam (Dantoan)/(Flickr Open)/Getty Images; page 357: Early morning in a bakery making moon cakes for the Moon Festival on Hong Kong Island © Oliver Strewe (Lonely Planet Images)/Getty Images; page 360: Political map © Sylvain Sonnet (Photographer's Choice RF)/Getty Images; page 361: sydney opera house at sunrise © David Messent (Photolibrary)/Getty Images; page 361: Rotorua, North Island, New Zealand © LatitudeStock -TTL (Gallo Images)/Getty Images; page 361: ULURU ROCK IN AUSTRALIA © Marc Romanelli (Stone)/Getty Images; page 361: Kangaroo road sign, outback Australia © Josie Elias (Photodisc)/Getty Images; All other incidentals are 99pages and Parragon images.